SO NEAR AND YET SO FAR

Bobby Robson's World Cup Diary

1982-86

WITH
BOB HARRIS

WILLOW BOOKS
Collins
8 Grafton Street, London W1
1986

Photographic Acknowledgements

All photography by Bob Thomas unless otherwise
specified

Willow Books
William Collins Sons & Co. Ltd
London ·Glasgow · Sydney · Auckland
Toronto · Johannesburg

First published 1986
©R. W. Robson/Bob Harris 1986

BRITISH LIBRARY CATALOGUING IN PUBLICATION DATA
So Near And Yet So Far. Bobby Robson's World Cup
Diary 1982–86
1. World Cup (Football championship: 1986: Mexico)
I. Title
796.334′66   GV943.5   1986
ISBN 0 00 218186 X

Photoset in Times Roman
by V & M Graphics Ltd, Aylesbury, Bucks
Made and printed in Great Britain by
Billing & Sons Ltd, Worcester

Contents

It is not the critic who counts,
Not the man who points out where the strong man stumbled
Or where the doer of deeds could have done better.
The credit belongs to the man who is actually in the arena;
Whose face is marred by dust and sweat and blood;
Who strives valiantly,
Who errs and comes short again and again;
Who knows the great enthusiasms;
Who, at the worst, if he fails,
At least fails while daring greatly,
So that his place shall never be with those cold and timid souls,
Who know neither victory nor defeat.

1. Taking Over

I was a proud man the first time I went home to Newcastle as manager of England. I could not have wanted a better first match as 36,185 packed St James' Park on that opening Saturday of the 1982–83 season to welcome the coming of their own football Messiah, Kevin Keegan. As a Geordie born and bred it was one of the greatest occasions of my professional career and I was as pleased as anyone in that ground when Keegan marked his arrival with the winning goal against Queen's Park Rangers. The England captain was cheered to the rafters and I was delighted by the warm response I received as well.

When I returned to the north east some months later I was abused, threatened and even spat at. My crime? I had not selected Kevin Keegan to play in England's opening game of the season against the up and coming Danes in Copenhagen on 22 September 1982. I was experiencing my first taste of the ups and downs of the hardest job in football and through it all I had to bite my lip and let Kevin have his say without responding and becoming involved in a slanging match.

Leaving Kevin Keegan out of my first international squad was the toughest decision I have ever made. I knew what he was and I knew what he had meant to England. Goodness knows I had seen him play enough and, as any of my players at Ipswich would have confirmed, I was a fan of his. I had, along with too few other League managers, attended almost every international match at Wembley and when I returned to Portman Road, Ipswich, I would say to my players that I had just watched a little fellow who was the bravest, most enthusiastic player in the country. Someone who was the epitomy of star material. I openly admit that I enjoyed every game in which I saw him play. He was busy, sharp, effervescent and a great finisher who had influence on any side in which he played.

Why then did I not select him to play against Denmark? The reason dated back to the World Cup Finals in Spain that summer when, under my predecessor Ron Greenwood, Kevin played no part until the final 27 minutes of the last game against Spain in Madrid when he came on as substitute for Tony Woodcock. I was in Spain as part of Ron's scouting

1

team and some of the stories that came my way were a little disturbing and I resolved to investigate them.

It was an important decision for me, for Kevin and, most important of all, for England. I spoke to a great many people involved and learned that, because of his back injury, he was being a little difficult and had lost some of his huge popularity with his team-mates. As he sought a solution to his personal troubles he became something of a disruptive influence. I spoke to his previous manager, fellow Geordie and good friend Lawrie McMenemy, who confirmed what a wonderful job he had done for Southampton but he also admitted that Kevin could occasionally be a little awkward to handle. I gathered that he liked to take over and yet I knew that it was vital that I should be in control from the first match against the Danes, especially as I knew it was going to be such a test of skill and strength so early in the season. Had I been sure that Kevin Keegan was still at his peak I would have had no hesitation in selecting him but I felt that he was beginning to play a little deeper and was no longer getting in where it hurt to win big matches, preferring the role of play-maker and provider.

That was why I went to watch him in that Second Division game against Queen's Park Rangers and, though I immediately acknowledged his impact on Newcastle United, the players around him and the supporters, I made up my mind that I would go to Denmark without him, thinking that I would initially see whether England could do without Kevin Keegan. After all this was a new age, a new era, building towards the 1986 World Cup Finals in Mexico and I wasn't at all sure what sort of role Keegan would play in that competition. I wanted to see who else was available in the country for the opening six months. I felt that it was my job to pick teams to get results and to drop players when I thought necessary.

At no stage did I intend to rid myself of Kevin Keegan altogether. If the team struggled he would have been straight back in and I knew that he would have a part to play somewhere in the development of the England side. What I did not expect was the dramatic reaction from Kevin that prompted him to spill his story out to a newspaper saying he was disgusted that he did not even get a telephone call to tell him that he had been thrown out and that he never wanted to play for his country again. It was all so controversial and caused so much unpleasantness when it could have been sorted out quietly between the two of us. I felt at the time of the newspaper article that his comments were unfair. I did not owe him an explanation because he had never kicked a ball for me. I am sure that had Ron Greenwood still been manager he would have done what Kevin wanted, but I felt that I was under no such obligation.

I deliberately remained silent and hoped that the fuss would die down. I still felt that I could repair some of the damage done and it was with this in mind that, on 29 September 1982, I wrote to Kevin Keegan explaining my point of view and finishing the letter, 'with all best wishes and kindest regards'. To make sure he received it I sent it to the then Newcastle United manager Arthur Cox with a covering note asking him to give Kevin the sealed letter. There was no response from Kevin at all and, added to what he had said about never wanting to play for England again, I permanently put him out of my mind. I could have made a big fuss about that letter (a copy of which is filed at the Football Association in Lancaster Gate) when pressure mounted for me to recall Kevin to the squad as he led Newcastle to promotion but it would have served only to prolong a row and would have done no one any good.

However, at least the incident gave me some inkling of what I had let myself in for as I turned my back on one of the best jobs in football at Ipswich and took a drop in salary to manage my country. It was no secret that I considered the task to be the highest I could go in football for, five years earlier, Brian Clough, Lawrie McMenemy, Ron Greenwood and I had been interviewed at the Football Association by the late Chairman, Sir Harold Thompson, for the same position after Don Revie had walked out to accept a contract in the United Arab Emirates. Both Cloughie and I were confident, almost like knowing we had done well in a school examination but, in the event, the job went to the right man, Ron Greenwood.

It was the right decision. In the intervening five years I turned down two offers from Barcelona, one from Bilbao, one from Everton plus a chance to return to the north east with Sunderland. There was also an approach from a major English club who asked me to keep their move confidential. Between 1977 and 1982 I believe I became a better manager, more fully equipped to tackle the daunting task ahead. I developed two teams in Ipswich during that time and, most importantly, went into Europe where I gained invaluable experience as we won the fiercely-contested UEFA Cup. In the meantime, Ron Greenwood was restoring confidence in our national team.

I once sat in my car an hour or so before the kick-off of a game listening to the sports round-up on Radio Two when Don Revie was interviewed and said that one of the reasons he had left the job was because the Football Association were about to dismiss him and had already made advances to me to ask whether I would like to take over. I would like to put that right straight away for all my dealings with Lancaster Gate have been conducted in a most proper manner and I can state categorically that I was never approached by anyone from the Football Association while Don Revie was still in office. As I said earlier, I was interviewed with others after his resignation and the first I knew of any discussion to take over from Ron Greenwood was in May 1982 when the Ipswich Chairman, Patrick Cobbold, told me he had received a telephone call from FA Secretary Ted Croker seeking permission to talk to me. He said that while it saddened him, he could not refuse and he left the decision entirely to me. All of this happened after Ron Greenwood's announcement that he would retire following England's final match in the 1982 World Cup competition in Spain.

Ipswich had just finished runners-up in the League for the second year in succession and I knew that I had done a good job with resources that were limited compared to the big city clubs over a span of thirteen and a half years. I was loath to leave a club I had come to love but the challenge of football's top job won the day and I thanked Patrick and told him I would like the opportunity to speak to the Football Association, which I did at an hotel in Luton in the company of Ted Croker, the FA Chairman Bert Millichip, Dick Wragg, the Chairman of the International Committee and long-serving Birmingham City Director, Jack Wiseman.

It was all very civilised as I was asked how I would feel if I were offered the job. Bert Millichip told me that there was no short list and that no one else had been offered the position, which was reassuring. The fact that no one else had been approached nor, according to these senior FA officials, thought about, was flattering and good for the ego and, even before any sort of terms were discussed, I was fairly certain that I would take it. As it happened they did not want to go any deeper on that first meeting. I was asked to go away and think about it and if I was interested we would talk business.

There was an educating diversion while all this was going on. Ron Greenwood and Don Howe were involved in a World Cup warm-up match against Finland in Helsinki and I was asked to take another England international side out to Iceland. It was a bit of excitement and the nice thing about it was that Ron knew exactly what was happening, namely that I was in line to be his successor and that I was more than interested in taking it. All I asked was that a decision be made fairly quickly so that, if we did agree, Ipswich would have time to find and bed down a new manager. This was important to me.

I talked it over with my club Chairman, Patrick Cobbold, at the beautiful Seckford Hall Hotel in Suffolk. He had a good idea of what I wanted to do but he was as dear and sweet as ever. We met on a warm, bright, spring day and after our usual chit-chat he turned to me and said: 'I feel extremely sorry. I do not envy you your decision but I want you to know that whatever you decide will be fine with us, whether you join

England or if you want a new, longer contract with us.' At no time did he try to press me to stay but I found myself wavering slightly as I considered how close we had come to winning the big prize of the First Division Championship, having finished runners-up to Aston Villa and then being pipped at the post by Liverpool. It was a matter of a one-match difference and had we won that then there would have been no conflict as my ambitions would have been fulfilled. Who knows what might have happened in another season for all the same players were available and I knew we could never be so unlucky with injuries again, having lost Paul Mariner, Frans Thijssen, Terry Butcher and George Burley for a total of 77 games in that one season. Even though we had won the FA Cup and triumphed in Europe, not to mention never having been out of the top six in ten years, I felt slightly dissatisfied.

I was happy, earned a fabulous salary, had an expensive company car, lived in a great part of the country and had a wonderful boss whom, I knew, would have happily appointed me to the Board of Directors though I already had all the privileges of being a managing director. I was part of a family and yet here I was ready to throw it all away for a job where your success rests on other managers' players. But I couldn't sit on the fence because it would not have been fair to either club or country and, supported fully by my wife Elsie, I went back to the Football Association and said that I was interested.

I had a brief meeting with Messrs Millichip, Croker and Wragg before they left for Spain. Everything was fine until we came to the question of salary. I was prepared, if necessary, to take a cut but I was disappointed by the figure mentioned. The difference became a matter of principle and, reluctantly, I told them, 'I like your job – I don't like your terms'. I mentioned what I was earning and it was their turn to be surprised. I then gave them my idea of a realistic salary and, after some discussion, they came back and said they were sure we could reach an agreement and we arranged a meeting in Madrid during the second phase of the competition.

I was also on my way out to Spain as part of a team which included Terry Venables, Dave Sexton, Howard Wilkinson and Eddie Baily. I went off to Oviedo and Gijon to watch a group that included Austria and West Germany – the team that England were to meet in a critical goalless draw in Madrid later in the tournament. I returned to Madrid to report to Ron Greenwood and stayed with the players for a day only because of the increasing speculation in the Press that I was about to take the job. Ron had enough problems on his mind with the games against West Germany and Spain coming up without me getting under his feet.

I went on to my meeting with Bert Millichip, having enjoyed my taste of international football, and the one obstacle we had come up against was quietly and easily overcome as the Chairman came up with an offer that I felt was acceptable. All other aspects were quickly agreed with first-class working conditions and clear evidence that there would be no interference in team matters, which would be entirely my province. We shook hands on it and I asked only that the news should be kept under wraps until I had personally told my Ipswich Chairman, Patrick Cobbold, and my wife Elsie. We agreed that no announcement would be made until England had run their full course in the competition and Ron had completed his service and retired.

Patrick accepted my decision like the gentleman he was while Elsie was full of encouragement even though I painted the black side of the job, with the long hours, the hassle and the many nights away from home. She and I returned to Spain to watch the semi-finals and final. As I saw Italy beat West Germany in the magnificent Bernabeu Stadium in Madrid, the excitement of the challenge ahead began to grip me as I contemplated the prospect of England being in a similar position four years later. All sorts of images were crowding into my mind as I tried to foresee what lay ahead and how I was going to change things.

I had been an international footballer myself. I had played 20 times in the midfield for England and so was only too aware of the special demands I was going to make on my players. I expected co-operation from them though I was more concerned about receiving the same sort of help from clubs. As a club manager with international players I was acquainted with those difficulties as well. I wondered just how strong the possibility was of cancelling certain Saturday fixtures before big games and how hard it would be to have the players I wanted, not just to have them available but fit and ready to give the extra 25 per cent that is needed at this level of football where you have to be just that much sharper because your opponents are as well. Tired players do not make the best international footballers and I could see that as the biggest problem ahead of me.

The first hurdle was the European Championships in which England was drawn in group three alongside Denmark, Greece, Hungary and Luxembourg with our opening game against the Danes in Copenhagen taking place before our season was barely a month old. Enthusiasm was high for England had done a lot better than many of the critics had predicted in Spain, finishing the competition undefeated, having conceded only one goal and that against the French in a 3–1 victory. I knew that we were good enough not only to win our group and qualify but also to go all the way and win the title in France but, even so, it was nothing more than a stepping stone to the greater stage of the World Cup. That was my great vision and that was what I was aiming for. It was the World Cup that had ultimately persuaded me to take the job and I had exactly four years to produce that side.

I knew that I would have to retain certain senior players to keep the side ticking over but, at the same time, build on it and introduce new blood. I began in defence where I drafted in Russell Osman from my old club. When Ron Greenwood had tried him, he had not played well in that disaster against Norway in Oslo but I thought that I would get more out of him as I recalled the stormers he had played for me in Europe where he formed a magnificent partnership with the current England centre-half, Terry Butcher. But while bringing in one Ipswich player I reluctantly left out another, my club skipper Mick Mills, who had captained England so well during Keegan's absence in Spain. It was a desperately hard decision to make but Phil Neal was a couple of years younger and I thought he had more chance of making it for the World Cup Finals four years later. Little did I realise that come 1986 both would be player-managers in the lower divisions.

Although we had lost the experienced Dave Watson, who had run his course as an international, and the injured Phil Thompson, I was not too worried about the defence, especially with the ever-reliable Peter Shilton behind them. I was more concerned about England as an attacking force because our failure to score goals had cost us a place in the semi-finals and who knows what else besides. I felt strongly that we needed to place the emphasis on our attacking play and the question I had to ask myself was whether we could afford to play one less in midfield to allow one more forward to achieve that extra bite that had been lacking in the goalless draws with West Germany and Spain in Madrid. If we could it would give us that critical edge. I knew then it was an edge we needed for while some of our football writers were describing the Danes as a team of grocers and bacon slicers, I had already watched them dismantle France 3–1 and it was obvious we had plenty on our plate.

But I had one major problem – where were the wingers I wanted so badly? The best of them, Steve Coppell, was injured while John Barnes, Chris Waddle and Mark Chamberlain were all still too young. In the end I settled for Tony Morley who had been left behind as one of the unlucky ones when England went to Spain. However, it was not our winger who took over the game but Denmark's, a little wisp of a player named Jesper Olsen. I had seen him play for Ajax against Ipswich in our UEFA Cup campaign but George Burley had handled him well. He turned the experienced Phil Neal over that night and so began a reputation which was eventually to lead him to Manchester United and a big international career.

With the benefit of hindsight that was one of three errors I made in that first match for not only did I underestimate the elusive Olsen but I also thought Russell Osman could handle Preban Elkjaer while Morley failed to provide us with the menace I had hoped for. It could have cost us the game but it did not. Although my team was not the right one on the night we might still have won it. Trevor Francis put us ahead, Hansen equalised from the penalty spot after Osman had tripped Olsen and Francis restored our lead with only ten minutes to go. To be fair only the brilliant goalkeeping of Peter Shilton had kept us in the game until then and it looked as though we would steal a win. However, the Danes scored a deserved second in the dying moments with a glorious solo from Olsen who beat Robson, Osman and Butcher on his way.

Sitting on the bench that night, the frightening responsibility for what the game and the result meant to the country suddenly struck me. The job had started. This was it. I felt on edge in a way I had not done for years and as the realisation swept over me, the hairs on the back of my neck stood on end. As much as I had contemplated the job in the past few months I still had not realised its full significance. If we lost this one it was going to be five weeks before I had my chance of putting it right and I was already unpopular enough in some quarters for leaving Kevin Keegan at home.

We were lucky. The Danes were the better side on the night and had it not been for Peter Shilton we would surely have lost. Managing was completely different from playing for your country when your responsibility is to yourself. When Walter Winterbottom selected me in 1957, it was because he thought that I was the best right-half in England. For the player there is sense of personal achievement to be picked at all which turns to pride when performing. You are concerned with winning, playing up to or above your club form and keeping your place in the side. I certainly did not, as a player, feel the weight of England's hopes on my shoulders.

This is probably a good point to digress a little to explain some of the problems I have encountered over the past four years as England manager. As an international manager you are acutely aware of the heavy responsibility for the players both off and on the field, not just in terms of their behaviour and performance but for your duty to return them to their clubs in good physical and mental shape. Perhaps because I had been an international footballer myself I had had an open-handed attitude to any requests for my players when I was a manager at Ipswich. I had tasted the thrill of playing in the World Cup, of appearing against the 'auld enemy' Scotland, of experiencing at first-hand the skills of Brazil and I believe it helped me to become a better player. I had wanted my own players to experience that because I thought it would benefit the club.

Running an international team in Britain – it is even harder for Scotland, Wales and the two Irelands – desperately needs the co-operation of the club managers and this is not always forthcoming. As England manager I am not asking club managers to do anything I did not do myself when I was at Portman Road. I willingly devoted my time to Ipswich six days a week but insisted I had Sunday to myself and spent it with my family. The only reason I would break this rule was for an injured player who had to report to his country on Sunday or Monday. The easy way was to tell the player not to travel but I always left it up to the international manager and physiotherapist. I would hold that same attitude whether it was Allan Hunter for Northern Ireland, Paul Mariner for England or George Burley for Scotland.

My biggest sacrifice at Ipswich was to England. In April 1978, we were on our way to an FA Cup triumph at Wembley but we were struggling to avoid relegation from the First Division after a season wrecked by injury. Of all teams, we were due to play Liverpool at Anfield, and all I could think of was what team to play against them when I received an urgent telephone call from Ron Greenwood telling me that he had been beset by withdrawals and found himself without a full-back for the game against Brazil at Wembley. He wanted my captain Mick Mills and without any consideration I told him he could have him. It could have rebounded on me but it didn't for we earned a 2–2 draw at Liverpool in front of a 40,000 crowd while Mills went on with England to show his character and leadership.

Unfortunately, not every manager has the same attitude, as I was to learn. Many pay lip service to England publicly and then stab the manager in the back. It makes the task doubly difficult for we are trying to run the biggest football club in the country without a single player of our own. Apart from the senior and Under 21 sides which capture all the publicity, I am also responsible for the Under 19, Under 18, Youth, Under 16 and the residential squad at Lilleshall. Unless we have help from the clubs it creates an impossible situation. I suppose 50 per cent of the League bosses go out of their way to help, 25 per cent do what they can and the other 25 per cent are obstructive.

Some clubs lay down their own rulings. Ron Atkinson has done so with Manchester United at Old Trafford. He says that if a player is not fit to play for the club on Saturday he cannot play for his country on Wednesday. However, what if someone goes down with 24-hour flu on Friday? Of course, he is unable to play on Saturday but he could be right as rain on Monday morning. It is a fact that fit people heal faster and with a professional sportsman three days is a hell of a long time to shake off a strain or a minor injury. Indeed, in this respect England can even be of great assistance to clubs for where else would you find a more talented and experienced medical team than ours with the likes of Fred Street, Norman Medhurst and Dr Vernon Edwards? We have taken on injured players and sent them back fit!

We have always been terribly careful about players who have joined the squad with injuries. We have endeavoured to make an early diagnosis and erred on the side of caution if there has been the slightest doubt. In this respect I have consciously tried to build up with a rapport with clubs in the hope that they will reciprocate. It worked ideally with Brian Clough at Nottingham Forest when England had both senior and Under 21 games which meant calling up Viv Anderson, Steve Hodge and Chris Fairclough, leaving Brian short for a club friendly abroad. Naturally, he wanted his most famous players at this prestigious match and as I had planned to use Viv only as a substitute I allowed his release. After that incident the controversial Forest manager gave me tremendous support. He has a powerful voice and was many people's choice for my job. He could have made life very difficult but didn't – until he attacked me for arranging a game in Egypt.

The public tend to notice only the difficulties we have with injured players for senior internationals but further down the scale it can be even more of a worry. When Watford's Graham Taylor managed our Youth side in the European Championships in England he had so much trouble persuading top clubs to release their players that virtually his entire squad came from the lower divisions and when Dave Sexton and Terry Venables steered our Under 21 side to the European Championships for the first time we had to use 42 players. Dave Sexton used only three less when he retained the title two years later. Let's put that into perspective. That same year, 1978–79, Liverpool won the First Division title using only 15 players in 42 games. We had to build almost four different teams to win our title in over just a dozen matches.

I felt those problems acutely for, shortly before we were due to meet the strongly-fancied Italians in the semi-finals at Maine Road in April 1984, we had our usual crop of injuries and Dave Sexton and I decided to turn to my old home town club of Newcastle for the services of their young strikers Peter Beardsley and Chris Waddle who were developing quickly under the influence of Kevin Keegan. Out of courtesy I telephoned the Newcastle manager, Arthur Cox, before making the selections public, expecting him to be delighted at the honour for the club and the boost for the growing support at St James' Park.

'I have picked Beardsley and Waddle to play against Italy,' I told Arthur brightly.

'You haven't, have you?' he responded, and then he staggered me as he went on to add, 'I don't know whether I want them to play. We are going for promotion and what would happen if they were injured? I am going to talk to Stan about this.'

'Stan' was Football Association Councillor Stan Seymour and, in his position, I was sure that he would sanction the selections. He didn't. He agreed with his manager and did not want to take any risks. I did not force the issue nor even make it public, but Dave Sexton was shocked. We called up Mich D'Avray from Ipswich and he did a great job for us but who knows what doors would have opened for Waddle and Beardsley had they played. Waddle had terrific potential and did not have to wait too long but it was not until 1986 that room was found for Beardsley. The same can be said for another Newcastle player, Neil McDonald, who we wanted for the UEFA Youth Championships, but he didn't play because he was wanted for a club tour of the Far East. Maybe I felt it all the more because I was a Geordie and this was the club I had worshipped as a youngster. Other clubs have been just as difficult, even to the extent of pulling out youngsters because of a South East Counties' Youth match.

It has also happened at my old club with physiotherapist Brian Owen not being released to travel with the Under 21s because he was required at a reserve match. Apart from the honour to Ipswich it was doubly useful in that he would have returned with some great information on the cream of the countries' young stars. As a club manager I would have been only too pleased to have let my staff go – and then to have picked their brains when they came back.

However, this was all to come. It was bad enough taking my first game and seeing us outplayed in some departments, relying on our goalkeeper to gain a result. There was a lot I was going to have to learn about the differences between management at club and international level. I was only just beginning.

2. The Learning Process

The Football Association had become increasingly anxious about the escalating costs of the pre-match build-up before Wembley internationals. Since Don Revie's days the squad had always gathered at the splendidly-appointed West Lodge Park, nestling in the Hertfordshire countryside. It was a glorious hotel with delightful grounds, an excellent restaurant and lovely rooms. But it was expensive. It was costing almost £100 per person per day and that meant £3,000 for every day we stayed and getting higher with every visit. I readily agreed to a change for, costs apart, I was not happy at having to use Arsenal's training ground.

I had looked over the National Sports Centre at Bisham Abbey and liked what I saw. The picturesque setting was, in my view, even better than that at West Lodge Park with the ancient Abbey standing on the banks of the Thames surrounded by grass and artificial surfaces, tennis courts, a golf course, residential facilities and a bar. It was a sporting environment used by athletes, hockey players and the Lawn Tennis Association. So why not professional footballers? It also satisfied the accountants at Lancaster Gate. It did not work. Certainly the amenities were perfect but I soon heard rumblings from the players. They were not happy and I was getting the feed-back. Eventually, a delegation of senior players came to tackle me about the situation, pointing out that they were not being fussy, nor demanding five-star hotel accommodation, but they were concerned about the cramped conditions and the lack of telephones with the privacy to call their homes or conduct business. They were perfectly within their rights and I listened to their complaints, appreciating their honesty in coming straight to me and not talking behind my back. What is more they were right. At international level you cannot offer players less than they are accustomed to with their own clubs. I looked around and saw that, with three separate small television lounges, the players were becoming cliquish and a particular worry was that the coloured players, who had fitted in well in every other respect, were tending to stick together.

There were other, smaller problems. The players, for example, liked to relax in a bath after training but, at the Abbey, there were only showers. When you added all these factors together it became more important that something should be done before it all began to have an effect on morale. However, we were lucky. We found an excellent hotel four minutes up the road in High Wycombe. It was a Crest hotel and the added bonus was that the manager, Richard Williams, was familiar with the needs of footballers and, indeed, was known to many of our players as he had previously been at the Wembley complex hotel. What is more, it meant that we could continue to use the outstanding facilities the Abbey offered. We could have the best of both worlds.

I suspect some critics saw it as a climb-down on my part. Of course, I have beliefs that I would defend to the death, but I cannot see any point in inflexibility, particularly when it could affect what happens on the pitch. I had been right about the amenities at the Abbey and wrong about the accommodation. It was not the only change I made. I was only too conscious of the short time I had with my players over the course of a season and I was determined that I would make the most of every minute and I began with my very first game against West Germany, the World Cup runners-up. We met on Saturday night and trained on Sunday. I even named the team that night so that they could work together without worry. I thought I could get all of the set-plays out of the way on Sunday and devote Monday and Tuesday to training together as a team. It was not long before the complaints began to roll in over this as well. Too intense, trying to cram in too much. I looked and listened. Times had changed since I played for England. In my 5 years I had won 20 caps. Now, in a similar period, Kenny Sansom had won 50. It was the same at club level, the demands were greater than ever and the players enjoyed going home on a Saturday night to see their families and having a pint in their local on Sunday afternoon. Once again I had to hold up my hands and it became more important later when three of our players, Ray Wilkins, Mark Hateley and Trevor Francis, would have to play in Italy on Sunday afternoon before joining us.

The lessons were coming thick and fast, not least of all on the pitch. There were the usual injuries and club calls that gave me the opportunity to look at some of the players on the fringe. Gary Mabbutt, for example, had impressed me by his whole attitude to football; David Armstrong was a good, hard-working player with decent touch; Ricky Hill was one of the most promising of the up and coming players; and Cyrille Regis looked to have all the qualities of a top international striker. They all had their chance against a team which had edged England out of the World Cup Finals a few months earlier. While we fielded a relatively inexperienced side, West Germany had seven of the team who had faced England in Madrid, not to mention a certain Karl-Heinz Rummenigge. In the end it was the blond-

13

haired striker who was the difference between the two teams and had we had him on our side we would have won.

There was little to choose otherwise between the teams as the new boys looked lively with Mabbutt hitting a post while Schumacher saved brilliantly from Hill's header. But it was Rummenigge who turned two half-chances into goals to show what an exceptional, world-class player he was and, though our substitute pulled a goal back five minutes from the end, we lost 2–1 and I suffered that dreadful experience of losing at home. Not even my first game had prepared me for this emotional upheaval. As I sat there on the bench at the side of the pitch it began to rain, adding to my deepening depression. It was a miserable feeling, one of the worst I had ever endured in football until that moment, worse even than losing in three semi-finals and missing the League Championship by a desperately close margin. I felt it not only for myself but for the nation. The England team does not belong to its manager but to the people and walking from the bench to the dressing room was a chastening feeling.

One of the hardest aspects was being unable to talk to the players and analyse the defeat the next day. Clubs, understandably, demand their players back as soon as possible and most of them were heading homewards straight after the game on Wednesday night. I had a month to wait and ponder before my next game, which was another difficult one against Greece in the European Championships to be played at the intimidating Kaftatzoglion Stadium in the northern industrial town of Salonika and, to make matters worse, I was without two of the players I had planned to build my side around, captain Ray Wilkins and Glenn Hoddle, who were both injured. I moved Mabbutt forward from full-back and gave little Sammy Lee of Liverpool his début playing him alongside Bryan Robson. I need not have worried, for the incessant rain dampened the spirits of the capacity 45,000 crowd but not as much as Tony Woodcock's opening goal did after only two minutes. Tony, playing in boots borrowed from physiotherapist Norman Medhurst, scored another and took the free kick from which Sammy Lee marked his first appearance with a fierce shot into the corner of the net.

It was a heartening result in every way and we used it as a springboard a month later, on 15 December, to score nine against Luxembourg at Wembley. The result not only lifted us to the top of our European Championship group but also put us in the record books, for it was the highest goal total by England at Wembley and England's biggest score anywhere since the ten-goal victory against the USA in New York in 1964. Coincidentally, the last time England scored nine against European opposition was in Luxembourg in 1960 and I happened to be involved in that one as well – as a player! Jimmy Greaves and Bobby Charlton scored a hat-trick apiece in that game as did Watford's Luther Blissett 22 years on when Phil Neal, Steve Coppell, Tony Woodcock and substitutes Glenn Hoddle and Mark Chamberlain also scored one each', plus an own goal.

Although I was forced into half-a-dozen changes for the game against Wales in February 1983 we still went on to win 2–1 at Wembley. We had our problems with the lethal Ian Rush scoring the first goal and then hitting an upright. Had that gone in we might have had even greater difficulties but Terry Butcher scored an equaliser and Phil Neal showed his remarkable composure when he scored from the penalty spot despite having missed one in a cup-tie for Liverpool only three days earlier. It meant a hat-trick of wins and I honestly thought we were on our way – and so did a lot of the Press, most of the public and all of our players. But football has a habit of kicking you in the teeth when you are least suspecting it and, of all teams, it was Greece who brought us tumbling back to earth.

However, I had been under no illusions. Despite the three-goal victory in the away leg, I knew from having watched the Greeks that they would be coming to Wembley at the end of March to try and restore their pride and that they would be giving us nothing. They were coming to defend, to get as many bodies behind the ball as possible and to hold on to what they came with, a goalless draw. The only answer was to meet defence with attack and though I was without both of my captains, Bryan Robson and Ray Wilkins, I thought that we would have far too much fire power for our opponents as I picked Steve Coppell and Alan Devonshire to play on the flanks with Trevor Francis and Tony Woodcock inside them. They all had pace, were neat on the ball, could turn and beat people and pass in quality balls from the flanks that would eliminate the need for the traditional big centre-forward down the middle. I read it exactly right for I counted seven of Greece's players who never even crossed the halfway line. It was like playing against seven dustbins and though we were nearly always in possession, perhaps too often, we could not break them down.

One goal would have brought them out but it would not come. Perhaps a big centre-forward might have made the difference, who knows? But I still thought I had selected the right team. I appreciated that a manager cannot blame his players but I remarked at the traditional post-match Press debriefing the next morning that in international football you have no dummy run and that you cannot put right on Tuesday night what went wrong on Saturday afternoon. You have one chance only. It is about performance on the day and on this occasion three out of the four forwards had performed at below their usual standards. Trevor Francis was the exception before he was forced out of the game by a series of bad tackles.

It was a long chat I had with the media over bacon and egg sandwiches that morning. There was a lot to reflect on, some of which was best left unsaid. I accepted that the buck had to stop with me but I still believed that I was right in going for skill. My midfield pairing of Mabbutt and Lee had plenty of possession but there is no doubt that we missed Robson, who was always likely to weigh in with a goal, and Wilkins, who could have provided that one telling pass as could have Glenn Hoddle, injured, and Trevor Brooking, retired. Because of injury, Coppell was not the same player for me that he had been for Ron Greenwood. I realised that night that he had lost half a yard of pace and was no longer able to explode past players. What I did not know was just how serious his injured knee was. That was to be Steve's last game for England and his loss was a terrific blow for he should be in the England side now.

I also pointed out to the Press that Alan Devonshire did not reproduce his West Ham United form and went into some technical detail. Somewhere along the line, my remarks were taken out of context, misinterpreted and suddenly the tabloid Press descended on Upton Park and even the player's house looking for a reaction to my supposed inference that Devonshire was the scapegoat. Nothing could have been further from the truth. I was concerned enough to want to put the record straight that instant and I telephoned Hammers' manager John Lyall to seek his permission to talk to Devonshire before he played on Saturday so that he would not go into the game under a cloud. I even switched my intended match that day in order to do so and I was fortunate that Lyall was and is such a good manager, and one of the most co-operative. We managed to clear the air.

Obviously, I had to do something about the composition of the team – and quickly. There was still no Bryan Robson so I called in Gordon Cowans to replace him and his Aston Villa team-mate Peter Withe to give us a little height up front. The problem was that with Coppell injured I did not have a winger to call on. It needed something different if we were to beat Hungary on 27 April and keep our qualification hopes alive. On the Sunday before the Wembley game Don Howe came up to me and quietly said: 'Mind if I tell you something? Two years ago when we needed to beat them in the World Cup we played "one-in-the-hole" with Brooking placed behind Keegan and Mariner and they did not know how to cope with it.' Don's advice confirmed my own thoughts. Who should play there? I toyed with the idea of Trevor Francis but decided against it because he was best at playing against the man-for-man system thanks to his experiences with Sampdoria in Italy.

But that was not the only problem. Ray Wilkins was back after injury

16

but I had already decided to stay with Mabbutt in that role. I had a practice match at Bisham and Ray played so well that he really worried me. When you have players for such a short span of time, those practice matches are vital and I was always looking out for the right attitude and a player obviously in form – or otherwise! I once left Russell Osman out of a team because of his approach in one of these games. Despite Ray's performance that day, I felt that I needed Mabbutt's 'bionic' qualities. I took Ray to one side and explained the situation, telling him I still needed him around. He took it well and showed immense enthusiasm and understanding, qualities that I was to appreciate even more as I discovered what a fine professional the man is.

In the absence of a first-class winger I eventually decided to play Withe and Francis up front with Luther Blissett in the hole. It was a decision which surprised a great many but, on the night, it worked. Withe was superb, a real war horse. The big man played his heart out for his country, broke his cheekbone, fractured his thumb and scored a great goal to make it 2–0 after Trevor Francis had put us in front. It was a good performance which pleased the crowd, the defence looked solid and Luther did well against a tough defence in a role that was alien to him. It put us back on course in the European Championships and gave us a breathing space for that was the last of the qualifying games that season with the home internationals to come against the Irish in Belfast and the Scots at Wembley. There was also what I saw as a morale-building tour at the end of it which would give me time to spend with my players and a chance to talk and work at various aspects both before and, more importantly, after games. I was deluding myself.

The game at Windsor Park gave me my first opportunity to play Glenn Hoddle in a full game, a player I had originally planned to build my side around only to be foiled by injury. I also called up his White Hart Lane club-mate, the resilent Graham Roberts for his début, while my search for a winger took me to Vicarage Road and a brilliant young West-Indian-born player named John Barnes whom I brought on as a sixty-ninth minute substitute. He might have won the game for us but for the usual calm assurance of the evergreen Pat Jennings who was winning his ninety-eighth cap. Although we had a difficult first half, with Peter Shilton saving Graham Roberts the embarrassment of putting through his own goal on his début, I was satisfied with the overall performance and especially with the development of Gordon Cowans. It looked as though we had discovered a rich vein in this quiet, purposeful, Aston Villa player.

Cowans convinced me even further that we had found a very talented midfield player when he scored one of the goals in a 2-0 win over the Scots to clinch my first Home International Championship. It was a memorable day for I remember looking around Wembley at the big crowd of 84,000 and thinking how important it still is to beat the 'auld enemy'. No matter how the game changes it really is, and always will be, a very special match. I had felt it as a player and now in a different way as a manager but the depth of feeling goes on and on. You can feel the tingle in the air even in the preparation for the match and when the game comes around the electric and intimidating atmosphere builds to a climax. Having said that, the Scots were a disappointment on the night with Bryan Robson hitting them with an early goal and, though he left the pitch soon afterwards with a groin strain, he had done his job and when Cowans scored the second we could have gone on and had four or five with any sort of luck. Both Francis and Lee had 'goals' disallowed for offside.

Graham Roberts showed the physical side of his nature when he came out of the pack early on to rattle Charlie Nicholas with a bone-jarring tackle. We did not see a lot of the talented young Scot after that for his mind seemed to be more on his preference for his pending transfer to Liverpool or Arsenal than on the game. One of the key areas for us was in the midfield where Cowans matched Gordon Strachan, one of the best of the Scots on the night, and showed that he had really earned his place in the side. He had been brought in because we did not have a suitable wide player and had matured very quickly to the demands of this higher grade of football. I was delighted with the performance and felt a sense of achievement.

It would have been an ideal platform on which to build with a close season tour but that, meantime, had turned into a disaster. Originally it had been planned to go away on a tough trip to South America and send a 'B' team to Australia for a series of three tests. As a newcomer I had inherited the situation and I was appalled when I realised that this was the one year out of four, following the World Cup, when the clubs had first call on the international players for their own summer tours. It quickly became obvious that we were going to struggle to find one squad, never mind two, and there was no question of undertaking games against the likes of Brazil and Uruguay with a severely understrength side and, in any case, we were already committed to Australia.

I had to make all the right noises about looking at fringe players and all the rest of it but, in truth, neither I nor England gained anything from this long, tiring trip where we were always on a hiding to nothing against a team desperate to prove themselves worthy of full status. Their manager, Frank Arok, was looking for a place in history by beating us and the Aussies went into the three games as though they were life-and-death World Cup Finals. But however you looked at it, this was not first-class football and after a long, hard season I had trouble building up enthusiasm and motivation in the team. What did please me was the dedication and commitment of the senior players, particularly those like Peter Shilton, Phil Neal, Terry Butcher and Trevor Francis who had played non-stop football for more than a year because of their involvement in the World Cup. There was a great deal of loyalty shown, too, with Neal and Sammy Lee coming on to join us from a club tour of Hong Kong and Bangkok while the Watford pair, the ever-willing Luther Blissett and John Barnes, came Down Under direct from a club tour of China!

Perhaps, from there, grew the seeds that were to develop during later England close season tours, but from short range all I could see were the bad points. Ideally, it was an opportunity to show the people of Australia a better brand of football and, for that reason, I picked attractive, attacking teams placing the emphasis on trying to entertain. That chance was completely missed for Arok and his Australians were intent solely on gaining results and they played hard, defensive football that was scarcely appealing to the fans and miserable for my players to take part in.

Soccer in Australia is always battling for a place in their sporting hierarchy, competing against Australian Rules, Rugby Union and Rugby League and, had Arok and I been able to discuss the situation, we could have shown off the game in its best possible light. As it was they defended, hit long balls and chased after them while we were simply neither good, relaxed nor motivated enough to knock it over them and exploit their weakness. Paul Walsh and Trevor Francis were our only scorers as we emerged with battered bodies and bruised pride from three games that ended 0–0, 1–0 and 1–1. In all we gave seven new caps to Mark Barham, Steve Williams, Danny Thomas, John Gregory, Paul Walsh, Nick Pickering and Nigel Spink with only John Gregory of them surviving to play in our opening game of the next season, a crucial match against Denmark at Wembley. The trip to Australia was of limited value and, on reflection, scant preparation for the European Championships.

3. Hard Times

Whatever I may or may not achieve in my football career, the blackest day will remain as 21 September 1983. It was the worst moment I had experienced at any level of football, no question about it. Before that I had considered myself fortunate in life and, in particular in football, with most matters going my way. I had never played in a Cup Final but I had managed a winning team in one and generally as a player and a manager I had had nothing to grumble about ... until that wet September night at Wembley. The 1–0 defeat was only part of it. The way the team played; the walk back to the dressing room afterwards; the abuse of the crowd; the feeling of total confusion all contributed to the desolate feelings. It was all such a blow to the country, our status in the world of football, my own credibility as a manager and the subsequent effect on my personal life. All I wanted to do was to go home to Ipswich but I had to face that gloomy dressing room and then the after-match Press conference with another the next morning in the Wembley Hotel. There was no sleep to speak of, just fitful dozing as the prospect of the next morning's headlines and comments kept running through my mind. It was all such a new experience, nothing that had gone before had prepared me for this moment and I was full of self pity, all I wanted to do was to turn the clock back 24 hours.

I looked at myself in the shaving mirror in the hotel bedroom next morning, feeling half numb and only semi-conscious. Perhaps, I thought, I live it too much, maybe I am too passionate about it. After all it is only football even if it was a result that almost certainly ended England's interest in a European Championship I had honestly thought that we could win. But there was no easy way out. The team I had selected did not play and I had to shoulder the responsibility for a result which affected every person who was interested in football in England. It was certainly never a case of underestimating the Danes, perhaps more the other way. I had watched them play and liked what I saw. They had a number of talented individuals who had the right experience through playing in the top Leagues in Europe. They were a formidable team as they had proved in the first leg in Copenhagen a year earlier when it was only thanks to two men, Peter Shilton and Trevor Francis, that we had held them to a fortunate 2–2 draw. They had had far too much of the ball which we could not get from them and my own feelings had been backed up by the experienced Don Howe who maintained that they were better than three-quarters of the sides who had competed in the World Cup Finals in Spain a few months earlier.

Where I had made my mistake was in exaggerating their ability in my own mind and then in putting it across to the England players. I felt that we would be in all sorts of danger if I did not outline the threat of certain of their players and emphasise what a difficult match it was going to be for us. I had hoped it would serve to increase the determination but, in the end, it seemed that all I did was put fear and doubts in the minds of my own players and they thought that I believed that we were not good enough to beat Denmark. I put the Danes on a pedestal and, in so doing, knocked our own confidence so that we failed to show our innate qualities on the night. We did not challenge or get among them. We did not work as a unit and were too easily separated. We neither disturbed nor frightened them. We were uncertain and for an England team playing at Wembley that was a ridiculous situation. Maybe it would have been slightly easier to accept had the Danes been truly outstanding but they came to the game as frightened as we were and we needed to play only reasonably well to have won by one or maybe two goals. As it was we lost to a single goal and that a disputed penalty when the ball bounced up and hit Phil Neal on the hand.

I am certain that it was our mental approach to the game that was wrong and not the team selection but even over that I took a considerable amount of criticism and suddenly earned the reputation of being indecisive. That rankled. For 14 years I had pitted my wits against the big names and the big clubs, making major decisions day after day. On this occasion it was one of the few times in my managerial career when I wanted to know my opponents before naming my own side. In the event Danish manager Sepp Piontek was hailed as a genius and I was held up for ridicule. I just wanted to be sure. I had already picked my team in my own mind but I did not want to give him a psychological advantage by making mine public first. I waited and waited until the whole thing became a complete nightmare. It was lunchtime on the day of the game that I announced my 11 players. My main doubts centred on our midfield where, for the tenth time in 14 games since I had taken over, we were without our influential skipper Bryan Robson. I picked Sammy Lee, John Gregory and Ray Wilkins, uncertain whether or not to play my 'bionic' man Mabbutt. I was also worried about Phil Neal and whether little Olsen would turn him over as he had done before. I told Phil that his sharpness would get him out of trouble and, that

21

unlucky penalty apart, he let no one down. I needed not have worried about him, but I did. I worried about everyone for that game.

As I walked out of the bitter after-match Press conference I bumped into one of their players, Soren Lerby, who was on his way to celebrate at the bar. I knew this big talented Dane quite well, having sat with him on a flight to Holland after watching Denmark and France in Copenhagen. He turned to me and said: 'You will be very disappointed at that result, I am sure. We are all amazed at winning at Wembley for when we came here we were afraid of England but on the pitch it was the other way around. Your team did not play tonight, they did not come at us all in the first half and when we went into our dressing room at half-time we felt sure that we could win the match.' I thought then just how much we had missed those special talents of Bryan Robson that night. He would surely have led the charge and been an example to the rest of the team. In circumstances like those it needs someone to set the others off, to light the blue touchpaper and of all the times he has been absent from my sides that was the occasion we missed him most of all.

I had Glenn Hoddle on the bench but, on the night, he was not what I needed. I wanted someone a bit spikey. It was a job I thought John Gregory could do for me. He had shown in those tough battles in Australia that he could put his foot in and that he was good in the air. I liked him and his attitude and had picked him specifically to replace Robson. What I had not counted on was his inexperience at this level. He played too deep and pushed in on Ray Wilkins, forcing him too far back and as Sammy Lee wasn't having his best game, our midfield failed to take control. There was no one willing to shoulder the responsibility and they were split into little units with no semblance of team play. At half-time we were losing by the Allan Simonsen penalty but in no way was the game beyond us even though they were the better side at that stage. I told the players not to let their opponents dominate them with possession. There was not a sound. Everyone clammed up. I told them to go out, fight and enjoy it but clearly, by then, the damage had been done.

I learned a great many lessons from this match, not just on the night but over the course of the build-up too. Most of all, it proved to me never to overestimate the opposition, to treat them with respect by all means but it taught me never again to overstate the case no matter how important the game. It also became clear that whatever you learned about the opposition and its individuals only certain aspects should be passed on to your own players. The information should be selective, positive and not confusing. The best that can be said of it was that it was an enlightening match for some of the players and for me. The whole unhappy episode could have also been destructive but I can honestly state that, as rough as I felt, I never at any stage thought about quitting, only that I would not allow it to happen like that again.

In the old days such games remained just a bitter memory but with modern technology it is permanently recorded on video tape, indelibly printed as it is on my mind. But you can turn adversity to your own benefit and that is what we tried to do. Our physiotherapist, Fred Street, is something of an electronics expert and he edited some of the 'low lights' together to produce a real Hammer Horror of a movie to show our players where we went wrong. It was ghastly as we stopped the film to emphasise the errors and we all cringed at one incident that showed two Danish players on the edge of our penalty surrounded by seven English defenders. The ball was 40 yards away. There was no place for the players to hide as we watched the video. It demonstrated to them that without the ball you cannot play. In tennis if you do not hit the ball over the net you lose the point. In football if you do not win the ball you get nothing. That is what we deserved that night against the Danes.

As a club manager a defeat like that would have left me brooding for 24 hours, put me off Sunday lunch and made me feel generally grumpy. By Monday morning it would have been out of my system and I would have been ready to prepare my players for the next game. This time it was vastly different and it took seven days or more for me to recover from the depression as I tried to take stock. I could not even hide myself away the next day for, after reading the papers and attending the Press conference, I was due back at Lancaster Gate to discuss the Centres of Excellence for children at a meeting with top executives from the Football Association, the Football League and the English Schools' Football Association. It was difficult putting on a brave face in front of bosses and critics alike but it had to be done for I was desperately keen to organise this scheme for youngsters from the age of 11 upwards. I have always felt that 14 is too late for a lot of kids to be taught the skills of the game. After all, if you want your child to learn to play the piano or the violin you don't wait until his teens to send him off for tuition, so why should football be any different?

I had been hoping for a good win at Wembley the night before as a psychological boost and to get the people who mattered to back me. I felt miserable and instead of concentrating on my arguments for the kids I still had the match spinning around in my mind. Fortunately, everyone at that meeting was sympathetic and shared my feelings that it had been a bad night for British football generally. I survived mentally and physically and came out of Lancaster Gate heading in the right direction. But I made up my mind then and there that, in future, that was last meeting I would attend the day after an international football match. I would be better off walking my dog and leaving the phone off the hook.

My first public appearance after the defeat was on the following Saturday when I went to Birmingham to watch Southampton play Aston Villa. The Villa Chairman Doug Ellis was very kind but as I took my seat in the Director's Box the electronic scoreboard at the Holte End of the ground announced: 'One of today's guests, England manager Bobby Robson'. Predictably it was greeted with a storm of boos. I was learning that in international football there were no greys, only black and white. Win and you are everyone's friend. Lose and God help you.

To have any hopes of appearing in the European Championships proper in France we not only had to defeat Hungary away from home but hope that they could also beat the Danes. On form that was impossible but then that is what makes soccer the great game it is. Our game came first and, just as we had done under Ron Greenwood in the World Cup, we beat the Hungarians in their own Nep Stadium on 12 October 1983. The midfield was strengthened by the return of Bryan Robson which allowed me to use Glenn Hoddle without any defensive responsibilities so that he could concentrate on his fluent passing. I wanted him to find positions to receive the ball rather than to chase after it. Lee, Mabbutt and Robson were our 'search and seek' team and I was able to tell Glenn to conserve his energy and think about their half only.

We were helped enormously by having the Saturday before the game to prepare without the intrusion of club matches. We had longer to talk and to practise together and as a result we went into the game feeling quietly confident. Glenn scored a great early goal to settle us down and what made it even more satisfying was that it came from a set piece that we were able to work on because of the extra time available! Sammy Lee scored a second from 20 yards and Glenn made a third for Paul Mariner. It put us back in contention even though the Danes had put six past Luxembourg on the same day. It hardly seemed likely that, after their poor performance against us, the Hungarians could upset the Danes but they did, by a single goal, in a game I watched from the warmth of the television studios on 26 October.

It left the situation delicately poised but with Denmark still in the driving seat. Deep down I could not see them losing in Greece and had we been in the same position I would have fancied our chances. However, as we arrived at Luxembourg's tiny stadium some wally of a fan shouted out to us that Greece were ahead. We all rushed to the dressing room where we had a radio link-up only to discover that the Danes were ahead and, indeed, went on to win 2–0 to leave them with an unassailable lead.

Although it had been expected it was still a huge disappointment and it was difficult giving touchline interviews before a game which was now meaningless. What we could not afford was a defeat for that would have only compounded our failure to earn a place in France. For a while the heads were down but Bryan Robson showed his captain's qualities by helping me to stir them up and by the time they ran out they were in a determined mood. We ran in four goals with Bryan Robson scoring twice, and Terry Butcher and Paul Mariner adding the others. It could have been seven or eight and even Brian Clough was moved to admit, in his capacity as television commentator, that someone had done a good job in lifting the players. The enthusiasm was heartening as was the World Cup draw, which was just around the corner.

The draw in Zurich on 7 December came at a critical time for English football, injecting new interest after our exit from Europe and giving the players and myself something to look forward to and plan for. As I sat in the conference room of the Zurich Hotel, I kept my fingers crossed for more than one reason. I was hoping for a place in a five-strong group where two teams would qualify automatically and where we would avoid neighbouring European countries which our supporters could easily travel to. That may sound a little cruel but we had left the beautiful Duchy of Luxembourg in deep shame because our rogues had terrorised the local inhabitants, thieved from the shopkeepers and behaved appallingly. They had disgusted us all by giving those lovely people a bad time for our second successive visit. Bert Millichip was rightly concerned because there was a growing lobby of countries who simply did not want us and there was a genuine worry that we would be tossed out on our ears.

It helped when we were nominated as one of the seeded countries, much to the annoyance of the Scots but I was hardly likely to refuse it, and then we were given what almost amounted to the perfect draw. We had the five-team group we wanted and each away game had its own specific hooligan deterrent. I could not see many of our lunatic fringe causing mayhem behind the Iron Curtain in Romania and anyone who had seen the film *Midnight Express* would have shuddered at the prospect of even a few hours in a Turkish gaol. Finland is an expensive country and a long way to travel to while Northern Ireland deals with far worse problems than violent soccer fans every day. My immediate thought was that it meant I would be able to concentrate solely on qualifying with time to reflect on and plan a campaign to see us safely through to the Finals.

It also meant that we went into 1984 in a fairly optimistic frame of mind. The disappointment of Denmark had receded a little with two successive away victories and the likelihood of the fans marring our World Cup campaign was small. Most importantly, we had a good programme ahead on which to sharpen our teeth with Europe's top team, France, to play in their own Parc des Princes Stadium on the outskirts of Paris; the Home Championships to defend; a home game against the dramatically improved Russians; and a very testing trip to South America to play Brazil, Uruguay and Chile.

France had been the darlings of the 1982 World Cup and were everyone's favourites to win the European crown in front of their own fans that summer, which was something they went on to do in great style. I decided that the game on 29 February gave me an ideal opportunity to experiment and, though Tony Woodcock and Paul Mariner were both fit and available for selection, I decided to try the talented Luton Town pair, South-African-born Brian Stein and his fellow striker Paul Walsh. I could have mixed them up and played Stein with Woodcock or Walsh with Mariner but I thought at the time that it would give them a better chance to express themselves if they knew their partners. I still believe in that concept but one of the lessons I learned from the game was that against really top opposition you cannot afford too many try-outs. Apart from the two young strikers, I also tried Steve Williams on his 'wrong' side, played Glenn Hoddle in the hole behind Stein and Walsh, gave Manchester United full-back Mick Duxbury his second cap and Spurs' defender Graham Roberts his third. There is a need to experiment in this type of non-competitive match, particularly now that the European qualifying competition takes two years and the World Cup the following two, but you can be penalised if you overdo it against a top side. We were.

At half-time it looked quite good. The game was still goalless and, though France had missed a couple of Platini-created chances, we were never under siege and Peter Shilton was no harder worked than Joel Bats at the other end who must have breathed a sigh of relief when Stein missed a good opportunity. I told Brian to forget it at half-time, that the worst part of his début was now over and that everything would begin to improve. The French midfield was as good as ever but they did not impress me up front and I thought that the first team to score would win the game. Unfortunately, it was Platini who scored it, eluding Mick Duxbury who was pulled out of position and could only watch as the ball passed over his head to leave the Juventus star with a free header. It was to be the start of an unfortunate period for Mick Duxbury, a talented player and everyone's choice to take over from Phil Neal, for every mistake he made in the next four matches was punished with a goal and it began to eat away at his confidence.

Any chance we had of getting back into the game was wrecked when we conceded a bizarre second goal. A misunderstanding between Shilton and Roberts left Shilton stranded a yard outside his goal and, instead of hacking the ball clear with his feet, he inexplicably handled to concede a free kick in the most dangerous of positions. Shilton was well aware of Platini's ability in this particular role and that he had left himself two alternatives. Shilton tried to cover both options and found himself caught half and half. He did not trust his wall and, as a consequence, left his near post exposed. Platini ran up to curl the ball over the top of the wall, the very ploy Shilton was most concerned about and as the English goalkeeper adjusted a yard the Frenchman spotted the movement, saw the gap and changed his mind in his last two strides. Platini was probably only one of two or three players in the world who could have done that to a goalkeeper as talented as Shilton.

However, that was not where or why we lost it. We were overpowered by the midfield of Platini, Giresse, Tigana and Fernandez. On the night they were absolutely superb and we never manged to get Glenn Hoddle going under the same terms as Platini who showed the Spurs player exactly the sort of role he could play for England over the next two years. But it was of little solace to me for, apart from a defeat, our so-called supporters had run riot again. It was so bad that our Chairman Bert Millichip told me afterwards that he had been able to watch only half of the game. I do not know what they were trying to do for they had certainly not helped the team in any way. They were unsettling and succeeded only in distracting and detracting. English boxing fans had disgraced themselves a few days earlier at a Tony Sibson fight and our reputation could not have been lower.

It was all very depressing allied, as it was, to our defeat. I knew we had lost to a very good side but that was of little comfort as I sat alone in my room in Paris to think it out. I felt that I was not much further on with my thoughts on our best players or our best formation than I was when I had started 16 games and one and a half years earlier. The problem was that I was still thinking as a Football League manager when that number of games would have taken you only to October in your first season, leaving time to sort it out and shape the side according to the talents of the players available. Suddenly, from thinking that I had a lot going for me, I was becoming unusually pessimistic. What I found upsetting were the inconsistencies of the job, not only players' form but also their availability, which was always such a lottery. I not only wanted to know where the team was going but where I was heading as well. It was a distressing night, an awful hotel and I did not sleep much. It bothered me that we had not been good enough to get back into the game after going a goal down and, at the end of

90 minutes, we were definitely two goals inferior. I was scratching my head about the qualities of my players and wondering about the next two years leading to the World Cup.

In retrospect, of course, I was being hyper-critical. After all we had lost to one of the world's best sides on their own ground while I was still in the process of learning my job and building a new team. I had been fairly satisfied at half-time so all this anguish was based on 45 minutes of football with a relatively inexperienced team. Instead of lying in the dark magnifying the problems, I would have been better employed going to the Left Bank and having a glass or two of Muscadet.

There was a slight improvement when we beat Northern Ireland in April 1984 by a Tony Woodcock goal. To my mind it was not a bad match but there was a little atmosphere, showing one of the reasons why the Home International Championship was being abandoned after 102 years. Naturally, the Welsh and the Irish were bitter about it for the revenue from this competition was important to their day-to-day running but, in truth, these games provided little unless they were part of the European Championships or the World Cup. We had outgrown them and I felt that foreign opposition would be more beneficial to us and to the Welsh and Irish as well because both have the talent to attract top teams to play in their countries and to bring in the crowds.

Needless to say Northern Ireland were a determined side and gave us a tough game with Ian Stewart doing well on the wing and providing chances that could have been turned into goals. We won but then we were expected to yet, to my mind, the Irish are one of the most difficult sides to beat because they have a settled style and a continuity of players. They showed the value of this in the 1982 World Cup Finals in Spain and many times before and since. Had that victory for us come in the middle of a successful run it would have eminently acceptable. It would certainly have been had we followed it up with a win against Wales in Wrexham a month later. Instead the match was a disaster and the knives were out with a vengeance. A series of injuries right up to the day of the game severely hit our squad and once more I was forced to take the field with a very inexperienced side. It would have been all right under certain circumstances for, with all due respect, Wales are not France but what we were lacking were our motivators. There was no Robson, Mariner, Butcher or Sansom, players who play a big part off the field in creating the right atmosphere. Winning an international football match is not only about the 90 minutes on the pitch but the build-up to it as well. What happens in the team hotel, at mealtimes, on the training ground, in the leisure moments and the dressing room. There is not a manager in the country who isn't looking for that sort

28

of player, the type that Howard Kendall found at Everton in Andy Gray and Peter Reid.

With England it used to be Trevor Brooking and Kevin Keegan, Brooking with his infectious laugh and Keegan the little hurricane who was always up to something and keeping everyone on their toes. The team that played against Wales did not have it that day. They were quiet in the hotel before we left, their heads were down as we walked into the ground and we never got going on the pitch. They played badly and hardly created a chance all night with Paul Walsh and Tony Woodcock looking a lightweight pairing. It was a pity, for Walsh had looked the better bet in Paris and had warranted another opportunity in a different environment. John Gregory, normally a talker, was too new to the scene to make his personality felt while Ray Wilkins looked as though he was missing his mate Bryan Robson. We performed like a team going nowhere fast and we were beaten by a couple of Manchester United reserves, Cup Final hero Alan Davies and a certain Mark Hughes who, that night, showed his qualities and a taste of what other teams were to suffer with a very well-taken goal.

The frustrations were enormous with selection the biggest nightmare as I struggled match after match to find the players I wanted. Only Ron Greenwood, Don Revie, Sir Alf Ramsey and those who have actually experienced the job can appreciate the difficulties of picking the team you really want. There is simply nothing in club management to prepare you for the job. At Ipswich I had almost 14 years of continuity because I managed to keep good players on long term contracts until I was surrounded by ten-year testimonial players. These are players you can educate in your own style and beliefs. When we lost five on the trot John Cobbold, the Chairman, came into my office, asked if I was worried and promptly added three years to my contract. I knew none of this was possible with England but what I did want was a bit of decent luck with injuries and some help in making players more available. Try this one, try that one and you finish up with a team of strangers and no time to work on them. At least I had the security of a five-year contract and there was no way I was going to duck out of that unless my employers decided differently. I was going to stick at it, put on a brave face and be cheerful. I walked into Thursday's Press conference, smiled and said that things could be worse. Sure enough they did get worse!

I became aware of a concerted campaign against me only when friends telephoned to tell me not to worry, to keep my chin up and that they backed me. I knew I had taken some criticism from certain sections of the media and with some justification. What I did not realise was that one of the popular daily papers had gone a step further and were actually offering lapel badges saying things like 'Robson out' and 'Clough in'. I am not a regular reader of the paper in question and it was not until former Scotland and Arsenal goalkeeper Bob Wilson telephoned to say he was horrified that I had found out what was going on. Bob told me that he was on my side, that he understood my problems and he urged me to stick at it. He went on to add that he was going to refer to the attack on his *Grandstand* spot, calling it the lowest of the low. It seemed to me to be dreadful persecution for something that was not entirely in my hands. It was all so damning and scurrilous. It was as if I had committed treason against my country and it even affected my family, particularly my boys Mark and Paul who had to suffer people saying to them: 'Why doesn't your Dad pack it in – he is no good.' My wife Elsie did her best to hide this sort of thing from me and we tried not to discuss it at home at all.

The strange thing was that, in retrospect, it probably helped. It certainly strengthened my resolve and the paper's tactics were so base that many were appalled and stood up for me. Managers telephoned to say that I was not to let it affect me and I found out who my friends in the game were. Happily, there were a lot of them and they all rallied around to offer their support. Even the attacking paper's chief soccer correspondent, Alex Montgomery, was embarrassed.

It was at this low point in my career that I was again approached by the Spanish giants of Barcelona. Twice before during my managerial career with Ipswich I had been tempted by offers from them though not quite so much on the first occasion in the late 1970s as when they came back again at the beginning of the 1981–82 season. Now they were proposing an easy exit from the inherent pressures of the England job with huge financial inducements but they had completely misread the situation.

Perhaps I should explain that Ipswich had twice been drawn against Barcelona in Europe and not only had we played well against them on each occasion but I had also come into close contact with their directors. This was because our Chairman, John Cobbold, would invite the opposition board to join their Ipswich counterparts for dinner on either the Monday or the Tuesday evening before the match and he always liked to have his manager there in attendance in case anyone was silly enough to talk about football instead of the quality of the wine. As it happened a senior Barcelona director, Señor Juan Gaspar, spoke good English and we came to know one another well.

While I was at Ipswich enormous sums of money were offered and particularly on the second approach. I was quite attracted by the challenge and the money, which, translated into sterling, read more like a telephone number with a three-year contract starting at £80,000 a year with minimum guaranteed bonuses of £35,000. On top of that were appealing tax concessions, a house and a car of my choice. John Cobbold gave me permission to talk to Barcelona and when I expressed some interest, John told them he would require compensatory payments of £200,000 to buy the remaining three years of my contract. Barcelona dug their heels in and refused to pay up but had they done so I would almost certainly have gone. However, I felt no bitterness even though I thought Ipswich had gone over the top. It would have made me financially stable, but at least it caused no major upheaval at home even though Elsie, as usual, had left it up to me. Although I would have enjoyed the testing nature of the job, it concerned me that I could not speak Spanish. Football may be a universal language but I thought it important to be able to converse with players and this was one of the reasons why I was able to put the big bid behind me and settle back into the job at hand. It was no great hardship. I put a high price on loyalty from players so why should I be any different? I could have resigned and taken the Barcelona job a month later but that was not my style.

I was proved right for the next season was one of my best and happiest in League football when our little, unfashionable club almost achieved the hat-trick. We were in the running right until the end of the season as we finished runners-up in the First Division, won the UEFA Cup and reached the semi-finals in the FA Cup. It did my reputation no harm at all and must have contributed towards me being offered the England job.

It was after I had been England manager for almost two years that Señor Gaspar was back again. After our desperate defeat by Wales in May 1984, I received a call at my Ipswich home telling me that Barcelona wanted to replace Cesar Menotti, who had led Argentina to the World Cup in 1978, and that I was the man that Gaspar and his President, Señor Nunez, wanted. This time they were determined to appoint an Englishman to run the club with a proper scouting set-up, youth scheme and all the ingredients that go to make a successful British club. Gaspar had done his homework well for he told me it would be a job without the problems associated with the England management and that he knew of the difficulties I had in obtaining the release of players and that I was expected to win every match we played. He went on to say: 'If you compare what you have now with what you lost when you left Ipswich you must consider it.'

Despite the badge campaign and the growing hostility from the media, I instantly told him that I had a five-year contract with three years still remaining and that I had no intention of quitting. I was not going to run away nor was I going to resign and the only way I would consider accepting Barcelona's offer was if I were sacked by the Football Association. Señor

Gaspar was not easily put off and responded by saying that the money would be even better than before and that they badly needed me. If I gave the nod the job was mine.

Gaspar telephoned me the first time on Thursday 10 May at the Football Association! He made his offer the next day in half an hour's conversation and was backed up on the following two days by a well-known First Division Chairman. The latter rang three times in 24 hours and told me that I could have a three- or four-year contract at thrice my FA salary, which would be tax reduced and paid into a Swiss bank account. I replied that there was nothing to consider and that my mind was made up. I was England manager and that was what I intended to remain. There was no way I was going to desert my country and when Gaspar came back to me on Sunday night he received exactly the same answer. 'If you offered me a million pounds I am afraid I would have to say no,' I told him.

The great irony was that Don Revie had left the England management under very similar circumstances, accepting his new position immediately before a tour to South America. The coincidence was not lost on me or on Señor Gaspar. He finally accepted I was not to be bought and, instead, began to ask me about managers like Ron Atkinson, David Pleat and Lawrie McMenemy, whether I rated them and was there any other Englishman I could recommend if I were sure I would not go myself? Obviously, it depended on what sort of manager they wanted.

The answer left me in little doubt that Barcelona wanted someone like Terry Venables of Queen's Park Rangers or my own assistant Don Howe and I told him so. I also added that this type of manager was recognised in England as well as Spain and that both were under contract and that any approach would have to be made through the proper channels. Gaspar knew all about Don Howe but was uncertain about the qualities of Terry Venables. I explained what he had done with Crystal Palace and Queen's Park Rangers and that, though he was young, he was a manager with great knowledge of the game and someone who was definitely on the way up. I felt certain he was a man who would be able to cope with the responsibilities. I left it at that.

With so much on my plate, I quickly forgot the conversation but was soon reminded of it when I read in the popular newspapers that Terry Venables was the surprise favourite for the Barcelona job and that he had already been seen in the city. I was busy preparing for the coming game against Scotland and, indeed, was about to leave the team hotel for a training session when I was told that there was an international call for me. It was my old friend Gaspar again to say that Barcelona had talked to Terry and were very impressed by what they had seen and heard. But was I sure he was right for them? I repeated that though he lacked a little First Division experience as a manager, having served only one year with QPR, he was intelligent, a good coach and had an infectious enthusiasm for the game.

The problem was that the local Barcelona Press had described Venables as an unknown and were casting doubts on the advisability of the appointment. Barcelona wanted my confirmation that they were not making a mistake, which I gave. Although Terry and I had never discussed it, Terry had clearly been preparing himself for the day because he had been taking a home correspondence course in Spanish for two years. I did not want his thanks for recommending him for he did that in the best way possible by winning for Barcelona the Spanish First Division title in his very first season there. Terry Venables was one of a new breed of young English managers who had impressed me immensely and I have no doubt that at some point in the future he will be a serious contender for my position as manager of the England team. The future looks quite promising for Terry is not going to have it all his own way with others like Graham Taylor of Watford and the former Notts County coach, Howard Wilkinson, coming through to compete with him.

However, to go back to England, something had to be done. I started by writing down all of the players I had used over the last year, crossing out those who were unfit, not on form and unavailable. I then went for players on known good form and telephoned managers to ask about the form of others. One, who will remain nameless, responded by telling me that he could not recommend any of his players because none of them was playing up to standard. Against Wales we had adopted the usual 4–4–2 formation and had hardly had a shot at goal and it was at that moment I made a surprising decision in modern terms by electing to turn the clock back and play with two genuine wingers. I wanted some imagination, I wanted England to attack, be exciting and to brighten things up generally, and to get rid of some of that gloom and despondency which surrounded all of us. To achieve this, I not only needed to find two good wingers but also to dig out two midfield players who could support the huge workload it would demand. I soon whittled it down to the names of Bryan Robson and Ray Wilkins and based my plans around them not only for the coming game against Scotland but also against the Soviet Union and the trip to South America.

The next question to answer was who to play on the flanks. Was it time to give John Barnes his head? He had been on the fringe of the team for a few games and I decided to keep him in the side for a run to see how he reacted. On the right there was Stoke City's Mark Chamberlain. He was a good crosser of the ball and was blessed with terrific pace. The die was cast, I was ready to give it a go by attacking the Scots on their own ground. All I had to do now was to keep my fingers crossed that the four players so critical to my plans would turn up fit on the day.

That should have been less of a worry than it was. The season was over but still I found obstacles being thrown in my path. Of all teams, Manchester United made an end-of-season trip to Hong Kong and insisted on taking both my key midfield players with them. While I was basing the future of the squad on Robson and Wilkins, they were risking their fitness by playing against Bulova Watches! They flew out on the Friday, played and returned the following Tuesday after a 22-hour flight with eight hours of jet-lag to recover from. It was the old club-versus-country controversy again but I could appreciate the difficulties Ron Atkinson faced with business contracts and guarantees signed. It was not his problem that his players were the only pair in the country I felt I could rely on at the time to do this job and cope with the extra running the system demanded. Until the whole England set-up is reshaped, these are the sort of troubles which will haunt every manager. Robson and Wilkins trained on Friday and I told them we would return to our old style if they felt they were not up to the task. Much to their credit they did not choose the easy option and fully backed me. I uncrossed my fingers.

The pair played well and I was heartened by a much improved performance all round. We played open, attractive football and came back from an early goal, when the unfortunate Duxbury let in McGhee for a header, to share a 1–1 draw. Tony Woodcock scored one of his best ever international goals. Mark Chamberlain chased to keep the ball in play and knocked it into space for Woody to run on to, turn Miller and take the shortest route for goal. As a second defender approached, Woodcock let go from 22 yards with the left-foot shot flying into the top corner. It was an uplifting goal and when Woodcock limped off it gave me the chance to blood Gary Lineker. Barnes particularly pleased me and looked a good bet for the future. Even though we still needed some fine saves from our world-class goalkeeper Peter Shilton to keep us in the match, the tactics had worked well enough for me to keep with it.

It was noted that there were 19 players unavailable for the Wembley game against the Russians on 2 June 1984. At least I had Trevor Francis back to replace the injured Woodcock and both Robson and Wilkins should have been that much fresher and fitter than they had been for the game against Scotland.

We did not play particularly well in the first half but we were not second best with both goalkeepers, Shilton and Dasayev, having an equal amount of work. Our passing was poor and you could sense the frustration building up among the 38,000 fans as our wingers failed to get going while Robson and Wilkins struggled to cover the wide open spaces of Wembley. What it needed was one of our back-four to come forward and help out and we talked about it during the interval. It could have gone either way but a freak error by Duxbury opened it up when he stood on the ball, fell over and set up substitute Gotsanov with a free run at our goal. It knocked the stuffing out of us, brought the crowd down on our backs and the new-found confidence seeped away. It was then that I decided to bring on Mark Hateley, a tall young striker who was playing with Portsmouth in the Second Division. He had done well in our Under 21 side and I told him to go out and take advantage of the crosses and bring a little physical presence to bear on the classy Dasayev.

Hateley did not have a lot of time and his entrance was somewhat overshadowed by a last-minute goal from another Russian substitute, Protasov. Hateley pushed up the sweeper and let the goalkeeper know he couldn't catch the ball without a challenge. He even lifted the crowd but that late goal killed them off, along with us and, in particular, me. It was the last straw and as I walked from my seat on the halfway line to the dressing room I was spat at, had beer thrown over me, and heard the growing chant 'Robson Out', 'Robson Out'. It's funny the things that go through your mind at a time like that but I remember thinking that I hoped my 81-year-old father Philip had left his seat in the stand before he heard it. He, as usual, had travelled down from the north east on the morning of the match, and I knew he would be upset enough at the result without hearing the abuse being hurled at his son.

There is no hiding place for a manager at a time like that. I cleaned myself up the best I could to face the television cameras and Jimmy Hill. He put me through it, pointing out our bad results and the absent players and asking what the point was in going to South America with a team like that; weren't we going to get bombed by Brazil and Uruguay and wouldn't it be best to pull out of the trip altogether and save the humiliation? Jim, an old friend and Fulham team-mate, needled me and I fought back, responding with tart comments of my own and getting a few things off my chest. I had no idea how it had come over and at the end of it I felt physically drained. I went home to Ipswich for a brief reunion with Elsie before leaving for Brazil. She had not been at Wembley because she prefers to stay out of it, but she knew what had happened and had watched my trial by television. I knew at that moment that I had survived another crisis for she told me how proud she had been of my reactions, adding: 'The job must be hopeless for you'. Depressed, short of players and heading for one of the toughest possible tours I knew what she meant. But there was no possibility of me running away for if I had crumbled then who would have taken the responsibility? As long as the people who matter give you their support and their loyalty you have a chance. Those who are simply out to destroy do not matter. I knew I had to dig my heels in and play for time. The new season was two months away and by then the injured would be fit and the recent bad results would be history.

I had gone through the mill but remained determined and proud to be the manager of England. Things had gone wrong and the results I wanted hadn't come but I still knew that I had the most important football job in the country and I was more determined than ever to make a success of it. Football management will always be difficult whether you are at Crewe, Halifax, Liverpool or Manchester United. Each has its different type of pressures but at least with a club side they are parochial. Few people in Ipswich care if Liverpool lose 2–0 but if England lose then the post master in Torquay and the newspaper seller on the Tyne Bridge worry and talk about it. I know because a great many of them write to me. I was ready for the task ahead and I just hoped that, at the end of a long season, my players were as well. Those who had said count me in when we sorted out our badly depleted squad had given me considerable encouragement – but I couldn't help wondering if some of those who had pulled out were being completely honest with themselves and with me. I tried to put those unsavoury thoughts behind me. Brazil were going to need my full concentration.

4. South American Tour

However, it is hard to sit on an aeroplane for 7,000 miles without letting your mind wander. I was angry at the way things were going for us, we were losing players, we were being punished for every mistake and our luck was deserting us. My concern that one or two players might be trying to hide was offset by the reassuring sight of Bryan Robson and Ray Wilkins sitting side by side. Had we lost either of them or had they not fancied it then we would have been in trouble, or more specifically, I would have been in trouble. When you work for the Football Association you should have the best bosses in football and, to all intents and purposes, they are. They have to set the standards the rest of football must follow and though I had reassurances from Dick Wragg, the Chairman of the International Committee, I knew that that was no guarantee for my future. Sitting there I knew that if I acted timidly it would all fall apart and I would lose my job.

Jimmy Hill had asked me what the point was in going. Both he and I knew that if I hadn't gone I would have no longer been the manager of England and two years of my life would have been wasted. To be sacked after losing a few matches is an accepted part of football. All you can hope is that the people you work for understand and can cope with the pressures brought on them from outside. If they cannot then you have no sort of job anyway. I knew my capabilities but I did not know about the players'. Their confidence had taken a pounding from the growing army of critics and if their determination had been undermined then we would have been in for a hiding.

I was gambling with my future – and knew it! I looked round the aircraft at my young wingers, John Barnes of Watford and Mark Chamberlain of Stoke, and thought how much rested on their youthful shoulders. It had been after our dismal performance against the Welsh that I knew we must be more adventurous. Barnes had performed well against the Scots while Chamberlain had struggled to find his feet. Against the Russians it was Chamberlain who had played well and Barnes who had been disappointing. I needed them both on form at the same time.

I looked around a little more, this time noting the vacant seats, particularly those of my strikers. Trevor Francis and Luther Blissett were wanted by their clubs in Italy; Paul Mariner and Peter Withe were injured; Paul Walsh had talked himself out of contention; and though Tony Woodcock was with us, there was some doubt about his fitness and mental attitude. Problems had followed me right up to the departure, even to the extent of losing Gary Lineker and John Gregory in a testimonial match for Keith Burkinshaw at Tottenham. I ended up grabbing Clive Allen and Simon Stainrod off a plane as they were about to depart on a Queen's Park Rangers' tour of the Far East thinking that, at least, they would have an built-in understanding, not that it had helped overmuch with Walsh and Stein against France.

There was also a tall, striking young man named Mark Hateley. He looked so much like his footballing father that I often called him Tony by mistake. He had appeared only briefly against the Russians but I knew from his Under 21 exploits that he was an intimidating player, good in the air like his Dad, as well as being strong, confident and difficult to handle. He was the sort of striker who would relish playing with two wingers who would get their crosses to the far post. There was no talk of Italy then as Mark was a Second Division player with Portsmouth and I wondered if it would be fair to risk him in such a vital game, particularly if I had to play him alongside a half-fit Woodcock and in between two kids who might just freeze at the prospect of playing against Brazil in the imposing Maracana Stadium. They looked so young and vulnerable and here was I ready to ask them to do a job that Stanley Matthews, Tom Finney, Bryan Douglas, Bobby Charlton or Steve Coppell would have found daunting. I would not have been human if I had not contemplated ditching the whole shooting match then and there. The questions rolled in one after another. Was it too big a risk? Were they too young? Was it fair to ask so much of them? It was not as if either of them had gone through the pressures of playing for a big club week in and week out to harden them to the job. Maybe I should play with only one? Those who had accused me of being indecisive would have had a field day had they been able to read my mind then.

However, by the time we landed I had decided. I was going to persist with the gamble and to hell with everyone who said it was suicidal. I made the decision in the full knowledge that we could get a fearful roasting if it went wrong. But the last thing I could allow was to let the players, the Press or even my assistant, Don Howe, sense my doubts. As for the Brazilians, they simply did not believe that any international manager could be bold or mad enough to take on their heroes with only two in midfield. The legions of Brazilian journalists who met us at Rio's airport let me know what they thought. 'Four-two-four?' they echoed shaking their heads in disbelief, 'Impossible. Everyone plays four or at least three in midfield

against Brazil. We don't believe you. It is impossible. We will wait and see.'
Having arrived on Tuesday, we rested on Wednesday and set out for our
first training session on Thursday evening to avoid the heat of the sun. The
Brazilians had let us down. The training ground we had been designated
was miles away and we had to sit on the coach for more than half an hour
only to discover on arrival that the Brazilian Olympic squad were using the
ground and that we had to wait another half an hour before we could use
what turned out to be a very bad, bumpy pitch. There were no floodlights
and we trained in the dark, working up a sweat only to discover that there
were no shower facilities. There was no alternative other than to jump back
on the coach and head for our distant hotel. The journey out had been
pretty bad but going back was a nightmare for we hit Rio's chaotic,
sprawling rush-hour. We sat and steamed for more than an hour and a half
in the humid atmosphere which made the muscles so stiff that some players
got off and ran part of the way back.

For the evening I had planned a team meeting in which we would watch
video film of our game against the Russians as well as some clips of the
Brazilians. Wouldn't you believe it, the systems were incompatible with
the hotel's and no one could find us a replacement! Instead we had a
meeting, a very long meeting. I gave the senior players the chance to have
their say and the likes of Shilton, Robson and Wilkins took the opportunity. The youngsters looked a little overwhelmed at what was going on but it
served to show them what the stakes were on this three-match trip. The
theme revolved around the importance of the trip after our recent
miserable time, what it meant to the country and to them personally. At the
time the English cricket team were going through a bad period as well and
I asked them how they felt about that to remind them how the people back
home suffered when the football squad were doing badly. It was a rally-
round-the-flag meeting and I could feel the response. It was hammered
home that this was not a game for the timid but for collective spirit and
attitude. We talked about the way we were going to play and how to get the
best out of the system we were to use.

We put the theory into practice the next day when we demanded that our
training ground be switched to a nearby stadium. John Barnes and Mark
Chamberlain worked in tandem with the one without the ball covering
back to establish three men in midfield when we were not in possession. We
were asking two players who could hardly be described as grafters for their
clubs to take on an extra workload and play a role that was basically
foreign to both of them. We were asking two boys to become adults
overnight. I had impressed on the whole team that it was not just about the
two wingers or the two midfield players because if we did not keep a tight

unit, the Brazilians' natural artistry would destroy us. The frankness at the meeting, the pointed remarks and the effort put into that training session began to convince me that maybe we would pull off an upset after all and it was especially reassuring to hear not only Bryan Robson but others like Terry Fenwick shouting and directing, which was in contrast to the silence in training before the game against Wales.

Just when everything seemed to be going well, Spurs' rugged and versatile defender, Graham Roberts, complained of feeling unwell. He was already training on his own because of a slight twinge in his hamstring but then he told our physiotherapist Fred Street that he felt ill and promptly proved the point by being sick. We sent him back to our hotel in a taxi and when we returned I went to see him along with our team doctor Vernon Edwards. He was worse than we had thought and the Doc gave him a thorough going-over before coming out to tell me that he had diagnosed appendicitis. He was right and within an hour a specialist had confirmed his opinion and Graham was rushed to hospital for an emergency operation. The Doc had done a wonderfully accurate job but, having already left the likes of Terry Butcher, Alvin Martin and Mark Wright behind, I now found myself left with two internationally-untried centre-backs in Terry Fenwick and Dave Watson. Watson, in fact, was making his full début while Hateley was also to play his first full match. Our relative inexperience, our poor results of late and my gamble in taking on Brazil on their own ground with only two in midfield meant that the first 20 minutes were going to be absolutely crucial to us and, while our entire concept was built on attack from our two wingers, paradoxically it was essential that we defended and did not concede a goal that would destroy all we had prepared for. We needed a good, bold beginning, with every player trusting those around him and, above all, great application from all of them.

Playing on their own ground, it was clear that Brazil were going to have a great deal of early possession which meant that my attacking formation would have to muck in and help when they did not have the ball, give nothing away and eliminate those individual errors which had cost us so dearly in our previous games. The pressure on young Manchester United full-back Mick Duxbury must have been frightening after his recent run of five mistakes and five goals. He had been having a nightmare without really playing badly, so I took him to one side and told him that I was keeping him in the side despite the demands on me to give Gary Stevens of Spurs his right-back's shirt. I had a long chat, boosting this likeable and talented defender's confidence, telling him what better place and what greater day to rediscover himself than against Brazil in the Maracana. I

40

could not have asked more for Mick and the other full-back, Kenny Sansom, were superb as they cut out the threat of Brazil's two flying wingers and provided us with the basis on which to build our performance.

All the senior players played superbly and none better than the mighty Peter Shilton. He more than anyone, knew how vital it was to keep an early clean sheet while his team-mates felt their way and he pulled out all the stops with one spectacular save from Renato and another good one from Zenon. You could see our confidence begin to grow and the Brazilians start to flounder, thanks in no small part to the massive pre-publicity given to our plan to play with two wingers and two midfielders.

Although the South American media had ridiculed us for our temerity it had clearly unsettled their team and I am convinced that they were concerned about coping with our strategy. They withdrew one of their midfield players, Peres, whenever we were in possession, leaving themselves with two in midfield against our two, Bryan Robson and Ray Wilkins. That was a mistake on their part for there are not two midfield players in the world I would back in a straight contest with our pair and this was certainly true on the day for, even in those early exchanges, we were not at all embarrassed and had our share of the ball. Much of that was down to our two full-backs who shuffled the wingers from side to side, coping with whatever the home team could throw at them and taking the pressure off the defence as a unit. I was still blessing Shilton for those saves for anything could have happened had we gone a goal down. Perhaps neither England nor I would have been making plans for Mexico two years later. It was that much of a watershed.

The players were emerging from the ordeal of having been booed off their own pitch at Wembley just a week earlier and began to look like the side I knew them to be. Indeed, we could easily have taken the lead when a typical run from Bryan Robson left the Brazil defence totally at sea and his final chip saw big Mark Hateley power in a header that goalkeeper Roberto Casto did well to keep out. It all had its effect and with half an hour gone I began to feel that a result was really on. Pires was going further and further back and we were beginning to take the upper hand. Duxbury became more sure by the minute while new boy Watson, after an understandably nervous start when he let the ball run under his foot, was winning everything in the air and the fierce Fenwick was mopping up all around him. But it needed a goal to put the icing on the cake, though none of us had the right to expect young John Barnes's contribution.

The timing could not have been more perfect for the goal that set us and English football alight. It gave us courage to face the next 45 minutes and was a reward for all the efforts of the first half. Terry Fenwick and Mark

Hateley began the inspirational moment with a pass out to Barnes who, but for his all-white strip, might have been a Brazilian himself. He surely looked like one as he started on a run from the halfway line, leaving a trail of defenders in his wake. I kept willing him to pass the ball as he seemed to run into one defender after another. Woodcock set off expecting to get the ball but, taking a defender with him, he left another hole for Barnes to go through. By this time everyone in the badly-positioned dug-out, which looked out on the giant Maracana at eye level, was on their feet. I thought to myself: 'What are you trying to do – walk it in?' Barnes did just that, eventually reaching the area to confront Costa, fooling him as he feigned to shoot and then leaving the great Junior sprawled on his backside as Barnes rolled the ball into the net.

The crowd did not know whether to be disgusted or delighted at this goal, which was the sort they expected from their own side, never the opponents. They were amazed while the British supporters and Press went quietly bananas. No sooner had they picked the ball out of the net than the whistle blew for half-time and, no matter how elated I felt, it was now my job to keep calm. I simply could not get excited for I had to impress on them that all the good work they had done so far could go to waste if they did not maintain their concentration, particularly at the resumption when Brazil would surely go for our throats. They were going to be angry and, if anything, we were going to have to play even better in the second half than we had in the first to contain them. I had to remind every player that it was, indeed, only half-time. But the goal had worked miracles. I am not sure that there will be a more important one in my England career. But, as expected, it had also fired up Brazil and they flew at us in the second half, battering us for the first ten minutes. My big worry was that they would release Pires to come forward and I had warned Fenwick at half-time that he might be required to come out of the back-four to help in the midfield. I need not have worried. The Brazilians were rattled and we were soaring. Another goal would kill them off.

Brazil versus England at any time and in any place will capture the imagination and this match was no exception. The game was not only being beamed back to Britain but all over the world. John Barnes had become a superstar with our first goal and in the second half he provided the opportunity for Mark Hateley to join him on that pedestal. I have no doubt at all that it was Hateley's performance and, in particular his goal, which prompted Italian giants AC Milan to pay almost £1 million to Portsmouth to take him from the obscurity of the Second Division to the most star-studded League in world football. Any debt Hateley owed me was paid off in the sixty-fifth minute of that game as he rose majestically at the far post in true 'olde-English' fashion to meet Barnes's cross, climbing above his marker and connecting with such ferocity that, though Roberto Costa got a hand to the ball, he could not keep it out.

We were now two up and in the driving seat. The players were 9 feet tall but I was painfully aware that there was nothing that I could do other than sit and watch though I knew we had to continue to defend well, work and give no loopholes for a possible comeback. They sent on Renaldo for the much-praised Roberto Dynamite and I was in the hands of my players and all I could contribute at that stage was to bring off the tiring Woodcock and send on young Clive Allen. It almost paid undreamt-of rewards for, shortly after, a touch by our substitute sent Bryan Robson screaming through a gap in the Brazilians' stretched defence to confront Costa one to one. Had it been 0–0 I am sure that he would have scored but our captain tried to disguise his shot and saw it pass the wrong side of the far post. Not that it mattered for, a quarter of an hour later, he was being presented with one of the biggest trophies you have ever seen, a trophy that had already been allotted its place in the Brazilian soccer headquarters.

As that final whistle blew everyone went crazy – except me. I felt surprisingly calm. Obviously I was inwardly both excited and relieved at a result that I had never needed more and one which no one had given us a chance of achieving. Seven days earlier we had been the whipping boys and now we were the toast of world football with a team bolstered by only four senior players and a half-fit Woodcock. That would have been a perfect moment to have finished the season with a few days on Copacabana Beach and then home to our families. We had beaten the team everyone wants to beat. We were experiencing the sort of feeling that the Hungarians must have felt when they beat England at Wembley. Not only were we the first team to win in Brazil for more than a quarter of a century but this was Brazil's first defeat anywhere by an England side since 1956 and their first ever by an England side on home soil. I took a great deal of pleasure in receiving the congratulations of people like Doc Edwards, Fred Street and Norman Medhurst, who had endured all the problems with me even though those barbed comments hadn't affected them and their families personally. They all came to me because they knew what it meant. I was chuffed for them, for my players, for my country and for myself. It was the lift we all needed.

There was an air of almost disbelief in the dressing room as the result sunk in. It was a happy scene, the best I had experienced as an international manager and there is no doubt of the effect it had on our future. Looking back, that was the moment our team spirit began to develop. The players had been drawn together in adversity and had come through the ordeal together. It produced a common bond and a shared pride that was heightened when the compliments and good wishes began to come in. Doc Edwards and I went back to the hotel via the hospital to see the recovering Graham Roberts and on my return the congratulations began to flow in from home including two telegrams, one from England cricket test selector Peter May offering heartiest best wishes on a magnificent result which he said had uplifted the country and our cricket team who were about to face the might of the West Indies, and another from the then Minister for Sport, Neil Macfarlane, telling us what a great result it was for the country. I kept them to myself until everyone was assembled at dinner and I could see the pride in their faces as I read them out. It emphasised what we had said in our long meeting before the game when I told them how important it was back home to give the people something to cheer about. I retired to my room feeling as though a great burden had been lifted from my shoulders. I left the celebrations to the others for all I wanted was a little peace. I was happy to be on my own and reflect on the fact that no other English manager had enjoyed such a result and that in real football terms it was probably second only to Sir Alf Ramsey's effort in winning the World Cup in 1966! It did not matter if anyone disagreed with me for those were my own private thoughts to enjoy on that special night.

It is a sad reflection on life that happiness is rarely unmarred and so it turned out on our departure from Rio to our next venue, Montevideo. There were one or two hangovers, mainly among the Press it must be stressed, but the atmosphere was all it should have been until we began to file through to the departure lounge. Our wingers John Barnes and Mark Chamberlain went through together with one of our senior sports writers only to be abused by a group of so-called England supporters. To the players' credit they walked on as though nothing had happened but they could not have helped but hear the racist remarks from a group who had previously been mixing with our happy players. The journalist involved quickly put the word around and, with hatred in their eyes, the rest of our party gave the louts the cold shoulder. It was incredible, they were even saying that we had won 1-0 because they did not recognise the wonderful goal scored by John Barnes.

I looked at them with contempt, restraining my natural impulse to react violently. One or two of the group were smartly attired though most were hooligans. I wondered to myself how they managed to afford such an expensive trip supposedly to follow England and then to reject probably the best goal they would ever see on account of the colour of the skin of the player who had scored it. It was not being hysterical to wonder who had funded their journey out to South America and what their part had been in previous England riots. That feeling was strengthened when they began to sing their racist songs on the aircraft. We left it to the football writer sitting directly in front of them to express the disgust everyone felt.

It was a pity that scum like that could sour what we had achieved and from the sun and splendour of Rio and its golden beaches we were plunged into a Uruguayan winter. The hotel had been picked out on a summer visit and I am sure that then it would have been a magnificent sight, a huge, ornamental building standing on the banks of the rust-coloured River Plate. The tourist season had long since finished and the hotel had been specially reopened to accommodate us. Some of the Press party took one look at the isolated and musty hotel, blanched at the time it took to make calls to London and promptly moved out into the bustling capital, Montevideo. It was a funny old hotel and even the dining room was opened just for us and the only area that was open to the public was the casino and bingo hall which were, of course, out of bounds to our players. Not all the usual services were available because of the skeleton staff and some of our party found their laundry being returned, still damp, in the early hours of the morning by the enterprising chambermaids who had done it themselves and wanted payment then and there.

We were made enormously welcome by the locals and by the large British community, especially at the nearby school where we trained. We were under constant armed guard because of the recent conflict with Argentina over the Falklands and, with Buenos Aires just a long free kick across the water, there were some jangling nerves, although the Uruguayans were convinced that our battle with their neighbours had stopped a possible invasion of their own country. We were taken to the area's leather factories where Peter Shilton dressed himself up like John Travolta in all the gear. The other players egged him on, telling him how terrific he looked and he bought the lot! I doubt whether he ever put the clothes on once he returned home. I also came across the cheapest food I have ever experienced. Don Howe and I went out one night to eat at a nearby restaurant with Bob Harris, David Lacey of the *Guardian* and Michael Hart of the *Evening Standard.* They had been to the restaurant before and knew what to expect but we were taken completely by surprise as we were served the biggest steaks you have ever seen, superb sweets, excellent wine and a total bill of about £7.50 for the lot of us.

We were all looking forward to playing the talented Uruguayans after our win in Brazil, with the exception of Arsenal striker Tony Woodcock. A combination of his injury and some personal problems he had left behind in London had caused him to come to me to ask if he could return home. In my opinion he was no worse than when he had arrived and while I wanted to hold on to the few experienced players I had, I was also aware that it would be unfair to the rest if I let him play in the plum game and then allowed him to go home. His club manager, Don Howe, agreed with me and we sent him for intensive treatment and tried to get his mind right but, even so, it was only on the afternoon of the game that he suddenly asked for permission to go for a run with one of the journalists and came back from this odd fitness test to tell me that he was ready to play if required as we left the hotel en route for the ground.

I have always held the football of Uruguay in the highest esteem, even if they can be a little over-physical at times. For a tiny country their football production line is nothing short of phenomenal. Footballers seem to be their biggest export and I understand that in the last 30 years some 1,500 have left to play with clubs in Argentina, Venezuela, Ecuador, Spain and Mexico. When we played them a number of their best players were unavailable and yet they still managed to turn out a remarkably strong team to beat us and our new-found confidence by a two-goal margin. The fact that they went on to win the South American Championship against the likes of Brazil and Argentina under the same difficulties indicated their inherent talent.

Mind you, they could not have complained had they lost that day. In the opening five minutes Clive Allen, yet another player to make his full début, showed his talent for being in the right place at the right time to leave himself with a roll-in goal. He hit it wide. Worse was to follow when, with only eight minutes gone, Acosta went across the outstretched leg of the defending Mark Hateley and the Paraguayan referee promptly pointed to the penalty spot. We couldn't believe it but the Uruguayan right winger Acosta could as he picked himself up to send Shilton the wrong way from the spot. Hateley was perplexed and upset. It was not the sort of decision which would have been given at Fratton Park, even in favour of the home side. The player had used him and Mark learned the lesson of being careful in the penalty area.

There was no question of England collapsing, especially in view of what they had gone through in recent weeks and we might easily have built up an unassailable lead by the interval as chances came our way with Chamberlain trying to emulate the Barnes goal in Brazil only to fail with his shot when it seemed that he must score, while poor Clive Allen missed a hat-trick of chances. Even Dave Watson joined the attack to see a couple of shots blocked on the line. It was a cracking game and we were in no way disgraced even when Perdomo got away from Sansom down the right and crossed between Watson and Duxbury for Cabrera to score a gifted goal. I sent on Woodcock for a run in the later stages but we were destined not to score. By the end of the game I was well impressed by the opposition even though I thought we could have won. Uruguay looked a better bet than Brazil and were not afraid to hit us in the tackle. I was pleased with our performance and delighted to get the feedback that we had received a good Press and had given a good account of ourselves on television.

We still had the opportunity to become the first touring England side to win twice on a South American visit when we left Uruguay for Chile and Santiago's Arturo Merino Benitez Airport. It was a game everyone in South America told us we would win for we were to play against what amounted to Chile's Olympic team, though there were no amateurs among them. We went without our most experienced striker Tony Woodcock, who was still complaining of injury and finally went home for further treatment, but with everyone else still happy and buoyant. We murdered them but could not score. We must have had 20 shots on target but goalkeeper Rojas possessed the unbeatable combination of good fortune and breathtaking agility. It was ridiculous. If we had won 6–0 no one could have complained and, while we hammered away at their goal, Shilton was called on to make just one save. Clive Allen kept getting chances to make amends but everything went towards his head while nothing fell to the waiting Hateley's. Ray Wilkins had more shots that day than in most of his internationals put together but the best was from a header and he came into the dressing room afterwards to lift the natural despondency saying: 'My head is like a 50 pence piece, it has seven sides and each time the ball hit the wrong one and went the wrong way.'

The one player who deserved a goal was our skipper Bryan Robson. I do not think I have ever seen him cover so much ground, he must have tackled each and every one of the Chile team, including their three substitutes. There was not a blade of grass in that stadium that did not receive the imprint of his boot. He went round the park like a man possessed and had eight or nine attempts at goal on his own without the slightest luck. He came into the dressing room with his shirt absolutely saturated and upset that he and his team had been unable to turn their superiority into the goals they deserved. Bryan Robson really came of age as England captain on that trip. He was a great example not only with his performances on the pitch but also off it as well. He had helped weld that essential spirit which was to serve us so well in the run-up to the World Cup Finals in Mexico and by the end of the tour they were more like a club side. There were no flights to England on the day after our game but, instead of moping around the hotel with its beautiful view of the Andes, Bryan insisted that the whole playing squad should go out for lunch together on that last day to a restaurant that had been recommended to us. They paid for themselves and had a marvellous time, laughing, singing and dancing much to the delight of the restaurateur and the locals who joined in and insisted on buying our happy players farewell drinks. They deserved it as well as their brief holidays that were to follow before reporting back to their clubs and the all-important World Cup qualifying competition.

However, there was no peace for the wicked. No sooner had we arrived back at Heathrow but I had to fly out with some of the Press again to France for the closing stages of the European Championships. We had time to catch our breath at the hotel near the airport. Manager Jim Fitzgerald laid on a quiet area of their dining room complete with oversize television so that we could watch Spain beat West Germany in Paris to earn a place in the semi-finals we were to go out and see. We enjoyed it but I am not so sure about the journalists' wives who had come to spend that one night with their husbands! We journeyed to Marseilles next morning to enjoy a little sunshine and to watch France play Portugal and then went on to Lyons the day afterwards to see Spain and Denmark. France came from behind to win a thrilling game 3–2 after extra time but their hoped-for clash with our conquerors Denmark in the final did not materialise as Spain won on penalties, again after extra time. It was Denmark's first major finals and my fears that they would not have the depth, the power or the resilience to cope with so many games in such a short space of time were realised.

The final at the Parc des Princes three nights later was a disappointment, apart from the incomparable Platini. France looked tired after playing five games in a fortnight and I was left to think about what might have been. That was the sort of situation our overworked footballers take in their stride and I am certain that had we qualified and gone to France for the Finals, we would have done very well and might even have won it had we played as we did against Brazil and Uruguay. But you cannot survive in football on what might have been and I felt that I knew what needed to be done now to make sure that we did not fail again where it mattered most – in the World Cup.

I finally went off on holiday with my wife Elsie in Zimbabwe to reflect on a season of contrasting fortunes. I was excited at the prospect of the World Cup and knew that if we got it right there was no one we need fear. The important objective was to qualify and that I was certain we could do after our performances in South America. A young, inexperienced squad had stood up to challenge superbly and I knew that, come the new season, I could only strengthen that team with the return of injured and previously unavailable players. They would have been sick at missing the glory in Brazil and would know that competition for places had suddenly increased. Outside Shilton and Robson, there was a scrap for every place in the team and that is how it should be. I was looking forward to the new season with some relish.

5. Qualifying

September is not always the best time to play an international football match as England – and I – have discovered in recent years. Players are still stretching their limbs after pre-season training, getting the feel of the ball after their summer break and have been away from their international colleagues for two, sometimes three, months. Ron Greenwood had suffered before me with that surprise 2–1 defeat against Norway in Oslo while I had been lucky to see my team draw in Copenhagen in my first match and then go down against Denmark at Wembley in 1983. It called for a dummy run and that is exactly what we had arranged. East Germany were to visit Wembley on 12 September 1984 to help us shake off the dust before we embarked on three successive World Cup qualifying matches. We knew they would provide a stern test for, while never being particularly imaginative, the East Germans will always be physically fit, well disciplined and highly organised in defence.

My first decision was whether to continue with my adventurous system involving two wingers. The boys in question had done exceptionally well for me on the summer tour but in the modern game a winger has to be very good to earn his corn and, while I would have no hesitation in playing two if both were outstanding, I felt that as well as leaving us a little short in midfield neither John Barnes, despite his outstanding contribution against Brazil, nor Mark Chamberlain, had truly asserted themselves. Barnes had been the more consistent and promising of the two and, though I picked both for the squad, I had made up my mind to leave out Chamberlain and bring in an extra midfield player. It was legitimate to gamble with my own future in South America but a different matter to take risks with England's qualification for Mexico. As it transpired the problem was solved without me having to make my intentions public when Chamberlain, along with several others, pulled out through injury. I still had some very difficult decisions to make, however, but once you allow sentiment to interfere you are in trouble.

The hardest decision of all was to leave out both Terry Fenwick and Dave Watson in order to bring in Terry Butcher and Mark Wright. It was obvious that Butcher would have to come back while young Mark Wright

50

was the up and coming young centre-back in the country and if he was going to gain the necessary experience for Mexico I would have to plunge him straight in now. Fenwick and Watson were great personalities and had stood up well to the challenge but at least I now knew what they could do and my job was to find someone who could play alongside my undisputed number one, Terry Butcher. It meant giving Wright his senior début and having another look at Southampton's Steve Williams who had been kept out of contention by that marvellous character Sammy Lee. Sammy had enjoyed a good run but had not maintained the promise he had shown at the start. I also relied on the experience of Paul Mariner and Tony Woodcock up front.

We were pretty comfortable at the back though the East German striker Streich, playing his hundredth international, struck the outside of Shilton's post with a 25-yarder. We had nice control of the midfield but lacked the cutting edge up front. As with most teams who visit Wembley, the East Germans' aim was to avoid defeat rather than to win and what was a useful work-out to us represented a cup-tie to them. Mariner and Woodcock had held the ball up well without ever getting in behind the defence and, though I had the feeling we were likely to score at any minute, I decided I had to make a change as I sent on Mark Hateley and Trevor Francis. Within a minute we had scored and despite the fact it would have been nice to take the credit I could not for neither substitute was involved as Sansom broke down the left and crossed for Ray Wilkins to pick out his mate Bryan Robson to score with a typical volley.

I was delighted for, apart from starting the new season with a victory, it was important that we should win at Wembley after two defeats in our previous three fixtures there. I had been worried that the squad might develop a phobia about playing on their own ground and that would have been a disastrous disadvantage to take into the World Cup with our opening game against the Finns a month later. They were sure to come and defend and were in good, confident mood having opened the Group Three programme with a shock victory over Billy Bingham's Northern Ireland team in Pori at the end of the previous season. What is more the Irish had then gone on to beat Romania 3–2 in Belfast on the very night we were beating East Germany. It meant that, without kicking a ball, we had got off to a flying start with our two biggest challengers both dropping points in their opening games. It was now up to us to consolidate that position and I went into my first World Cup-tie as a manager with every confidence. There were no nerves, for South America had done us all a power of good and the game against the East Germans had provided exactly the sort of loosener we wanted. I did not believe the Finns had the firepower to score against us at Wembley. I could not see them controlling us in midfield and I did not believe that they could handle us in the air in front of their own goal.

I kept the same shape we had had against the East Germans. Mariner and Francis had withdrawn because of injury and though I called up old faithful Peter Withe and, to a lot of people's surprise, the then relatively unknown Leicester City striker Gary Lineker, I decided to start with Hateley and Woodcock up front. We wanted them deep in their own half right from the start and despite the fact we created half-a-dozen chances it was not until midway through the first half that we finally broke through as Barnes hit the underside of the crossbar and Mark Hateley followed up to score his first-ever Wembley goal. The home fans had found a new hero in the big, bustling Hateley and another in Tottenham's Gary Stevens who made his début when he came on for the injured Mick Duxbury. We went on to score four more times with Hateley confirming his ability with a second goal and Woodcock, Robson and Sansom adding the others. We even finished the game with two wingers when Mark Chamberlain came on to make the last goal for Sansom as Robson went off with an injury. The game was dying and Kenny was the only one I could reach. I shouted to him that we wanted one more. He obliged and everyone was happy.

It gave us exactly the sort of start we wanted and I was further encouraged when I watched our next opponents, Turkey, lose at home to Finland. That was a bonus because the Turks were the dark horses of the group and no one was very sure how they were going to perform. They were not particularly good on the night I watched them but everyone was at pains to tell me it was the worst they had ever played and that they could not possibly play as badly again and that this was, in fact, just the kick up the pants they needed before they played us in Istanbul in November. This was backed up by the Northern Ireland manager, Billy Bingham, who told me not to underestimate them as the Irish had struggled to beat them 2–1 in Belfast while losing by a single goal in Ankara in the European Championships a year before.

Billy was convinced that they would give us a tough game and warned us that they would be rough and tough. I was not so sure. I could see weaknesses that could be exploited, particularly in the air at the back. There were disappointments in the build-up when we lost first Mariner and then, on the Sunday as we arrived in Istanbul, Hateley, who had been injured playing for AC Milan in Italy that very afternoon. Fortunately, we had Peter Withe with us. He may have been getting old in international terms and he may have two suspect knees but I knew that he would not let us down. This man has a Union Jack tatooed on his heart and he had been dying to play again ever since his courageous performance against the Hungarians at Wembley in April 1983. Maybe he would not be as mobile as Mariner or Hateley but I knew that he would be every bit as intimidating and that was what I needed.

They call Istanbul the Gateway to Asia and we enjoyed the unusual experience of crossing the huge bridge over the Bosphorus to train in one continent while playing the game in the other the next day. There was certainly no time for boredom in this fascinating city and we took the opportunity to visit the Blue Mosque and to look at the carpets in the Bazaar. The atmosphere at the stadium was one of the most electric I had come across and, clearly, the Turks were looking to mark their first game against England at this level with a victory. Had we started badly we would have been in trouble but they were never in the race. We pressed them back from the start, hustling them and not allowing them to settle on the ball. Bryan Robson opened the floodgates with a brave header from a corner after just 14 minutes and when Terry Butcher came charging out of defence to catch one of their defenders in possession and sent in Woodcock for a goal it was all over bar the shouting. Robson went on to hit a hat-trick with Woodcock scoring again, John Barnes getting two and Viv Anderson his first ever for England, as we won 8–0 to give us a 100 per cent start to our World Cup campaign with the bonus of 13 goals scored and none against, which was worth an extra point if it came to the crunch of goal difference. It was also England's biggest away victory since we had beaten the United States in New York 20 years earlier – and we had shown our critics that we could score goals without Mark Hateley. The only disappointment for me was that Withe, who had led his line with skill and courage, failed to score. The lads did their best to set him up but the ball would not go in.

I had settled again for one winger and kept faith with Steve Williams, asking him to forget his usual club duties and to keep shape on the right. He played well but he is one of these lads who wants to play his own way and, though it worked while goals poured in at the other end and Arsenal's Viv Anderson played well behind him, it posed a question mark against his discipline when we met a stronger team who would take advantage of any weakness or lopsidedness. It may appear pedantic but when you see players so infrequently you have to take everything into account, not just the fact that we had scored eight and missed another five. We were in the driving seat but wanted to stay there.

Then we hit a brick wall! Just when we were getting into full swing we were brought to a shuddering halt. After our runaway win on 14 November 1984, the next time I was reunited with my players was for the game against Northern Ireland in Belfast on 27 February 1985 – a huge three and a half month gap, which is longer even than a club manager loses his players during the close season. The Football Association did their best to help me as I tried to organise a gathering of the squad without a match for Bisham Abbey in January. All I wanted was three days, Monday, Tuesday and Wednesday but, by the time the bad weather had interfered and games had been rearranged, I was left with a grand total of eight players out of a selected squad of twenty-two. I had no alternative but to cancel. Goodness knows what would have happened had we arranged a game against foreign opposition for that week!

When the game did finally come round, I had lost both my skipper Bryan Robson (again!) and his Manchester United team-mate Remi Moses whom I had brought in to cover Robson. Poor Remi, not only did he miss that chance to force his way into the squad but he was knocked out of the World Cup reckoning altogether with an injury which would not clear up. It was a pity for I had been impressed by Remi's improvement. I had seen a lot of him while watching other players at Old Trafford and I realised that he was a great ball winner who got his foot in and that he had developed into a good passer. With Gordon Cowans sidelined for some time and Robson and Moses out, I turned to the versatile Spurs' player Gary Stevens to fill that midfield role little knowing that he, too, would be joining the long-term casualties in the near future.

Mark Wright and Steve Williams had also been left out for disciplinary reasons by the Football Association after problems with Southampton, so a little more shuffling was necessary as I called up Alvin Martin to support Terry Butcher in the back-four and gave a first cap to the lively little Everton player, Trevor Steven. I was pleased to have Mark Hateley back because I knew that this was going to be one of our most testing games in the entire competition. You had only to look at the Irish record over the past five years or so to see how dangerous they were, with the most recent reminder being their 3–2 win over Romania at Windsor Park. Not many teams have beaten them at Windsor Park and I have seen Ireland get the better of Scotland who had talented players but not a better team, a fact more than amply displayed with Ireland's double triumph over West Germany and their brilliant results in the last World Cup in Spain.

I was glad I did not have as few to choose from as Billy Bingham for, with my injury problems, it would have been hard to raise a team. But Billy has always been able to turn the small numbers into an advantage by building continuity of tactics and personnel. They could always be relied on to produce a sound, collective performance and I knew we were in for a harrowing time unless we stood up to them. Any sign of weakness and we were likely to be knocked over, both physically and result-wise. I had sent the shrewd, former Luton Town boss, Harry Haslam, to watch them beat Romania and from his report it was evident that it was going to be an uphill task, with the ball often in the air and no time for clever football. These facts were confirmed by the non-stop rain that fell in Belfast that day and throughout the game.

It was both frantic and frenetic with little chance for anyone to settle on the ball or build passes through midfield. Butcher was the pick of the bunch in our outstanding defence but, even so, Quinn headed against the crossbar while Butcher cleared off the line from Whiteside and Armstrong. Butcher also had a big hand – or rather a big foot – in our goal when he gave Pat Jennings' long clearance a massive kick back upfield for Mark Hateley to avoid the lunging O'Neill and beat Jennings for a superbly-taken goal. It took a physically strong man to achieve that in the deep mud. The players trooped back to the dressing room exhausted. Ray Wilkins, who had been caught up in the frenzy of the game and had been unable to bring his influence to bear as much as he and I would have liked, said: 'It's a change to play like that and win, for all too often we have lost games in the past when other teams have battled harder.' Ray was right. We took a lot of criticism in the Press next day for our performance but how often have Liverpool won by the odd goal when they have been off form? Seven results like that in a season had won them the Championship on more than one occasion and so far as I was concerned this was likely to be one of our most important results in Group Three, especially as it gave us six points from our three matches.

It was a night when result and attitude were more important than polished skill. The Irish have always been thought of as something special when they pull on those green shirts, especially in Belfast. This time it was a dozen Englishmen who had fought and won. They gave it everything they had and were still condemned for it by their critics. No one, next morning, gave us a chance in Mexico even though all we were concerned with at this stage was actually qualifying and there was clear evidence that the players were determined to do so – with or without Bryan Robson. There was never any possibility that we would play that way in Mexico. The English papers were full of how well the Irish had played and how lucky we had been but the truth could be found in the Irish Press. They felt that, with ourselves and Romania to play away, Ireland had blown their chances. As for me, I was both happy and confident.

We were not scheduled to play our next game in the group for two months but we did have a friendly game against the Republic of Ireland to fill the gap, which is always a good testing fixture because of the quality of players like Lawrenson, Brady, Whelan, Stapleton and McGrath. It also gave me a chance to look at one or two players in a less pressured situation, though I knew that anything less than victory was unacceptable. It meant I was able to award Gary Bailey a rare game, débuts to Chris Waddle and Peter Davenport and second caps to Trevor Steven and Gary Lineker.

I had watched Waddle a great deal at Newcastle and felt that he had the ability and pace to get behind defences. Potentially he was one of the best wide players in the country and had come out of the Second Division to practise it where it mattered most in the First and, what is more, had improved while doing it. Lineker had long been on my mind. I had watched him closely at Leicester and when I had included him for the Welsh game little was known about him. Now the big clubs were taking an interest in him and while Tottenham were to fail in a bid to land him, Everton eventually won his signature for more than £750,000. He possessed the pace and the desire to score goals that made him a natural for international honours, though I considered he needed a gentle introduction. Peter Davenport was another I picked out myself for he was never personally recommended to me by his manager Brian Clough. I was interested by the way he could hold up the ball and wait for support and by his control and his speed on the turn. He is also very unselfish as he showed in the Republic of Ireland game after he came on as a substitute for Hateley; he rolled a perfect ball for Lineker to finish to put us two up after Trevor Steven had stolen one in the best Steve Coppell tradition. It was a pity that injury put Davenport out of contention at a crucial time for him, which allowed others like Kerry Dixon to overtake. But his time will come, especially if he remembers what he learned at Forest when he takes advantage of his move to Manchester United.

My only disappointment that night was that, just before the end, we conceded our first goal in nine hours of international football when Brady exchanged passes with Stapleton, finishing with a cross-shot that squeezed under Gary Bailey's body. Even so it was our fifth successive victory and all had been achieved by different line-ups against different types of teams. It put us in perfect heart for our next big test against the Romanians on their own ground. This was two months later, on May Day 1985 when 70,000 people including such noted celebrities as tennis star Ilie Nastase, packed the August 23rd Stadium knowing that their team needed to win to get back on course for Mexico. That was the last thing we wanted after our promising start and it was crucial that we came out undefeated to keep the pressure firmly on the other countries in the group to chase the runners-up spot rather than the top position we intended to keep. But, even though we lost both Hateley and Davenport from my original squad, we did not go behind the Iron Curtain intending to defend.

However, defend we did and that was all down to the ability of the Romanians. I had seen no need to readjust the team or our tactics. Any such move would have been considered regressive and had I done so I would have undoubtedly been asked to explain why, especially if we had lost. Romania were good. You have to give credit where it is due and we were not playing a team of dummies that afternoon. They were chasing points, they were at home and they knew they had to get among us. Their way back into the World Cup was to beat England. Without detracting from the ability of the Irish, there is no doubt that in terms of technical skill the Romanians were second in the group. Shilton, as ever, played well while Viv Anderson, marking the dangerous Gheorghe Hagi, had his best game for England. He kept the shape down that flank and forced the talented youngster to move around in search of space. It was a fine team performance and we might even have won it when Bryan Robson headed a John Barnes free-kick against the cross-bar while Paul Mariner, in the side for his experience, missed the best chance of the game from a Robson pass. But I was satisfied with the point and though the game had finished goalless it was still a good spectacle for the fans. There were a lot of good footballers out there, a good deal of cut and thrust and inevitably some cancellation of similarly talented players.

It was a creditable performance and only total capitulation in our remaining games, three of the four being at home, would see us fail in our bid to reach Mexico and, as a bonus, we had a further two games to look forward to in May and a close-season tour to Mexico City and Los Angeles, which were all the more meaningful with the World Cup Finals as much a certainty as anything in football can be. I would not have felt quite so at peace with the world, however, had I known what lay ahead. Certainly Finland should not have presented any problems and though they did it was only a warning of what was to come from totally unexpected directions. Finland asked us as many questions in their Helsinki Olympic Stadium as any of our other rivals. They embarrassed us in midfield and caught us out with an early goal, using one of our own set-pieces, as a long throw-in from the right was headed into the area where Lipponen fired in a header that Shilton palmed against the woodwork only for Rantanen to score from close range. Worse still, we could have gone two down as Butcher cleared off the line.

After that it was all uphill. We had our chances and might have had a penalty when Francis was brought down. I began to relax when Mark Hateley added to his growing England goal tally just five minutes into the second half, but the winner would not come and it seemed as though fate had decreed that we should not score again when Hateley looked set to convert Barnes's centre only to be knocked out of the way. Once again the East German referee said no penalty. Considering the thrashing we had given the Finns at Wembley you had to admire their fitness and physical strength. They were good athletes, denying us possession and space. The inevitable Wilkins reminded everyone: 'That was the sort of game we were losing not so long ago.'

It was our last World Cup game of the season and though qualification was on points – we needed four from our remaining three home games to be absolutely sure – it would have been nice to have erased even those last lingering doubts. But our record: played five; won three; drawn two; lost none; for fifteen; against one; points eight, made fairly comforting reading on the trip to Mexico. But first there was the slight domestic matter to be settled against Scotland at Hampden Park. The game should have been at Wembley but the Prime Minister Margaret Thatcher, no less, requested that it be moved from London because of the transport and other problems it would cause on a Bank Holiday when police resources would be stretched without the added burden of a football match. It was an unhappy sign of the times and another blow to the game.

For the first time the two protagonists were competing for a trophy named the Sir Stanley Rous Cup in honour of the great administrator's recent ninetieth birthday. It wasn't, though, as if England and Scotland needed any excuse to play each other and, whatever happens before or afterwards this is still the one that matters, the most prestigious fixture in Europe. The result is all-important and every player knows he is in for a hard, gruelling dogfight of a game where a yard to play in is a luxury that you have to make for yourself. This one was no different. Scotland manager Jock Stein packed his midfield and gave advance notice of what we were to face. We were pretty close to full strength despite losing the services of the four Everton players who were wanted for their final game against Coventry City because of the backlog of fixtures.

We had our fair share of a good game but I was surprised to read afterwards that there had been a massive total of 34 goal attempts, 20 of them by us! The more relevant statistic was that Scotland scored the only goal of the game after our full-back Gough met Bett's superb cross beautifully. But the key to the Scottish success was the midfield performance of Graeme Souness, who looked ready to end his run of never having been on the winning side against the English on his own. He certainly took on both Bryan Robson and Ray Wilkins that afternoon, chasing and tackling them all over the midfield.

I did all I could to change the pattern and might have been successful when I sent on the languid Chris Waddle for John Barnes. The Newcastle winger displayed all his qualities in getting to the by-line but, with Hateley waiting unmarked, he made the wrong selection with his final ball and the chance was gone. I took some criticism when I replaced Glenn Hoddle with Gary Lineker for Hoddle had played well and observant watchers noticed that I changed my mind while waiting for the ball to go out of play as it was the No. 8 of Trevor Francis that was being held on the touchline. I admit that it was an impulsive act and had the ball gone out of play earlier, Hoddle would have remained on the pitch. My change of mind was no reflection on Hoddle. I suddenly decided to push Francis wide and play Lineker in that 4-2-4 system which had worked so well 12 months earlier. It was not as if we had played badly or been second best, simply that the goals which had come so easily at the start of the season had dried up. Naturally, I was concerned that we had scored only once in more than four hours of football but that had to be weighed against a season in which we had taken ourselves to the very brink of qualification and lost only once in eight games for the loss of three goals. It was still a nice record to carry to Mexico, or so I thought!

We were due to fly out to Mexico on Tuesday 28 May, which gave us all a couple of days with our families. My Sunday was wrecked when I received a telephone call at home from a London journalist saying he had something to tell me that I would not like. He was very embarrassed and I asked him to spell out what he was trying to say. 'We are carrying a front-page story tomorrow saying that you must go,' he answered.

I must have been a bit slow on the uptake for I asked: 'Go where?' before it dawned on me that one of the biggest circulation newspapers in the country was demanding that I be sacked from my job as England manager. The journalist asked if I wanted to respond. This is an old ploy to get double mileage out of one story but I was too shocked to take in what he was saying and told him to ring me back in an hour. When he did he read out some of the worst bits to me. I told him I had nothing to say. Next day the paper did, indeed, lead the front page with the banner headline: 'Robson Must Go' under the Saturday scoreline with a stern-faced picture of me and a caption spelling out the message a second time: 'Time for him to resign'.

Not content with that the *Daily Mirror* even elevated me and my job to their leader column telling me to prove them wrong. It was probably unprecedented in British journalism to give such prominence to that type of story and I was furious. In fact, no other newspaper bothered to follow it up and the story died a lonely death. But it still hurt. I could only assume that I was the victim of the tabloid newspapers' circulation war and, in fact, it was just the beginning of several more articles against me that were going to appear over the next 18 months. The players were equally disgusted. Bryan Robson said that he hoped I would take no notice of such rubbish. It was nice to know I had the backing of the people who mattered.

However, all I could do was bite my lip and say nothing in print. There were more urgent matters at hand in Mexico where the World Champions Italy and hosts Mexico were lying in wait for us with World Cup runners-up West Germany not far behind. The medical advice was that we should get to Mexico and relax for a few days while we adjusted to the jet-lag, the heat and the breathless atmosphere. What better way to relax than to watch the European Cup Final between our own great champions Liverpool and the brilliant Italian team, Juventus. We settled down and waited for the match to begin, little realising that far from preparing ourselves for the World Cup challenge in 12 months' time our whole future would be hanging in the balance with no guarantee of returning to Mexico or anywhere else.

6. In the Wake of Brussels

It was our first full day in Mexico City and all of us were looking forward to watching the European Cup Final which was to be shown live from Belgium. With the seven-hours' time difference it was around lunchtime when we began to gather in the coffee bar area of our luxurious Mexico City hotel, the Camino Real. It was open to the public as well and the hotel had erected a big screen because of the interest, not only from ourselves, but also from the curious locals who were well aware that Liverpool's clash with Juventus was a prelude to our own game against the World Champions Italy in the Aztec Stadium, which was to be the scene of the World Cup Final itself in a little over a year's time. The entire scenario was being repeated just down the road by the Italian manager, Enzo Bearzot, and his squad who were waiting for the Juventus players to bring their team up to full strength.

We assumed that there was some technical delay as kick-off time came and went with the screen frustratingly blank. No explanation was forthcoming and, for 90 minutes, we waited and wondered what was going on. We did not see the horrific pictures that were relayed into British homes and it was only as some of the Press and players made telephone calls home that the drama began to unfold. News began filtering through that two groups of unsegregated supporters had been fighting and that the kick-off had been delayed while the police sorted it out. We heard that there had been deaths but we dismissed this as gross exaggeration when suddenly the giant-size television screen flickered to life showing the two teams preparing to kick off. Certainly, we could see the debris in the stadium but, as far as we were concerned, a match was in progress and we were simply not aware of what had happened. Surely, we thought, if the stories we had heard from home were true the game would not have gone ahead.

The nagging doubts were confirmed only later with the news items on television and further telephone calls to England. We were outraged as the news came through that 38 people had died, bringing shame on everyone connected with the English game. I slowly began to realise the possible implications and that from this moment on my role was much more than that of a football manager. There were going to be many repercussions

61

and, with our game against the Italians only days away, if it went ahead at all, I was at the sharp end. An awful lot was about to happen and I told myself that I had better make certain that I did and said the right things, particularly in the absence of Bert Millichip and Ted Croker who were on their way to Mexico at the time, having stayed behind for discussions on the very subject of hooliganism with the Government.

I had been told, when I took the job as England manager, that it was more than simply looking after a group of footballers, that it carried added ambassadorial duties and that when I signed my contract I would be joining the diplomatic service. The next morning I was to discover the truth of that statement when it seemed as if the entire world had turned against England and especially against anyone who was involved with football.

The hotel was besieged by Mexican, Italian and West German journalists who were looking for statements and were particularly anxious to interview Trevor Francis, Mark Hateley and Ray Wilkins who all earned their livings playing in Italy. The situation rapidly deteriorated with every successive bulletin bringing worse news on the events of the previous evening in the now infamous Heysel Stadium in Brussels. There was immediate talk of a world-wide ban on English clubs and on our own national team with our game against the Italians under serious threat. In fact, at that stage, it looked an impossibility.

I thought I would be relieved of some of the front-line duties when Messrs Millichip and Croker arrived – they had been intercepted at Miami Airport when they changed aircraft. They had been given the dreadful news and interviewed for their reactions. Of course, when their plane touched down in Mexico City the Press were waiting for them along with an urgent message from the Prime Minister summoning them back to London on the next plane. It was left to me to carry on handling the highly inflammable political situation which seemed to be worsening by the minute. I was fortunate that I had such good backing from the three members of the International Committee, Chairman Dick Wragg, Lionel Smart and Jack Wiseman. It would have been easy under those circumstances to have panicked and made rash comments that would later have been regretted but we were able to sit down and talk about it without anyone making silly statements to the Press.

Our priority was to contact our opposite numbers in the Italian headquarters down the road. We wanted to express our sympathy, apologies and anger at everything that had happened even though we had been powerless to do anything about it. I cursed inwardly when the difficult task fell to me. I knew that our respective governments were involved at the very highest level and that the consequences were grave to say the least. I also knew that there were signs that if England played Italy so soon after the deaths of 38 football supporters it would further exacerbate the situation. However, this was not the line I intended to take with Enzo Bearzot when the meeting was arranged to take place at their hotel.

Dick Wragg, Lionel Smart, Jack Wiseman, Liaison Officer Alan O'Dell and Press Officer Glen Kirton and I met and concurred that if Britain and Italy pulled away from each other at that fragile and important moment there would be an irreparable breach. I believed that the game should go ahead in a spirit of mutual understanding. Had the fixture not been on the neutral territory of Mexico, it would probably have been impossible to play but I knew that there would only be a handful of supporters from the two countries at the game and that in a stadium which held over 100,000 people it would be extremely unlikely that there would be violence of any kind.

That was how I felt but if the Italians were as hostile as other countries then I did not stand a hope and the game would be off. However, the Italians were terrific. They could not have been more understanding or helpful. They gave us a genuine welcome of friendship and told us how gratified they were that we had made the initial approaches to set up the meeting. They, like us, wanted to go ahead with the game. Bearzot said that we must keep our dignity and maintain our calm. We all agreed that Heysel was the most shocking incident in the history of football but that we were unable to do anything about it other than start building bridges as soon as possible. There was no animosity at all between the two groups and they were only too aware that, in today's violent society, the situation could well have been reversed. I believe that they put themselves in our shoes and that is why they reached the same conclusions.

It was a big help that the game was not scheduled until 5 June for it gave us all time to show proper respect to the dead and we weren't seen to be progressing with undue haste. One of the items both sides readily agreed to was a memorial service in Mexico City for the casualties of Brussels, attended by players and officials of both sides. It sounds a simple duty but it is hard to imagine what a difficult and delicate time is was for everyone. The English had lost a tremendous amount of respect and I know that I felt as if I were personally responsible. They were our fans and therefore it was our fault.

The main topic of conversation in every Mexican bar, in every newspaper and on television, whether Mexican or American, was the English football hooligans and what football was to do about them. To ban the lot was the concensus of opinion and, indeed, that was the trend, according to the reports that were reaching us, with news of English teams being barred from every competition and with us on trial for our future in Mexico. Every Press conference covered these questions and I used to leave them feeling exhausted, having answered the toughest questions of my life with the most frequent one being, 'Why didn't we pack our bags and go home?'

Although we had agreed with the Italians to play the game there was still no guarantee that it would go ahead. We both knew that either the Mexican authorities or the international ruling body, FIFA, could call it off at any minute. We were in a state of limbo as the arguments raged over the future of English football. If our game did not go ahead then it was obvious that the tournament would be ruined. It was rumoured that if the Italians refused to play us then the Mexicans would also cancel and there was hardly any point in hanging around for a couple of weeks waiting to see whether the West Germans would follow suit.

At least I had plenty to keep me fully occupied but it must have been a very unsettling time for the players. We held a team meeting and stressed the importance of keeping calm and staying out of trouble. We had to be seen to be whiter than white. However, the lads were my least worry for I trusted them completely. They were fully aware of the gravity of the situation and I knew they would let no one down. The three Italian-based players, Francis, Hateley and Wilkins, were under the most strain for the news initially learnt was that they would not be allowed back into Italy. Their biggest concern was for their families. I told them that if there was the slightest sign of any problem they were to tell their wives and children to get straight on a plane back to England and that the Football Association would take care of the cost.

The only place where we could escape and relax was at the marvellously-appointed Reforma Club on the outskirts of the city. It was worth that coach ride out there every day for, apart from excellent football facilities, there were tennis courts, a huge swimming pool and even a cricket pitch. The club had been formed by the wealthy British community and, though it was now an international club and run by Mexicans, it still retained a delightful, colonial atmosphere. It was the one place where we knew we could find friendship and hospitality while the rest of the world seemed to be set against us.

The players responded magnificently. One way to get the terrible scenes out of their minds was to work hard and that it is exactly what they did. Once we felt that they had rested sufficiently to recover from jet-lag and had learned what altitude was about, we put them through a series of gruelling tests which were designed to discover how they were coping with the complex combination of heat, rare air and smog. That was what this trip was all about, not the games, important though they were, but rather about which players coped well with the conditions, and those which did not.

We also wanted to take the fear out of the World Cup Finals. The challenge ahead was going to be tough enough without having our performers concerned about how they could cope with the abnormal conditions. We had to destroy a few myths for them as well as for ourselves. We needed to show them that their hearts were not going to seize up if they did too much running nor that blood was going to pour from their ears and noses. On a more basic level 'Montezuma's Revenge' did need dealing with. We certainly could not afford the sort of stomach upset that had cost Gordon Banks his place against West Germany in León 15 years earlier.

We had done our research well for, while Beckenbauer's West German team suffered a spate of tummy upsets, we had only two during our entire stay in Mexico City. Strangely, it was room-mates Trevor Francis and Mark Wright who suffered from something called altitude nausea allied, we suspected, to Trevor consuming too much Vitamin C from the orange juice we encouraged them all to drink. When Trevor did get out of bed to play he was outstanding. The stress symptons were similar to morning sickness in a pregnant woman and as it apparently afflicts one in every forty visitors, our record was not too bad.

In fact, we had begun our preparations long before we left for Mexico. Dr Edwards, as usual, had done his homework well. Our preparations had started four months before leaving for Mexico when Vernon put the players on iron tablets to increase the oxygen-carrying qualities of the blood. After we arrived, the doctor took blood and urine samples and constantly checked weights with great care. From a physical point of view we gave all the players a simple test comprising a carefully measured and timed 600-yard run where we asked them to give their very best because any cheating would have made the tests useless. I started each group of four and encouraged them to go hard while the doctor, Don Howe, Fred Street and Norman Medhurst waited on the finish line to check their pulse rates, which had been taken earlier at rest.

The object of this was to determine the rate of recovery, which was a crucial factor when comparing England with Mexico. It was a difficult test. I took Kerry Dixon's pulse myself and he was turning over so quickly at the end of his run that I could hardly keep count. It was a little disconcerting at first but they all showed remarkable powers of recovery that indicated their very high standard of fitness and conditioning which is a credit to their clubs and the English game.

It would have been interesting and useful, had we been able to conduct more of the tests during our stay, to monitor the changes as the body adapts to the new environment but with three fixtures against top-class opposition in the space of nine days we had to be wary of how we balanced our programme. We settled instead for the tried and trusted 'Cooper Test', which is a sustained 12-minute run that we threw at the players on only the second day of training. We started them off in a pack this time and asked them to give it all they had. As usual, they gave their most and finished on their knees completely exhausted as the effects of the altitude took their toll.

We measured the distance each player achieved on his individual laps and then on the fourth day of training we made them do it all over again. We explained what we were doing and why because for many of them it was harder even than their pre-season training. We wanted to prove to them that they could run and play at altitude if they had prepared themselves properly in terms of their day-by-day diet and health programme charted by Dr Edwards. Everyone in the party had been informed before we left of the basic do's and don'ts of living in Mexico City. Things like: the twice daily streptotriad tablets; the banning of salads, strawberries, water melons, oysters and ice cream; the exclusive use of bottled water for drinking and cleaning teeth; and washing hands in Phisohex to kill any bacteria. It may have seemed petty to the players but the results of the Cooper Run proved the sanity of our methods to them when we recorded the enormous improvement.

Obviously, however, there were problems. In the first few days we all suffered from sore eyes, nostrils and lips, dry throats and coughs. These had been expected and were alleviated by the hotel room mini-bars being stripped of all alcoholic content and replaced with fruit juices and boiled sweets with the direction to drink as much as they wanted. The proof of the attention to detail came with every training session and practice match. Every single player stood up and did everything we asked – even the three goalkeepers. These individuals have different fitness demands from the other players, for they are often big men and are not usually built for running.

Meanwhile, the plans for the game against Italy, which would be our first real test of our fitness at this altitude, were going ahead. Bert Millichip had, by this time, returned to Mexico after his deliberations with the Prime Minister and the then Minister for Sport, Neil Macfarlane. He was naturally concerned but he backed the decisions we had taken with the Italians. It had been further agreed with Enzo that, to help reduce nationalist tensions among supporters during the game, the teams should walk out in two lines of alternating Italian and English players who would stand shoulder-to-shoulder in a silent tribute to the dead and their families before the kick-off. Enzo and I were worried about how the two small groups of English and Italian fans would react.

We knew that there would be more than enough police on duty to curb any violence but what they could not stop was the verbal abuse that would be recorded and relayed around the world by the news-hungry media.

Bert Millichip made a point of coming into the dressing room before the kick-off and demanded, rather than asked, for perfect discipline, with no flare-ups, regardless of any provocation, and positively no bookings. The players were left in no doubt of what would happen if one of them stepped out of line for any reason whatsoever. Irrespective of the excuse they would be disgraced and put on the very next flight home.

Imagine the pressure on those young men as they walked out with the Italians. They had been shut away in training for days, frustrated by the uncertainty of the past week and bursting with energy and enthusiasm to take on and beat the World Champions Italy. Yet they were having to tread on egg-shells. But, at least, our concern over the fans seemed to be without foundation. Admittedly, a group of Italians greeted us with chants of 'murderers' and 'animals' but it was in their native tongue and passed unnoticed by most. I looked anxiously around for Union Jacks and though there were a few in evidence the English fans were hugely outnumbered by the Mexica Guardia with their riot sticks and guns. It was only later that I heard our old 'friends' from South America were in the stadium but, apart from hurling abuse at the English journalists, they were engulfed by the emptiness of a huge stadium scattered with 13,000 spectators. It was undoubtedly the greatest strain imposed on an English international football team, greater even than the 1966 World Cup finalists for at least they had known that they succeeded or failed on their own football ability. We were playing the World Champions without a friend in sight. I told them before they went out that the world was anti-English at this precise moment and that they could expect nothing from the crowd and nothing from the Mexican officials. I told them that decisions were certain to go against them but that they must bite their lips, smile and get on with the game, for if there was any misbehaviour of any sort Bert Millichip's threats would not be idle ones. It would be goodbye with no sympathy from anyone.

They handled it brilliantly, just as they had done off the field and I was proud of them. They did everything that we had asked and a little more beside. It was difficult to discuss the game in normal terms but we had to look on it that way if we were to make use of all the effort that had gone into the preparation. We had been in Mexico for eight days and needed to know how the players were reacting under match conditions. It quickly became evident that the Italians were far more acclimatised for, while we had been at altitude for eight days, they had been in Mexico City for two weeks. It immediately destroyed the fallacy that time was not needed to prepare for the 1986 World Cup Finals and it was clear that it would take a while to adapt to the unusual conditions as players overhit passes and misjudged crosses. Under normal circumstances Mark Hateley might have had an early goal or two had the centres travelled at normal speed. It was even worse for the ever-reliable Peter Shilton who allowed a swirling centre from midfielder Bagni, from way out on the right, to sail over his head into the net.

With only 15 minutes left and some of our players gasping for breath but having ignored some distinctly iffy decisions given against them by the Mexican referee, they showed their tremendous character by coming straight back and equalising through Mark Hateley. Had it stayed like that everyone would have been happy; a 1–1 draw would have been the perfect result and would have helped us both to start repairing the damage. But it was not to be and I still maintain that it was the sour taste of Brussels that cost us an honourable and deserved draw in the Aztec Stadium that day.

The game was in its death throes when Gary Stevens did exactly the right thing by rolling the ball back to goalkeeper Shilton but as he did so Sampdoria sweeper Vierchowod, arriving late, threw himself over the Everton defender's outstretched leg. To everyone's dismay the Mexican referee Marquez pointed straight to the penalty spot and Altobelli duly converted. It was the sort of decision we had feared and one which would have caused all sorts of problems in an ordinary match. This one was anything but ordinary and the protests were muted to say the least.

If that decision was not enough then seconds later we suffered a second to test the players' temperament to the full. Although there was nothing left on the clock other than injury time, our bottled-up anger and aggression swept us towards the Italian goal and Gary Lineker, who had replaced the outstanding Trevor Francis, was well positioned in the box until his legs were swept from under him. It was the perfect opportunity for the referee to put the record straight and give the game a perfect result, but with even the Italians waiting for the inevitable, he waved play on and seconds later blew the whistle to give us a defeat we simply did not deserve. Fortunately, the result was almost the last thing that mattered on this particular day and when the players trooped sadly into the dressing room I told them that they could hold up their heads and face the world. They had represented their country in the finest possible manner. They had done the game of football a service world wide.

From a footballing point of view, it was also pleasing. I was satisfied that, given the same preparation, we could play the World Champions anytime, anywhere with a very good chance of winning. We had also learned a good deal for future reference. Although it was to be emphasised later, we detected that the first 15 to 20 minutes after the interval were the most difficult in terms of adjusting to the conditions. There was an obvious reacton after sitting down at half-time and it took a long while for the players to get going again. It was a problem we needed to solve in the next two games against the Mexicans and the West Germans. Everyone had suffered from overhitting the ball and misjudging its flight. It showed how important it was going to be in a year's time to enjoy the correct acclimatisation period while showing me that the careful use of substitutes was going to be critical. There were other bonuses. Francis had played exceptionally well against the sort of marking and the players he had been used to meeting every week in Italy while Everton's Gary Stevens had made a more than useful début at right-back with no blame at all attached to him from that ridiculous penalty. I was also gratified with the way our midfield of Trevor Steven, Ray Wilkins and Bryan Robson had performed with Glenn Hoddle looking perfectly at home when he took over from Steven.

In a bid to simulate the sort of programme we would face 12 months hence, we were due to play the World Cup hosts, Mexico, just three days later. It was tough on the players because the tests we needed to put them through meant precious little rest but we needed to make use of every day we had them together. While we were still looking ahead this was also a major public relations exercise as general opinion was still vehemently anti-English with substance being added to the rumours that our game back home was going to find itself in total isolation with no guarantee that we would not be going down the drain with it.

Italy had been the acid test of our character but this one was going to be equally tough against the locals who were carrying the Mexicans' hopes on their shoulders. This time we had a West German referee, the highly-respected Volker Roth. I made a few changes to see how some other essential members of the squad coped. It was important to give Gary Bailey a taste of the thin air while Viv Anderson replaced Gary Stevens, Fenwick and Watson came in for Butcher and Wright, Hoddle continued in place of Steven and John Barnes took over from Chris Waddle in their on-going tussle for the number eleven shirt.

The Mexicans were taking their training seriously and, under their Yugoslav manager Bora Milutinovic, had been brought together from their clubs in readiness for a full year's work. The clubs simply had to get on without them, though it must be said that they were without their most talented forward, Sanchez, who was developing his talents with those Spanish aristocrats, Real Madrid. The gap between the locals and ourselves from sea level was immediately obvious. While we were forced to pace ourselves and play in little bursts, they ran around like a dream with all the energy in the world. Although we had now spent 11 full days there, they still looked sharper and their engines considerably better tuned than ours. With the game being shown live on television there was again a lack of atmosphere with only around 15,000 in the stadium.

Our opponents also displayed good technical ability and might have taken a couple of goals in those opening 20 minutes but settled for the one when Flores scored past Bailey off the post. We could have had goals ourselves but the inspired goalkeeper, Larios, saved superbly from Francis and dealt with our crosses surprisingly well. When we did find our way past Larios via a Wilkins left-footer, sweeper Quirarte was on the line to clear. We did equalise in the second half when Viv Anderson bravely beat Larios to score with a superb header. Larios arrived late, bundled into Viv and then collapsed dramatically on the ground, rolling about in agony. While we celebrated our deserved equaliser, referee Roth was giving the home side a free kick for a foul on the goalkeeper. It was the third time in two matches that vital decisions had gone against us and I was grateful that the games were being shown on television for not only would it show the injustices to the people back home and in Mexico but it would also display how well our players took those reversals. In fact, I learned later that day that we had met with sympathy from all the media and consequently by the public.

The honeymoon was short-lived for the record books revealed that no other England team had lost three internationals on the trot since 1959. The likes of my England assistant, Don Howe, Jimmy Armfield, Billy Wright, Ron Flowers, Jimmy Greaves, Bobby Charlton and Johnny Haynes had lost to Brazil, Peru and Mexico on a similar summer tour, ending the run with an 8–1 victory over the United States. It was the season before I came back into the England side so I was close to being involved in that as well! This time we also had the United States waiting at the end of the trip but the difference was that we still had a tough game against our old rivals, West Germany, who would be only too pleased to rub our noses in the Mexico City grass.

The previously sympathetic Press were not slow to catch on and at our breakfast Press conference the next morning, I was asked by one of the more friendly national newspaper men: 'Do you realise, Bobby, that if we lose to West Germany it will be the worst-ever run by an England

70

manager?' What England manager had ever had a sequence like this? Not only had we coped with the heat and altitude but we had also played some good football against teams who were better prepared. The emotional stress on our players was nothing short of horrific after the Heysel disaster and we had been the victims of a series of cruel on-field decisions. But the journalists were right. There are no excuses or reasons recorded alongside the results in the FA Year Book and I have to accept those stark facts.

By this time our three Italian-based players had returned home to play in the Italian Cup – Trevor Francis to help Sampdoria win the competition for the first time in their history – after I had played them in both games against Italy and Mexico to use them to the maximum. Changes were forced and I was once again under terrific pressure to produce a victory in a friendly against the World Cup runners-up whom England had beaten only once in eight meetings since that historic 4–2 victory in the 1966 World Cup Final at Wembley Stadium.

But against this I felt that I had other things going for me. Such had been the antipathy against us and everything English that people suddenly began to turn the other way and say, 'Hold on, these people in Mexico had nothing to do with what happened in Brussels. They have been polite and have taken bad decisions and their beatings like real men with no moans and no complaints.' You could feel the atmosphere lighten, especially after the Italians completed their tour and returned home. I could also see just how well our players had settled into their new routine and how well they were coping with the conditions.

The other big advantage was a little more intangible for the West German manager, Franz Beckenbauer, had kept his players behind in Germany to train. He contended that there were two ways of approaching the conditions. One was to arrive well in advance as we and the Italians had done, the other was to, as he preferred, train hard at home and then fly in shortly before the game. They had turned up only two days before we met and I was certain from our own experiences that they would suffer. I guessed that, like any West German side, they would begin strongly and put us under some severe pressure but if we survived this then we could fight back and beat them. They would not be aware of that awkward period straight after the interval when it takes time to get the legs working properly again after relaxing. By then, we were using oxygen to revive our players during the break while keeping their limbs moving and supple.

I recalled Peter Shilton, Gary Stevens, Terry Butcher, Mark Wright and Chris Waddle while giving Everton's Peter Reid and Chelsea's striker Kerry Dixon their first full caps with the brilliantly-promising Gary Lineker playing alongside Dixon. The players were well aware of the crucial nature of the game and were determined that they would not be party to the unwanted record. Thanks to the brilliant medical work by Doc Edwards and his team, we had a clean bill of health and time had not only healed a few physical scars, like Reid's damaged hamstring, but also a few mental ones as well. All we wanted now was a fair crack of the whip.

The Mexican referee Leanza was all we could have asked on the day and in front of another sparse crowd but a television audience of millions in Mexico, England, West Germany and a great many other countries beside, everything began to fall into place. On 12 June we recorded a worthy three-goal victory. It was England's biggest margin against their old rivals for 50 years and what is more it could easily have been five as the tiring and dispirited Germans folded in the second half. We had read it exactly right for the Germans had looked fresh and eager in those early stages as they tried to make use of the thin air with a succession of long-range shots. Dixon and Lineker took time to get used to their new partnership but gradually we began to settle down and eventually took command as Lineker almost bundled in a Dixon centre while Bryan Robson, of all people, lifted the ball over the bar from Sansom's perfect centre. Bryan Robson had set a magnificent example as England captain before the game. Despite struggling with a nasty groin strain, which completely justified him to sit this one out, he was as enthusiastic as ever and determined that he should take his place in what he saw as an important game for his country. You never see Robson's head drop in an international and his early miss had no effect whatsoever and, indeed, just a few minutes later he had fired us in front as Dixon chested down a superb Hoddle pass for a delightful goal. It was the first time we had been in front for six games! It was no more than we deserved, but all the good could have been undone four minutes before the interval when the young and still inexperienced Mark Wright brought down Rahn. This time there were no complaints and the referee was left without any option. But the magnificent Shilton displayed his remarkable, quick reactions to save Brehme's spot kick and keep us in front at the break.

It was important for I was still convinced that the Germans would be at their best in that first half and would struggle if we could go out and play high-pressure football. We did, however, have difficulties. Lineker, who was suffering from cramps because of all the running he had done was replaced by John Barnes, and Bryan Robson by Paul Bracewell because the last thing I wanted to do was to send him back to Manchester United with an injury. Everyone did their duty that day and when Terry Butcher broke forward, he found himself supported from nowhere by the goal-hungry Dixon. Unselfishly, Butcher waited until the perfect moment to release the ball and Dixon, in his anxiety to score his first international goal, almost missed the biggest sitter of his lfe. But it went in off an upright and not long afterwards he was on the far post to convert a Barnes' centre for what the world has come to know as a typical English goal. Mill had shot against a post in between Dixon's pair but, that apart, the Germans crumbled and it was only their controversial goalkeeper, Toni Schumacher, who kept the score down to three.

It was an excellent all-round performance and I was delighted that the likeable Kerry Dixon had started his England career so well. There had been some doubts over his ability to make the step from club to international level and I must confess that I had not been at all sure how he would cope. The only way to find out had been to play him and he proved his worth against the highest-quality opposition. He seemed to be a natural goalscorer with the essential lucky streak that every top striker needs. Peter Reid, who looks like a little old man with his stooped shoulders and greying hair, had also established himself as a genuine contender for a regular place showing that he could have the same influence with England that he had in helping Everton to win the League Championship and UEFA Cup in 1985 and a narrow Cup Final defeat by Manchester United.

The victory was a tonic after our undeserved defeats in the previous two games. Justice had prevailed and we had finished the Mexican section of the tour on a high note and headed for Los Angeles and our final game with some relief after the earlier traumas. We had gained a great deal in team spirit and in our understanding of what we were to face in 12 months' time. There was a lot of muttering from outside the squad that the game against the Americans was a needless burden on already tired players but we had been pressed by the US Football Association who had been good friends to us in the past and it was on our way home. More importantly, it was a good opportunity for me to stay on an extra couple of days after the rest had gone home for I had my eye on some training facilities that would be ideal for our preparations immediately before our opening World Cup games.

It was very relaxing being in Hollywood among friends but the danger was that we would become a little too comfortable. I had to impress on the players that all the good work they had done would be worth nothing if they lost this one. The Americans had failed not only in their bid to stage the World Cup Finals but had also missed out on their much-needed qualification. Everyone kept reminding the players of the time we had lost to the Americans in the 1950 World Cup Finals at Belo Horizonte in Brazil when players of the quality of Bert Williams, Alf Ramsey, Billy Wright, Tom Finney, Wilf Mannion and Stan Mortensen earned one of those unwanted places in the history of football. I warned them that it could happen all over again if they did not approach the game in the Olympic Stadium properly.

Although there were a good many distractions I need not have worried. They were as professional as ever and were feeling the benefits of all that altitude training. They made it an easy match and even contrived a diplomatic scoreline! We won by five clear goals, which was enough to satisfy those at home and not too many to shatter the Americans' confidence. It was Gary Lineker who emphasised why I had always thought so highly of him when he relieved any possible anxiety with an amazing goal, chesting down a Hoddle pass, turning and hitting a right-foot volley for a goal that would have been raved about had it been against any other opposition. He and the eager Dixon, who had scored 35 goals for his club that season, scored two apiece while Dixon was also brought down for a penalty which goalkeeper Mausser did well to save as Glenn Hoddle tried to increase his internationally tally. Having given the patient Chris Woods his début in goal, I was also able to test Bryan Robson and juggle the remaining players around by using four substitutes. Two of them conjured up another fabulous goal for the enthusiastic crowd as Bracewell acrobatically knocked the ball down for his Everton club-mate, Trevor Steven, to score our fifth and final goal.

It was a happy coach ride back to our hotel. A long season was over at last. The boys could have a beer and relax knowing that they would soon be off on their holidays with their families. Sadly the atmosphere was soured when first one, then another, and another came down from their rooms with stories of missing money, credit cards and personal stereo units. The night out was delayed as the hotel manager and the security staff were called and lists made of the stolen property. Someone had known we were going to be out all afternoon and they had made a hasty sweep of the rooms. The concerned officials of the American Football Associaton could not have done more for us. It was a heart-stopping moment as everyone wondered what they had left in the room but, fortunately, because I had some of the Football Association's money with me I had put all my valuables in the hotel safe.

My wife Elsie had flown out to join me and we saw off a fine group of professional footballers who had done themselves and their country proud by their conduct. We enjoyed a few days in and around Los Angeles with an old friend, Mike Shapow, before heading off for a visit to the Rocky Mountain resort of Colorado Springs. However, this was anything but a holiday. From the moment I had known that the World Cup Finals had been switched from hard-up Colombia to high-up Mexico I had been anxious to discover somewhere where we could acclimatise. I had heard of

74

the good facilities and clean air of Colorado Springs from the stories of skiiers and particularly from one of my own favourite athletes, Steve Cram. I had been further influenced by the Scottish Youth Coach Andy Roxbrough who had taken his team there before the World Youth Championships in Mexico in 1983. When I had telephoned him he confirmed what an outstanding centre it was and then went into some detail when we met up in the South of France for an Under 18 tournament in Cannes.

He went into raptures over the place and, in particular, the American Airforce training base that was situated at 7,350 feet, which was almost the same height as Mexico City. He added that there were no health hazards and there were plenty of good hotels for us to stay in. It sounded perfect. Going to Mexico too early would be a mistake for too long in the same place makes only for boredom and staleness with professional sportsmen of any kind and in this footballers are a special breed who need that change of environment. I wanted to see the resort for myself and this was an ideal time to slip quietly away. It was good of Andy to tell me so much about it when the Scots might well have wanted to use it themselves but from what he had said there was room for both of us to live and train without ever seeing each other. In the event we got in just in time for others were quick to follow. The Canadians used their local knowledge to book the facilities early, while South Korea also moved smartly through their obvious American connections.

I had spoken to enough knowledgeable people to realise that we would not be able to make our final preparations at home, for not even my local Geordie mountain of Tow Law was high enough even though referee George Courtney had to make do with it before going out to Mexico as England's sole representative. My contact in Colorado, where the USA Association had their offices, was another former referee Keith Walker who had gone there to supervise the NASL's officiating and had then used his experience as former secretary with Sheffield United to work for the National Association. Unfortunately, he had been called away to some meeting in New York and had left his wife Brenda to look after us. She did a wonderful job, driving us round in her jeep so that we travelled 150 miles and looked at seven hotels. Had we been on our own it would have taken days. I knew as soon as we saw the famous old Broadmoor Hotel that this was the one for us. It was not because it was in the deluxe class for that is not always the best setting for footballers, but because of its amazing range of facilities and general feeling of space.

The other six hotels were all terrific but had no grounds in which to move around. The Broadmoor not only had its own grounds so that the players would be breathing the crystal clear fresh air instead of car fumes but also there was a lake, a pool, sunbathing areas, tennis courts and two golf courses. It was situated at 6,200 feet and ideal for preparation. Players need to get out of their bedrooms and be occupied with things other than simply training if their minds are to stay alert over a long period. I am not of the school of thought that bans all other activities including swimming and sunbathing. I have no hesitation in telling players to go out and have a game of golf, a swim or even a spell in the sun if I think it will do them good. Providing the sunbathing is monitored and not abused I believe it can be beneficial, for after all, players are going to be training and performing under similar conditions for spells of up to two hours. I know that Alf Ramsey banned the 1970 squad from lying in the sun before they played in Mexico but Bobby Charlton convinced me that I was on the right lines when he told me that he had suffered sun burn on his bald patch when he and the others suddenly emerged into the fierce Mexican sunlight with its enhanced burning properties due to the thin air. The only thing I was determined to draw the line at was...ice skating! Yes, our proposed training quarters even had an ice-rink.

But even this incredible hotel hardly compared with the American Air Force training base at Colorado Springs. Overlooked by the towering 14,000 foot Pikes Peak, it stood at the ideal altitude of nearly 7,500 feet and had everything a football manager and his team could want. The young Americans were spoiled for choice with every possible kind of sporting facility from baseball through grid iron to 35 tennis courts but, far more interesting to me, was the superb selection of football pitches. We were made immediately welcome with no reference made to Brussels or any of the other unsavoury things which had dogged us ever since we had left England. Everyone we met at the Academy was diplomatic, friendly and helpful, aware of England's status in world football as the founders of the game. They made it clear as they showed us around the multi-billion dollar sports complex that we would be made more than welcome with the promise of the two best of the dozen or so pitches if we decided to go there. The Colonel in charge of the physical recreation side of the base, could not have been more co-operative while soccer coach, Luis Sugastume (pronounced like socertome), was thrilled at the prospect of having us on his doorstep for two weeks. He was a fan of the English game and even held one of our FA coaching certificates from Lilleshall. He was like a dog with two tails when I told him he could not only attend all our training sessions but also take as much video footage as he wanted for his own use.

I simply could not believe what I was seeing and they told me that all the Football Association needed to do was to apply in writing and the use of

Top: World Cup 1982; Ron Greenwood was in charge with Terry Venables and me in support

Above: Here it was at last, my first game as manager of England in September 1982 and how proud I felt as the National Anthem was played. Ninety minutes later I was happy to have escaped with a 2-2 draw against Denmark

Top left: Dad and me. My father, Philip, 51 years a miner in the north-east of England, after making the trip to Wembley at the age of 81 to watch my first game as England manager. He caught the milk train back home!

Top right: One of my favourite players, Kevin Keegan. What a shame we never worked together at international level

Above: With two players as big as Terry Butcher and Paul Mariner, you can begin to understand why the team thought the rooms were a bit on the small side at Bisham Abbey

Top: Not even the best goalkeeper in the world, our own Peter Shilton, can stop this one as three times European footballer of the year, Michel Platini, heads past him for France's first goal in a 2-0 win in Paris

Above: Mark Hateley heads the golden goal that clinched our spectacular victory against Brazil in the Maracana Stadium, Rio de Janeiro in June 1984. Mark's performance that day convinced AC Milan to gamble £1 million for the Second Division centre forward

Above: Bryan Robson in my favourite pose – celebrating an England goal – after Tony Woodcock had scored against Finland at Wembley in October 1984

Centre: A sight, however, I saw far too often during the build-up to the World Cup as Bryan Robson leaves the pitch early. This time he is being carried off with an ankle injury, supported by physiotherapists Fred Street and Norman Medhurst, during our 2-1 win over the Republic of Ireland in March 1985

Left: Deep in discussion with Ray Wilkins, a player who has made an enormous contribution to the England team over the years. In the grounds of our Belfast hotel, we discuss the key World Cup qualifying match against Northern Ireland in February 1985

Right: Maybe it's the sun I'm pointing at above the haze of Mexico's smog or maybe I'm calling on divine intervention as the Press grill me after three successive defeats and a match against West Germany next at the Aztec Stadium in June 1985. An important part of the England manager's job is keeping the public informed through the media

Centre: With a venue like Mexico, the medical back-up is vital and in this respect England have the best. Here, Dr Vernon Edwards and physiotherapist Fred Street take a blood sample from Terry Fenwick with room-mate Dave Watson in the background

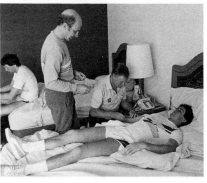

Below: In a bid to show international footballing unity following the Heysel disaster in Brussels, when Italian and England fans clashed, the players of the two sides lined up together a week later for a minute's silence in remembrance of the dead before the game. Left to right: Giovanni Galli; Mark Hateley; Bruno Conti; Trevor Francis; Pietro Vierchowod; Mark Wright and Salvatore Bagni

Top left: Off the field Kenny Sansom can always make the players laugh with his clever impersonations. On the pitch, however, he is a brilliant defender as he shows here marking one of the world's top wingers, Gheorghe Hagi, against Romania in Bucharest

Top right: Gary Lineker on his way to a hat-trick against Turkey in October 1985. A player I picked out as a future international long before he received the acclaim that brought him a big transfer to Everton

Above left: Glenn Hoddle always had the talent to be an outstanding performer in Mexico

Above right: Mark Hateley (right) and brave Trevor Francis, who made a despairing, last-ditch attempt to earn his ticket to Mexico by playing against Scotland at Wembley with a double fracture of the cheekbone

Top left: Ted Croker and me in front of the board displaying the draw in which we had just been paired with Poland, Portugal and Morocco in the heat of Monterrey. We could afford to smile for we had just missed going into the toughest group of the lot, Group E

Top right: 'Here come the animals.' The headline leaves no doubt what the Mexican Press think of our fans. The cross I continually have to bear

Above: Real Mexican hospitality. AeroMexico pilot Captain Hector Alcocer brought his aircraft back to the ramp to pick up my fellow late passengers and me for the flight to Saltillo after the draw ceremony in Mexico City

Top: If the Sphinx knows anything at all, he is saying nothing. Somewhat less inscrutable are the England squad

Above: This is not a sight you see very often in the corridors of the Football League grounds. Tony Woodcock and Viv Anderson, along with liaison officer, Les Walker, look in amazement at two Egyptians kneeling in prayer outside their dressing room

the complex was ours for a peppercorn rent. I knew it was right for us. Even Pikes Peak had its uses for, though its summit was too high to do more than walk on, lower down were routed four- and six-mile runs at around a breathless 8,000 feet. I told Luis these were fine as long as he found me a bike. I was not joking for these sort of runs are only any use if run at the right pace and they always go at the rate of the slowest man. That would be me. He promised not only bikes for Don Howe and me but also a couple of his own athletes who would take the players through at the best pace and make sure no one got lost.

Brenda Walker even took us to a local school where the headmaster, who was a football fan married to an English wife, offered us the use of a couple of football pitches along with a smartly-appointed dining room. The pitches were of a high quality but the problem was that they were down at below 6,000 feet, though they were always available for a change of scenery and for a very pleasant public relations exercise.

My mind was well and truly made up. This was the place for us and all I had to do now was to clear it with the Football Association back home, for after all, they had to foot the inevitably large bill at one of America's finest hotels. Bert Millichip and Ted Croker were as delighted as I was that we had found the right place so quickly and they backed me fully knowing that there was no way I would have chosen a luxury hotel unless it was for very good reasons. There was no argument, only agreement. Although final confirmation of our qualification was a point or two away, I had a very good idea of how I wanted to prepare for the World Cup Finals.

The only problems were the imponderables. Injuries to key players, overcrowded fixture lists, bad weather, the behaviour of our fans who could get us banished from the Finals without our even playing a game if there were any further outbreaks of violence and, of course, the draw scheduled for December when we would know where we would be based. We had been told that we were unlikely to be one of the seeded teams and that in all probability we would be in the industrial northern city of Monterrey. That was disturbing news for it was one of the hottest areas in Mexico and was also the ground nearest to sea level. It would thus pose many added problems for the teams who qualified when they suddenly had to move a great deal higher into thin air in the latter stages of the competition.

There was no doubt that we were walking a tightrope where the problem of hooliganism was concerned for, after world-wide discussions, it was decided that we were the only English team who could travel abroad to play matches of any kind, and this included even visits to Scotland, Wales and Ireland. It was equally clear that if the England followers played up

again we would also be banned from World and European Championships alike. This we could cope with to some degree by choosing our
fixtures with great care while the preliminary stages of the European
Championships to be drawn in January would not begin until after the
World Cup Finals.

In a perverse way I also thought that the ban on English clubs could give
us a head start in our bid to win the World Cup. I had idyllic visions of a
shortened season with no European dates to keep free, the possibility of
extra international matches and even an April departure date for Colorado. Perhaps our luck had turned at last. Or maybe I was deluding myself.
Just about everything that could happen to hinder our progress was to be
thrown up by friend and foe alike.

7. Expectations

When I began to recover from the shock of the English club ban, I realised that maybe it could be turned to England's advantage. No European dates and no money-making trips to the Middle East meant that our previously overcrowded domestic season had suddenly eased. I had visions of the season being shortened so that we could leave for our high altitude training before the end of April and, being greedy, maybe fit in an extra international game or two. At worst, I thought we could have additional squad training in those barren months between November and February.

I was so excited at the prospect that I took the opportunity of speaking to the League President, Jack Dunnett, who had flown out to join us in Mexico. I explained that though it was a terrible blow to the country and to the international development of the England players, who would miss the chance of playing against top continental opposition, we could turn it to our advantage in terms of World Cup preparation. With our domestic structure it would have taken 25 years to have planned something similar.

I was whistling in the wind. My illusions were quickly shattered for Jack Dunnett was not thinking along the same lines. Quite understandably, he was still recovering from the body blow of the European ban which would cost his financially overstretched clubs a great deal of expected revenue. So far as Jack Dunnett was concerned there were no compensations and I had the distinct impression that he had taken offence that I had seen it that way. I immediately resigned myself to the fact that all I would gain was maybe one extra fixture in mid-winter and, at least, the minor satisfaction of the season finishing on time. I should have learned by then not to be even mildly optimistic.

By the time the season began the situation was worse than ever. The gaps had been filled not by one but two competitions. I could not believe it after all the complaints of overcrowding. The clubs who would have qualified for Europe had entered something called the Screen Sports Super Cup while everyone else in Divisions One and Two were asked if they wanted to play in the Full Members Cup. I thought both ideas ludicrous and decided then and there not to lend my support to either and not to attend any of the games. It was a deliberate decision because I knew that, one way or another, they would ruin my plans either by injury or fixture build-up. Now I had lost on two fronts with my players unable either to gain European experience or to enjoy extra training days with the national squad.

I could not even get the date of the Cup Final changed. I thought, at least, I would be able to travel out to the States with all my players if the Football Association could change the Wembley date from 10 to 3 May but there were far too many obstacles. My bosses at Lancaster Gate were sympathetic but, because these things have to be planned so far ahead, they felt they were unable to do anything about it as Wembley was booked for the Rugby League Cup Final on the previous Saturday. I tried every argument I could think of such as swapping dates with the Rugby League or even playing the match on Sunday, 4 May. I know this would have created problems but I was prepared to tackle them if someone would back me. After all, the National Exhibition Centre seemed able to cope with two major events in two days, so why couldn't Wembley cope with two 100,000 sell-outs in 24 hours? What was there to lose? They could only say no.

Unfortunately, nothing happened and a golden opportunity was thrown away. Was I one of only a few people who could see the benefits of England reaching the later stages of the World Cup? Surely it would have been to everyone's advantage if a fit, well-prepared England team went out to Mexico and lit up the television screens back home. With all due respect to Liverpool, Everton, Manchester United and the rest, whoever wins the League or the Cup will not restore the crowds to grounds in any place other than their own back yard, whereas if England performed well in or even won the World Cup, it would be a wonderful boost for the country and our beleaguered game. Remember what happened in 1966? Alf Ramsey's success with England halted the declining gates, added on an extra three million spectators and made people talk about football again in pubs. Maybe we wouldn't have quite the same effect but we would surely add a million and revive interest in an ailing game. It would rub off on every club, large and small, because the public's interest would be matched by the sponsors who recently have found football's image a little too tarnished by the events of 1985.

Other countries prize their national team and do everything they can to help them prepare but, despite the events of the previous season, nothing changed and far from looking for new benefits I found myself praying that the weather would not cause the usual pile-up and that my players would not suffer too many injuries or be too tired from playing 42 League games plus the FA Cup, the Milk Cup, the Full Members Cup and the Screen

Sports Super Cup. All of them, it seemed to me at that time, were taking precedence over the World Cup.

The World Cup action was due to come around quickly with Romania the visitors to Wembley on 11 September. Although everything had gone pretty well I knew that a defeat here would bring criticism from the media and possible uncertainty for my players. If we won no one could catch us and if we drew we would still be nicely on course. Having already performed with great credit in Bucharest, I was confident that Wembley would hold no terrors for England.

The crowd, which had dwindled after one or two indifferent performances, was coming back. I desperately wanted to see Wembley filled but I knew that would only happen with a consistently winning side. It is an awful place to play when it is only a third full and both the players and I were looking forward to the atmosphere of a 60,000 audience. Wright and Fenwick continued at centre-back with Terry Butcher again out with injury while I took the opportunity of giving the midfield of Robson, Hoddle and Reid another chance, which sadly meant leaving Ray Wilkins on the substitutes' bench. This was still one of the few areas I was wrestling over in my mind – Wilkins or Reid? I was hoping that this was one of the games that would help me to decide. I wanted two ball winners and I wanted the talented play-maker Boloni snuffed out. I knew that Reid would get his foot in more often than Wilkins. Robson had other duties and I wished Glenn Hoddle to have a little freedom to show the Wembley crowd what he could do. I picked what I thought was a team to win but I still had Mexico very much in mind. With perhaps two exceptions that was the team I was considering for our opening game. In fact, I felt I was very close to my ideal squad even though there was a full season to go before the World Cup began. I had 18 or 19 players out of the 22 I needed to name some time late in April. I had to be decisive for there were players whom I urgently required to gain international experience.

The Romanians have a good record at Wembley and, once again, they gave us some problems with the young and very talented Gheorghe Hagi twice hitting the woodwork before we took control with a piece of pure invention by two of our outstanding players, Kenny Sansom and Glenn Hoddle. I would like to be able to claim that the free kick was of my making and that it had been well rehearsed in training but, in truth, it was nothing of the kind as Sansom made a fine decision when he saw Hoddle making an unchallenged run. The delivery from Sansom was perfect as was Hoddle's control and turn before he coolly shot past goalkeeper Lung. It was a rare goal, the sort that even Platini would have been delighted to score. In short, it showed exactly the type of flair and imagination we would need in Mexico.

The game was close but we stayed in the driving seat, seeing a lot of the ball and looking for the second goal before Camataru squeezed between Fenwick and Stevens to beat Shilton for the equaliser. However, the television cameras showed that the tall, powerful Romanian striker had controlled the ball with his hand to beat our two defenders and Shilton, who after confidently appealing, was too late to recover when he realised that the referee was masked and had allowed play to go on. Camataru, like the quality international he is, slid the ball under Shilton's diving body. Such are the decisions that make or break teams and reputations. Fortunately, it did not mean disaster for us, though it was a body blow to the Irish who had not helped their own cause with a goalless draw against Turkey in Izmir.

I sent on fresh legs in Barnes for Waddle and Woodcock for Lineker but it made no difference and we were still a point away from officially qualifying. Frustrating and disappointing, yes but displeasing, no! The team had given its all and performed well against a good team. I could see the need for improvement but that was only going to come with more experience of playing together. To our credit, we were not leaking goals and the midfield looked balanced. Like every other manager in the world I was still seeking the elusive finishing power that transforms ordinary teams into good ones and good teams into great ones. I was sure we could score more goals if better quality centres were fed to Hateley and Lineker on the far and near posts respectively.

The sad news was that Reid finished the game hobbling, which was an injury that was to keep him out of action for a long time. It was a blow to Champions Everton and to ourselves. We did not at first know how serious the injury was because Peter just gritted his teeth and kept going. It was typical of the man but small consolation for his club manager, Howard Kendall, and for me as I have always felt bad about sending players back home injured.

At the end of the day we had maintained our pole position and had seemingly not upset too many people in the process for we received a reasonable Press. All we needed now was to beat Turkey at home for everyone to throw away their calculators along with any lingering doubts. As it happened we did not even need that last point as the unpredictable Irish upset all the odds by beating Romania 1–0 in Bucharest before we had even kicked off. It was smashing for Billy Bingham and his boys to give themselves that unexpected chance but as I listened to the game on my radio in my hotel room in High Wycombe, I thought it was a pity for the

Wembley crowd that they would not see us do it that night and for our players who would have to remotivate themselves.

What should have been an enjoyable romp took on serious overtones, for, while the players responded superbly to my pre-match exhortations to play properly and give the fans something for their money, our influential skipper Bryan Robson pulled a hamstring to start a chain of events which were to haunt him, Manchester United and me right up to the World Cup itself. Having won by eight goals in Turkey, a great many of the 52,500 Wembley crowd were expecting us to run up double figures and while that was hardly likely, we wanted to give a performance and were looking for a convincing three- or four-goal victory. For an hour it looked as though the supporters would be right as Chris Waddle set us off with his first goal for England, which was a spectacular solo effort that brought the house down. Lineker next scored with two fine headers followed by a fourth from Bryan and at half-time we were on our way to another massive scoreline.

What really delighted me was the way the midfield performed. Wilkins was back for the injured Reid and, along with Robson and Hoddle, played well. Although the opposition was scarcely world class, I thought the integration between the three was superb and likely to improve. Turkey simply could not handle the power of Robson, the solidity of Wilkins nor the intuition of Hoddle, who was settling into a position that was somewhat removed from his normal club one. Obviously, I needed to test it against higher-quality opponents as I thought ahead to the matches against the Soviet Union and Scotland, but at least I felt that I had solved another of the riddles.

There was further confirmation in the opening quarter of an hour of the second period when we carried on where we had left off with Lineker completing his hat-trick with a right-foot shot but then Robson, chasing a lost cause, charged after a long cross to the far post and pulled a hamstring. Five up, he could have let it go but not Bryan, who was looking for number six. Off he limped and with him went our sparkle. The whole game had died long before Hateley was tackled and limped off. It was something that was picked up both by the crowd and in the criticism that followed. I could understand it and those players must be the only internationals who have ever come off after a five-goal victory and received a severe dressing down from their manager.

We had played well for an hour and finished badly and I went into the dressing room to say, 'It is hard for me to moan after a win like that but if we had kept going and scored even one more you would have all been hailed as heroes instead of walking off in silence.' Their heads were down but they were not so concerned as me for once again things had gone adrift when the skipper was missing. We did not fall apart or anything like that, we just stopped playing and let our supporters and ourselves down. If we were that reliant on one player we might as well not bother going to Mexico. It was a problem I had to find an answer to.

The news the next morning about Robson was bad. He was going to be out for a while after making a magnificent start to the season. He had been at his best as Manchester United threatened to win the First Division Championship by Christmas, never mind Easter. They simply could not lose and I had these visions of Bryan lifting the First Division Championship, winning the Footballer of the Year trophy and then leading England to victory in Mexico. The dream began to turn into a nightmare that night at Wembley as he was missing far too many England games. He is our best outfield player and it would have been nice to build towards Mexico using him as much as France did Michel Platini.

Having now qualified it was the right time to visit Mexico to make further plans. Even while we had been on tour in Mexico in May we heard that Mexico, Brazil, West Germany and France would be four of the six seeded teams and that they would be in Mexico City, Guadalajara, Queretaro and León respectively and that it was more than likely that the holders Italy would also be seeded and share the capital with the hosts. That left one spot and the story was that we would be given it and be based in Monterrey. If possible, we wanted confirmation of the rumours, for Monterrey presented a completely different set of problems, being not only the hottest by some 20 degrees but also the lowest at 1,800 feet, making it extremely difficult for the team when it moved onto a high altitude centre in the second phase.

There were other difficulties. On Thursday, 19 September there was a tragic earthquake in Mexico City which killed thousands. Naturally, it put the whole competition in question with suggestions of a change of venue, a 12-month delay and even the possibility of cancellation. It had happened once before when Chile was devastated by an earthquake but that was two years, not ten months, before the Finals. The television film and newspaper reports suggested that a third of Mexico City had collapsed and that the World Cup Final city was virtually destroyed.

However, my second visit to Mexico was not going to be a sightseeing tour. It was Work with a capital 'W', beginning with an early call for Ted Croker and me to catch our flight to Mexico City via Miami. We were already tired having paid a flying visit to Manchester the day before to look at Umbro's range of leisure and training wear for the team, which was important in view of the high temperatures. It was the start of a hectic schedule.

When we arrived in Mexico City on 1 November we were surprised to see little apparent damage. Obviously, there were pockets of devastation where one in three buildings were damaged, some of them having collapsed and others in an unusable state with the rest being completely unaffected.

We met Brian Gay in Mexico City. He had been liaison officer for Alf Ramsey in 1970. Fortunately for me, the Football Association had kept in touch with him and so we had a man on site who knew the country intimately and spoke the language. The first trip we made was to the headquarters of the Organising Committee to see if we could discover whether or not we were seeded. If others could be informed why not us? We told them we had been tipped off about Monterrey but they could tell us nothing. They knew nothing.

The afternoon was spent inspecting the Mexico City hotels after hearing that our favourite, the Camino Real, was earmarked for the Press and FIFA officials as were the El Presidente, the Sheraton Isabella and the Gallery Plaza. The best had already been taken and we had to look at the rest. It was not as easy as it sounds for the hotels designated for team use were widely scattered, with some being situated in the Pink Zone, full of nightclubs, and others in the earthquake area. I couldn't have the players disturbed by noisy late-night revellers nor could we stay in an area surrounded by devastated buildings. The earthquake had caused a completely new set of problems.

We still felt that there was a chance we would be seeded and if we were the venue would be in Monterrey so, next morning, we were off again with a 4.30 a.m. call for an early flight north where we spent the day looking at hotels and training facilities in Monterrey and much higher up in the university town of Saltillo. The only other place we could stay if we were seeded was Mexico City itself and we felt that it was important that we should book the training facilities at the Reforma Club that had been so popular with the players and the backroom staff on tour. We joined the President of the Club on the evening of 3 November for drinks to confirm arrangements after yet another tiring day of looking at hotel bedrooms, possible kit rooms, recreational facilities and the rest. It was all run of the mill, very tiring but extremely necessary. We were given no special treatment by hotel managers who were keen to have England and certainly we were not offered any bribes. They knew they were going to be able to fill their rooms without us. We were lucky to be given a cup of tea! But the Mexican people themselves presented a different face. They had their own enormous problems to deal with but they were clearly gratified that we still had faith in them and their ability to stage the World Cup. The fact that we had bothered to visit at all was reassuring to them for they wanted the Finals and were quick to tell us they could cope.

One problem the Mexicans and their visitors were going to have to face in June, however, was the Mexico City traffic. It made every trip a tiring excursion and lengthened the day interminably. On the morning of the 4th, Ted and I visited the headquarters of the Mexican Football Association to add our name to the growing list of World Cup teams who wanted to arrange fixtures in the ten- to twelve-day period immediately before the Finals. We told the Secretary we were prepared to play local First Division club sides or visiting Central American teams. We were not the first to ask and would not be the last. In the afternoon we visited the Mexico City grounds and even more hotels.

We had another early start on the fifth day of our visit when we caught a 6.30 a.m. flight with Brian Gay to León where we looked at six hotels, several training grounds and met the local Press – an important public relations exercise. We visited the hotel that Alf had used and even had breakfast with the manager. It was certainly convenient for it was only a mile from the stadium, but there was no privacy. We also looked at the hotel the West Germans had used before they beat us in that famous quarter-final 15 years earlier and then went 17 miles out of León to Juan Quato where the Brazil squad were booked for a month's stay before going to Guadalajara. By the end of the trip I quite fancied León which said a lot for the place considering we saw it after a 17-hour day that ended in the coffee shop with a midnight snack.

The next day Ted Croker and I left Mexico City for Colorado via Houston. Now we had qualified I wanted Ted to see the training centre and the hotel I had chosen and to meet Lieutenant-Colonel David Schichtle – I wished to confirm the Academy and to see if we could negotiate a decent price at the luxurious Broadmoor Hotel where the standard rates were well in excess of £100 per night. When we disembarked at Colorado Springs we were told that Concorde was due to arrive on a courtesy visit and if we wished we could stand on the tarmac to watch it land. The whole airport was crowded with people waiting to see that beautiful aircraft land and as we saw it a spontaneous round of applause came from the Americans. Both Ted and I felt proud to be British at that moment.

Ted, an ex-RAF man, took an immediate liking to the Lieutenant-Colonel. The base facilities clearly met with his approval as well but, under the guidance of the former English referee Keith Walker, we had to look at the options as, after all, the hotel would be very expensive. We also discussed the possibility of another match with the USA while we were there. The next day we visited the USA offices and inspected the Clarion

Hotel before rushing off to catch a flight to St Louis for our connection to Gatwick.

We arrived at Gatwick on Saturday, 8 November, and I drove straight to Stamford Bridge to watch Chelsea play Nottingham Forest. I knew Mark Hateley was struggling and felt that I needed to have a look at Kerry Dixon and maybe compare him with Peter Davenport. I drove home to Ipswich that night but only to change my suitcase, say hello to Elsie and leave the next day to join up with the squad for the final qualifying game against Northern Ireland. I had left the names of my squad with Dave Sexton and I was pleased to see that there were very few changes because of injury, though I was without two of my most important players, Bryan Robson and Mark Hateley. I had already decided to give Kerry Dixon his Wembley chance and I opted for yet another Everton man, Paul Bracewell, in place of the captain. Paul had been in the squad for a year having served a sound apprenticeship with the Under 21s. He had proved himself to be a good footballer, neat and tidy, industrious and a good link between attack and defence. He had also been a superb squad member, which was typical of the whole group of Everton players who were a credit to their club. It was one of the reasons why they had become such a force in the English game.

The build-up to the match was dominated by insinuations from Romania that they suspected that the game would be fixed to help the Irish to qualify. Romania were playing Turkey half-an-hour before our kick-off and even if they won the Irish needed only a draw to join us in Mexico. We were already group champions whatever the outcome. I used the accusations as part of my pre-match motivation. I pointed out to the team that we had worked hard to bring the crowd back and it would be criminal if we were to take it easy or cheat on them in any way. I can state categorically that the Northern Ireland manager, Billy Bingham, never once approached me for any form of favour and I would no more have expected him to than I would have done myself if I had been in the same position.

Romania, as expected, beat Turkey 3–1 in Izmir before our match had finished. We drew 0–0 with Northern Ireland in front of a 70,500 crowd, some of whom chanted 'fix' at the end, a thought which was echoed in Turkey and Bucharest that night but not in many other places for we received a clean bill of health from the FIFA observer and everyone else who saw the game on television. To accuse us of arranging the result was an insult to that great goalkeeper, Pat Jennings, who at the age of 40 was playing his 113th international that night. Jennings made spectacular saves from a swirling Glenn Hoddle shot and another from Kerry Dixon's header. You cannot make shots or saves like that to order, no one is that talented.

To be quite honest, the Irish were fortunate that night. They fought as though their lives depended on it and earned everything that went their way after being their own worst enemies in the earlier group games. If the Romanians wanted someone to blame it should have been themselves for having lost twice to the Irish. Bingham's team had done him proud, conceding only one goal in their final five World Cup games. We had so much possession that Shilton did little more than pick the ball up a couple of times while we gradually built up the pressure. Jennings and McDonald were outstanding because of the work they had to do, though the QPR defender was fortunate when he clearly handled the ball in the penalty area on the blind side of Swedish referee Fredriksson. When Jennings was not saving or the Irish defence clearing off the line, we contrived to miss the opportunities we were creating, especially Lineker who put his effort the wrong side of the post and Dixon who completely missed the ball in front of goal. Those misses brought more murmurings but can you imagine the goal-hungry Lineker deliberately missing? Or Dixon, with all his family present, mis-kicking in front of goal on his Wembley début on purpose.

Whatever happened that night at Wembley we could not win. If we had lost we would have been pilloried and accused of selling the game while a victory would have had others saying, fancy stopping a fellow British team getting through at the expense of an Eastern European one. In the end we were disappointed not to have won but I admit feeling pleased for Billy, his team and especially for Pat Jennings. I admired the way they had stuck to their task. So far as I was concerned they had made it to Mexico entirely through their own efforts without help from us or anyone else. What is more they had done it by beating the Romanians twice, which was something England had not done even once.

I did not say very much to my players after the game because there wasn't a great deal to say. They had not disgraced themselves, far from it. Maybe, if we had needed one or both points, we could have coaxed another five to ten per cent out of them but World Cup qualifying must be judged on the whole competition and not just on one 'dead' match. There was a period in the game when we went for their throats and had we scored then they would have been out. We did not manage to get that goal but we had completed our eight-match programme without a single defeat. We were the only European team to reach Mexico with such a record, having conceded just two goals. It was a performance no one could equal. My players had done a more than reasonable job and the whole country should have been delighted that we had done it so well. We had approached each match professionally, progressing all the time and never relinquishing our place at the top of the group. We had never been in a difficult position and had achieved qualification for a World Cup Finals by the most comfortable margin in our history.

Yet not everyone was satisfied, not by a long way. It was my misfortune to be caught in the middle of a newspaper circulation war and I was well used to some football writers who had not even attended our games attacking me and criticising our players. That is their prerogative. It is what they are paid to do and it is up to their conscience and their professional integrity how they tackle it. But what I cannot stand is when my fellow professionals jump on the bandwagon.

They were at it after the Irish game with, as usual, the *Daily Mirror*, right at the forefront. Their latest weapon against me was former England captain, Emlyn Hughes, who pulled no punches. He began by saying: 'I don't go around kicking people when they are down. That's why I'm not going to put the boot into Bobby Robson.' He went on to add, 'But, like I've been saying for a long time, England are not good enough.' He then attacked me personally: 'Robson worried me. Anybody who goes up to Mark Dennis of Southampton and says "How are you, Paul Walsh?" would, wouldn't they?'

It was not the first time he had had a go and it wasn't to be the last. I took offence at some of the things he said. Straight criticism I can take, but downright lies, no. The Mark Dennis story was ridiculous. I have only occasionally met the lad but I would certainly recognise Paul Walsh if I saw him and if Emlyn had stopped to think he would have known why. Had Emlyn ever bothered to call me and ask for an interview I would have been happy to talk to him as an ex-international but he seems to go out of his way to avoid me these days. It hurt that someone who played for a club as professional as Liverpool, a player who had represented his country and someone who had tried football management should be so sour about the game that had been so good to him. It is a pet hate of mine for people who have enjoyed a good living from football to want to knock others for either notoriety or money.

It was the second time in a few days that I felt hurt by a fellow professional for when I returned from Mexico and the United States, I was shown extracts from Steve Perryman's book in the *Sunday People* where he said, 'I've played only once for an England team under Bobby Robson and I was horrified by what I saw and heard. Everything about it was so amateurish I could not believe that was how England did things.' This was written on the strength of one appearance for what was little more than an England 'B' side, though players were awarded full caps. I looked after the team with Dave Sexton because the senior players, on their way to Spain for the World Cup, were playing Finland in Helsinki that same day. Ron

Greenwood picked the squad and the team and I just met them at the airport on the way out to Iceland. One of my instructions from Ron was to bring Perryman on for a cap in the second half because he had been such a good honest professional for so many years without being quite talented enough to make the international grade. Perryman's response was to say that playing for England was a laugh and, on the strength of those few minutes in Iceland for a 'B' team, he had learned enough to state, 'It seems to me that since Alf Ramsey was in charge there has been a lack of organisation and direction.' I know that neither my players nor I are above criticism but it would have been nice to have had the backing of my fellow professionals. Goodness knows the job is hard enough as it is and I need all the help I can get.

It was not, however, as if I had a lot of time to consider the slings and arrows for, having seen the Press and spent a little time at home, I was off on my travels again on 16 November headed for Paris to watch France play Yugoslavia at the Parc des Princes in a World Cup qualifier that the European Champions needed to win. It was a nice feeling to know that we had qualifed and were well ahead with our plans while teams like France were still worried about getting there at all. What is more the better side lost on the night for only two goals from the marvellous Platini separated the teams at the end of the game and it had to be said that the French were a mite lucky.

It was important that I saw as many of the World Cup finalists as I possibly could, particularly when they were being fully stretched as the French were that night. Next morning I left Paris for Munich to see West Germany play Czechoslovakia in bitterly cold conditions at the Olympic Stadium. Even with a sheepskin coat I needed the two blankets my hosts lent me and it was so icy that *Daily Mail* football writer Jeff Powell and I had to give our taxi a push start to even get to the game at all! A late goal from Karl-Heinz Rummenigge gave the West Germans a fortunate result that failed to impress either me, their own manager Franz Beckenbauer or the lowest-ever attendance at a West German home international.

The next day I flew from Munich to Nice to watch the England Under 16 team complete their commitments in a major tournament involving West Germany, France and Italy. These were my 'babies' and I was as interested in them and their match as I was in the senior internationals I had just watched. They had done well and were due to play France in the final the following day. It was luxury to spend a night knowing there was no plane to catch the next morning. The boys went out on Tuesday, 19 November and beat the French 2–0 to receive the cup from Prince Rainier himself. It was a proud moment and especially for Dave Sexton and Mike Kelly who were in charge of the team. The French coach came up to me afterwards and said that it was the best performance he had seen from 16-year-olds and that some of our FA/GM National School of Excellence players were among the most promising youngsters he had ever seen.

However, the respite was brief for there was my usual 5 a.m. alarm call on Wednesday, 20 November for a flight to Amsterdam. By lunchtime I was in Rotterdam ready for the play-off between Holland and Belgium. It was another important game as I had not seen either team play for two years and we could end up playing the winners in Mexico. Holland won the game 2–1 but lost their chance on away goals when Grun scored six minutes from the end. Teams reach the World Cup Finals on merit, not reputation, and out went the runners-up of both the 1974 and 1978 competitions. How glad I was at that moment that we had managed it without any problems other than that unwarranted cricitism.

However, there was little time to consider the result in depth as I had arranged to fly back to London the next morning to pick up my car and drive to Manchester where I was due to speak at an Altrincham FC dinner, keeping a long-standing promise I had made to their Chairman, Noel White, well before I knew I would be taking nine flights in the space of six days. I started my speech by saying that I hoped I was in the right place at the right time and dressed appropriately, having carried my evening suit through half-a-dozen countries, adding that my wife Elsie sent her best wishes and the message that I should be at home instead of with them. It was a light-hearted comment, but there was more than a grain of truth in it. I did eventually get home the next day before driving to London on Saturday for a guest appearance on the kids' show *Saturday Superstore*, taking in the local derby between Watford and Luton that afternoon. I had spent three out of the last twenty-five nights in my own bed.

8. The Draw

I was beginning to get to know Mexico City. By the time the draw was made on 15 December, I was there on my third visit in the space of 12 months. It may sound rather extravagant and some critics even questioned the validity of my going to Mexico simply to see who we were to play six months later. Let me say straight away that not a minute was wasted on any of those visits nor on the subsequent trips to the States.

Having failed to discover where we would be based on our previous visit, we were concerned this time to be well situated not just for the preliminary round but, it was to be hoped, for the later stages in the competition. This meant avoiding Monterrey for, as I explained to journalists on the day before we left, it was a bad choice because it was close to sea level which would make life doubly difficult in terms of acclimatisation before and after the three first-round matches. Unfortunately, these comments were misinterpreted in Mexico where they thought I was criticising the city and its people. Now we had another reason not to go there.

There were all sorts of rumours and counter rumours including one by a South American newspaper which alleged that the entire draw had already been arranged behind closed doors and that the world-wide televised event was just a sham. To emphasise their point, they even printed what they claimed to be the full draw. The visitors were amused but the Mexicans were outraged. All anyone knew for certain was that Italy, Mexico, West Germany, France, Brazil and Poland would be the seeded teams and that we were among the second group, along with Argentina, Paraguay, the Soviet Union, Spain and Uruguay and, while all the South American teams had been split up, it was quite possible that we could be in the same group as Scotland and Northern Ireland. How ironical that would have been after the scrapping of the Home International Championships!

We had a couple of days to spare before the draw and this we spent looking at yet more hotels. If we were going to be successful I knew we would eventually have to make our way to Mexico City but, because of the question marks surrounding the venue for the knock-out section of the competition, all sorts of allowances needed to be made. I had already been assured of the use of the magnificent Reforma Club. It was not only a fabulous place away from the grime of Mexico City but we were used to it and had been exceptionally happy there during a very difficult period. For me it was the best training centre in Mexico and I wanted to find a hotel to match it. I had seen Mexico play Hungary in Toluca and had been impressed by the hotel there which, at 8,000 feet, would have been perfect if it did not take us more than two hours travelling each way. We eventually settled on the Holiday Inn out by the airport – after assuring ourselves, of course, that it was suitably soundproofed!

Our immediate concern, however, was the first-round draw and we were only too well aware that we could find ourselves in any of the six groups which were to play at different places all over Mexico. The Mexican Organising Committee had told us that there would be no panic over booking hotels and other facilities and that, after the draw, there would be a special desk at the Camino Real Hotel which would supply air tickets to wherever we wanted to go. We wanted to be better prepared than that and wanted no second or third choices. Our previous visit had provided us with an insight into each venue, which hotel we wanted and where we wanted to train. We told no one and everyone else was naturally playing their cards close to their chests for, after all, the other three teams in the group may have had exactly the same ideas. Our provisions were made. We had a man in Guadalajara sitting in a chair next to the manager's office watching a television set, another was waiting with a filled-out cheque in León ready to claim our headquarters for the French group, Ted Croker had written out a personal cheque for the Camino Real's sister hotel in Saltillo if we drew Monterrey and consul Ted Lawrence was lurking outside the manager's office to confirm the booking if necessary. Someone else was in Toluca and we had our own ideas if we were in the capital.

All in all we felt that we had been pretty foxy for, as an extra precaution, we had decided that the moment our name came out I would start off for the airport and Ted would remain for the rest of the draw. We were calm and ready for any eventuality. I was quite excited for this was the moment we had been working for since I had taken over and very soon we would know exactly what we had let ourselves in for. There was a terrific feeling of expectation and enthusiasm about the place and my immediate hope was that we would be one of the ones to be drawn out first. The alternatives went through my mind. Mexico City I didn't mind because of the Reforma Club and the facilities at Guadalajara were so good that I did not even care if we drew Brazil, which would have been quite a coincidence in a repeat of the 1970 draw. I also liked the idea of León and the possibility of an early encounter with France just as Ron Greenwood's team had done so successfully four years previously in Bilbao. However, my fingers were crossed that we avoided the heat of Monterrey.

The groupings were no major problem either for anyone with an eye on the final knows they have to beat the best to win but, like everyone else, I was none too keen on having Denmark as the 'weak' team of the group. They should never have been placed with the likes of Canada, Iraq, South Korea, Algeria and Morocco but there had been little choice because the Danes were such an emergent soccer nation that this was their first ever qualification for the final stages of the World Cup and they, and whoever they drew, had to accept the principle. I just hoped it wasn't us.

The draw was cleverly done and very well presented. As the names came out of the hat I kept thinking to myself, 'that group will do us very nicely', only to see someone else step in. So it went on, and on, and on. For a moment I wondered whether we had been kicked out. Eventually, there were only two names left and my hopes of an early getaway vanished as I loosened my collar feeling the heat of the camera lights. The only other remaining team were the South American Champions Uruguay and here I was contemplating the prospect of either being in the toughest group or playing at what I considered the worst venue. Suddenly, Monterrey did not seem so bad. I recalled my earlier visit and remembered how pro-English the people had been, how passionate they were about their football and what a good crowd they would be to have behind us. Monterrey began to look a distinctly attractive proposition compared with the alternative of joining West Germany, Scotland and Denmark in Querétaro and Neza. Or would it? Before I had time to change my mind, Uruguay's name had been picked to join the West Germans while ours was now the very last of the 24 teams and there was no longer any doubt that we would be in Monterrey along with seeded Poland and outsiders Morocco and Portugal.

There was no time to reflect on our misfortunes or otherwise. The race was on and, after a quick television interview broadcast live into the BBC Sportsman of the Year studios in London, I was jumping in a taxi and heading for the airport where I had arranged to meet Ted Croker. He had dashed back to the Camino Real to pick up Brian Gay and the promised air tickets. Even after the television interview, I arrived at the airport with a good half an hour to spare before the flight left for Monterrey though I was surprised that I was there before Ted and Brian. The flight departure time drew dangerously close as I searched the sea of faces for our rivals from Poland, Portugal and Morocco who had given us no indication of their plans. Brian eventually turned up looking red-faced and upset. There had been no ticket desk and no hostesses at the hotel to organise flights and neither had seats on the planes been arranged as promised. To say that it was a shambles would be an understatement but, undaunted, we chased over to the check-in desk to try and gain access to either the Monterrey or, better still, Saltillo flights which were both due to take-off within a quarter of an hour or so.

'No chance,' said the girl looking pointedly at her wristwatch.

'But, miss,' I said, 'We don't have any luggage and if you point us towards the gate we can be there in moments.'

'Sorry,' she replied carrying on with her paperwork.

Still not knowing whether Ted Lawrence had been successful in booking our hotel in Saltillo, mild panic began to set in and as I again searched for a glimpse of our rivals, I spotted Manus Goldsmith, James Goldsmith's son, who was not only a football fanatic but also the Mexican Youth team administrative manager. By this time we had been joined by the Northern Ireland manager, Billy Bingham, who was in exactly the same predicament as he wanted to board a soon-to-depart flight to Guadalajara. As much as I like Billy I couldn't, at that moment, have given a fig whether he caught his plane or not, and I waited impatiently as Manus explained in Spanish that we were very important guests of Mexico. The hostess eyed us up and down, made a brief telephone call and began slowly to write out our tickets.

It was now beginning to resemble Brian Rix farce as ITN Sportscaster, Jeremy Thompson, and his crew, Mike Borer and Tony Hemmings, arrived with all their equipment asking if we could help them as they wanted to fly out with us to film the venue and the hotel. To add to the confusion, photographer Bob Thomas turned up wanting to do the same thing and, as politely as I could in my anxious state, I excused myself and left the whole thing to poor Manus. I was off at a run with Brian trailing behind me as we searched for gate six, found the walkway and sprinted down it only to see the nose of the plane start to move as we reached the end. We had missed it by that much. The walkway was sealed off and the aircraft was reversing out of its concourse position ready for take-off. Six of us stood there in total dejection as we watched the cockpit come into view in which the pilot was clearly visible talking to the control tower. When he glanced in our direction, his eyes widened in astonishment as I held up my hands to pray.

Incredibly, the aircraft began to nose its way back. Within seconds a ground steward came rushing down what should have been an empty walkway, shaking his head as he saw the six of us, along with a mass of photographic and electronic equipment, waiting to board a plane that should have been heading down the runway. But the door opened and on we climbed. Fortunately, for Jeremy and his crew, the plane was only half full with lots of room to spread out. The faces of the other passengers as six heavily-perspiring Englishmen boarded their flight were worth remembering. Brian Gay explained who we were to one of the stewardesses and what the panic was about and, after she had served our drinks, I asked her if she would thank the pilot for his help. She came back to say that the captain had not realised who we were but now that he knew he was delighted and wondered if I would like to join him up front for the landing.

I thanked Captain Hector Alcocer of AeroMexico not only on my own behalf but on that of my fellow travellers and the England football team. He could be our guest any time he wanted! I posed for pictures with him and promised we would meet up when I returned. His actions meant that I had had the head start that I wanted and, indeed, by flying to Saltillo instead of Monterrey I was going to be ahead of my original schedule. We reached the hotel to discover that Ted Lawrence had done his job and that our booking had been accepted in principle and all we needed to do was to discuss terms. It had been arranged for me to look around the hotel and the rooms and to meet with the manager and the sales director over a working breakfast at 8 a.m. the next morning.

We had a busy programme to cram in the next day. We wanted to meet the Press to rectify those comments about Monterrey being the short straw, talk to the local Organising Committee, and inspect the improvements that had been made in the training facilities to see which suited us the best. But the working breakfast came first and our cloak and dagger style haste seemed totally justified when halfway through our breakfast in the boardroom there was a discreet knock on the door. It was an assistant to inform the manager that representatives of Portugal and Morocco were outside demanding to see him urgently in order to book the hotel. I held my breath as the manager told his assistant to explain that he was busy with Mr Robson, that the hotel had been reserved and that they were too late. I learned later that the manager turned down several financial inducements from our rivals.

That was easy compared with the Press conference later that morning for not only had my comments been twisted but also representatives of the local media had been more than well informed about the hooligan element of our fans and the headline which was stuck under my nose was translated as: 'The animals are coming.' Added to my remarks about the city and the inhabitants being misinterpreted, I was off to a rather bad start and the tone of the questioning by the local Press reflected the early animosity. Once again it was down to Robson the diplomat rather than Robson the manager and I set about trying to right a few wrongs. I called attention to the distortions and said that it was the sort of sensationalist journalism that was equally prevalant in our own country. I pointed out that there was every chance that there would not be a single incident involving our 3,000 supporters, crossing my fingers as I said it.

Remembering the problems Alf Ramsey had had in 1970 when the Mexican people made him and his players suffer because of his comments about the food and hygiene, I worked hard at making friends with the local media just as we had done with the Mexican people in the capital a year before when smiles, politeness and a few souvenirs had resulted in a fond farewell from lots of admirers as we left the Camino Real. This time I was appealing to the citizens of Monterrey through their newspaper men, telling them how pleased we were to be in such a friendly place. I told them that we wanted to be accepted as their team, that was why we were going to travel down from Saltillo every day to train so that they could identify with us and know who the players were that they would be watching in their own stadium. I promised that I would make as many of the training days as possible public. The early hostility had dissipated and I flew back to Mexico City that night feeling a lot happier. I had liked what I had seen but I made a note to return in the near future to ensure that the promised improvements had been made to the training areas and to bring Dr Edwards with me to make his checks. I wanted to leave nothing to chance and if I could counteract the natural disadvantages, our chances of success would be considerably greater.

On the long trip home I had time to reflect on the draw as a whole rather than on our own little corner. We could not complain even though we were in the hottest centre of all. The poor old Scots had the rough end of the stick in the group that we had so nearly landed, with seeded West Germany, who had been runners-up four years earlier and were always a team to be reckoned with when World Cups come around, the South American Champions Uruguay and Europe's best team of the moment, Denmark. The only consolation for manager Alex Ferguson was that Scotland always seemed to produce their best when the opposition was at its toughest. There was no doubting, even at this range, that Scotland were the rank outsiders of Group E.

There were other interesting clashes with the holders Italy matched against the 1978 winners, Argentina, for the fourth successive time with Italy undefeated in the sequence with two wins and a draw. Bulgaria, always difficult to beat, and the unknowns of South Korea made up Group A. No doubt the Italians shuddered when Korea came out of the hat for they will certainly recall their amazing defeat by North Korea in England in 1966.

I had no doubts at all at that stage that the hosts Mexico would progress, having been drawn against two teams who qualified only as 'lucky losers', Belgium, who beat Holland in a play-off and Paraguay, who beat Colombia and Chile after losing their initial group. The fourth team, Iraq, posed little threat to a team that had been preparing together for over a year.

One of the more interesting combinations came in the León-Irapuato group where European Champions France, the seeded team, paired with the emerging Hungarians, the powerful defence of the Soviet Union and the remarkable Canadians who under English coach, Tony Waiters, must surely have been the only qualifier not to have a National League from which to pick their team. With the collapse of the North American Soccer League, many of Waiters' players were out of a job or playing indoor football in the United States.

Billy Bingham seemed happy enough at Mexico City Airport when I saw him on his way to Guadalajara. He managed to reserve a luxurious hotel he had had earmarked and was not at all put off by being paired with the Brazilians who were immediately quoted as the 5-2 favourites for the competition. Billy liked the venue having been there a couple of years earlier for the World Youth Championships while the Irish had to play Spain, whom they had beaten four years earlier in Spain, and Algeria before meeting the favourites.

As for myself it was time to look at the positive side rather than the negative. We had booked the hotel we wanted, which was high enough for us to maintain the effects of our altitude training in Colorado, all three of our games were to kick off at 4 p.m. local time instead of under the midday sun and all three were to be played in Monterrey while Morocco and Portugal had to play their final group game in Guadalajara. As for the opposition, we could have done worse. You can underestimate nobody in a World Cup Finals but the last time I had seen our seeded rivals Poland play was in the 1982 World Cup in Spain. They had reached the semi-finals, having topped the eventual winners Italy in the first phase, before putting out the USSR and Belgium to reach the last four where they bowed out to Italy and two-goal Paolo Rossi. Their success was built on solid organisation, which was a hallmark of their performances over the years as England well remember from 1973 when they held Sir Alf Ramsey's team to a 1-1 draw at Wembley to deny England a place in the Finals at West Germany.

They have always produced two or three outstanding players in every squad but never quite enough to take them all the way. Even without seeing them I knew instantly that they would be fit and well prepared and with the stamina to ensure that no one would outrun or outgun them. The modern generation of Polish footballers has been brought up in a climate of adversity and they are a new breed of hungry fighters exemplified by their outstanding striker, Zbigniew Boniek, who is not just one of the best strikers in Europe but in the world. He was certainly good enough to persuade the Italian giants Juventus to part with a huge amount of cash to secure his services when they had the pick of the world's best. He repaid them by helping them to win the European Cup before departing for AC Roma and another big pay day. He is quick and will obviously have to be watched.

My knowledge of Portugal, our first opponents on 3 June, was a little more recent for I had been impressed by them in the 1984 European Championships finals. That was a tournament for the players to show their flair and attacking skills. The dull sides had been eliminated by the time I arrived from England's tour of South America and the first game I saw was the semi-final between the hosts France and Portugal in Marseilles. It was a wonderful match and I am sure that had it been played in Portugal or even on neutral territory we would have had a different result.

Portugal, after going a goal down to Domergue, came back to equalise late in the second half and then take the lead in extra time with two goals from the dangerous Jordao. It was not until six minutes from the end, with a frantic crowd roaring them on, that France scored a second from Domergue with the inevitable Michel Platini putting the brave Portuguese out in the very last minute from Tigana's run and centre. It was breathtaking and the underrated Portuguese took a large share of the credit. There are a lot of those same players still around, capable of beating anyone on their day as they amply displayed when they qualified by winning in West Germany, the first to do so in a World Cup qualifying competition. They are quality opposition with a striker in Gomes who has earned international repute.

As for Morocco I knew nothing of them at all. Here were the prospective giant killers of the group, part of the emergent third world of football. African soccer has been on the up and up for some years, ever since Zaire had had their fingers badly burned in West Germany. Since then Tunisia had made their presence felt in Argentina, (where they beat Mexico and held West Germany), Cameroon in Spain (with three draws against eventual winners Italy, semi-finalists Poland and Peru) and Algeria in Spain (winners over West Germany and Chile). You can't ignore performances like that.

Professional football has gained in stature and popularity in the interim with the emergent countries importing top coaches to train their players and top opposition to play against. I had mixed feelings about Morocco for this was a potential football trap, the game everyone expects you to win at a canter but one of those when they might, on a good day for them and an off day for us, beat us. Goodness knows there have been enough examples. It was important that I did my homework. I urgently needed to discover their fixtures and find out what they were up to.

9. The Last Lap

I celebrated the New Year 1986 – by watching a football match! I suppose that was predictable and even as the old year went out and the World Cup year came in, my mind was far away from the convivial crowd at a friend's house in Ipswich and on the challenge that lay ahead. It was everything that I had worked for over the past three years. At last the thousands of miles I had travelled and the hours of football I had watched were taking on their full meaning. I did not let these thoughts interfere with the party but Elsie and I soon left for home for it was a morning kick-off at Highbury where Arsenal were due to face Spurs on New Year's Day and several of my prospective World Cup players were taking part.

It must be said that football eventually took a back seat as, in the evening, we took some American friends to see the Royal Shakespeare production of *Les Misérables*. It was wonderful. The theatre doesn't often make me emotional but at the end of this spectacular musical, I admit I stood up with everyone else to give the cast a standing ovation. It was probably the best show I have ever seen. Trevor Nunn must have been proud to see such a responsive audience and it was something I could appreciate as it was the same sort of reaction that I wanted in Mexico.

I was aware that it was not going to be an easy run-in and that there were many pitfalls ahead. But at least I was prepared for them now. I felt I had served my apprenticeship and I was not only ready but excited by the prospect. The immediate hurdle was a fixture to fill that huge gap between our game against Northern Ireland in November and our meeting with Israel at the end of February. The Football Association had tentatively agreed, though mindful of the possibility of disruptions through weather and FA Cup replays. It was not as easy as it should have been.

What we needed was a game against opposition that would stretch us in a climate that would ensure no cancellation and would be a welcome escape from the English winter. We had a chance to play European Championship runners-up Spain in Seville. It would have been perfect but we had to to turn it down because of our spectator problems. We simply could not afford the chance of disruptions with the European Championship draw to be made in Frankfurt on Valentine's Day and we had to give

Spain the same answer as several other close European countries. What an unnecessary burden to carry because of lunatics who claimed they were on your side.

Instead Ted Croker sent off a batch of telex messages to Algeria, Egypt, Yugoslavia, Sweden, Switzerland (though that brought back some bad memories of violent supporters) and Greece. Yugoslavia seemed the favourites but they kept us waiting so long that we simply had to look at other alternatives. In the meantime, I continued with my usual round of games, functions and meetings with any expert who could offer help, ideas or suggestions on the task that lay ahead in Mexico. I visited Ipswich, Charlton, Crystal Palace, Spurs and Chelsea in the space of six days. In the middle of this usual activity, I had a most useful lunch with Ron Greenwood, whom I like and respect enormously. He is one of the nicest men you could meet. We spent three hours talking about Ron's experiences in the World Cup Finals in Spain four years earlier. His information was invaluable for he had been there in the driving seat and knew what it entailed. We were not discussing club football for this was the game at its best and most difficult and only he and Sir Alf Ramsey had managed at that level for England in the past 20 years and, at that stage, I planned to speak to my Ipswich neighbour, Sir Alf, at a future date.

Ron gave me much advice, telling me how important it was to handle the Press properly, to keep cool under the continual harassment, to make the time to answer their questions and to give them access to the players at certain times. I could see the logic in this for some of my players had been telephoned at all hours by reporters, though not by those that follow England around regularly for, in the main, they behave responsibly and are sensitive to what we are trying to achieve. At the big event it is the fly-by-night news reporter who doesn't care whose toes he treads on to get his story because he won't be back again. Ron went into some detail about the injuries that had eventually stifled England's challenge in the quarter-finals, and especially the problems affecting world-class players Trevor Brooking and Kevin Keegan. He felt that, in the end, his team had been just a bit short up front and I made a mental note not to gamble with injured players in Mexico.

There was a diversion from England's progress when, on 13 January, Señor Gaspar telephoned me from Barcelona. This time it was not to offer me a job, Terry Venables was doing well enough. He wanted my opinion on the Welsh and Manchester United striker, Mark Hughes. It was not difficult. In the first three months he had been untouchable and, linked with Ian Rush for Wales, they were as good as any pair in the world. Although Mark had gone off the boil a little, there was no doubting his ability. I was surprised that Gaspar should seek my opinion but £2 million was such a lot of money that you could not blame him for wanting a second view. 'I would back Terry's judgement,' I told him, 'You have done so until now. Hughes is worth what you can afford if he is the player you want. You have watched him while he has been having a thin time but you must look beyond his present form. He is so young that he cannot help but improve.'

We were still only a few days into World Cup year but already the demands on my time were growing by the telephone call with requests for television interviews extending well beyond BBC and ITV. There was an 8 a.m. camera call in Bray for a Manpower Services advertisement, a job I was pleased to do because the fee was paid into a pet charity of mine, the Charles Palmer Trust, which eventually raised £250,000 for the mentally handicapped. I then rushed back to Lancaster Gate for interviews with Polish Television and the Egyptian football authorities, for we had agreed to play Egypt later that month in Cairo, the first time the countries had faced each other at senior international level.

There were so many drawn cup ties on the Saturday that I lost a whole team of 11 players and I was at Sunderland myself to see our skipper Bryan Robson, just back after injury, sent off and then ruled out of England's game against Egypt when United's ten men drew 1–1. I do not normally sympathise with players who are sent off but I really felt for Robson this time as he was unlucky to go. I drove from the north east to London in time to catch the Chelsea-Liverpool tie, only to see another of my players, striker Kerry Dixon, carried off on a stretcher and thus also ineligible for the trip to Cairo.

It prompted me to bring back Gordon Cowans of Bari, Ricky Hill of Luton and Danny Wallace of Southampton. I also invited young Newcastle striker Peter Beardsley to join us and the squad began to take on an unusual shape. It provoked some observers to say the visit was not worth it. Emlyn Hughes, for one, strongly criticised the trip saying: 'What on earth are England doing in Egypt? What do the Football Association and Bobby Robson think they are playing at?

'It is ridiculous arranging a fixture right in the middle of January at a time when players are already extended by Cup-ties and replays. It's death on the Nile.

'There's another joke trip lined up next month when England go to Israel. We won't learn anything from that match either and by the time Mexico comes round everyone will be burned out.'

I was also disappointed that Brian Clough, who had been a tremendous supporter, added his considerable weight in the same paper by calling our trip laughable, adding that there were ten places up for grabs in the

England team in front of Peter Shilton. Brian is sometimes a man of whim and I can only imagine he was caught at an inopportune time for there is no greater 'tourist' than him when it comes to taking his team abroad to earn Nottingham Forest a few bob. At least our motives were right. I knew that it was a risk to play a match in cup week, but it was one that Ted Croker and I were prepared to take rather than leave a gap of three and a half months between fixtures. Which would have been worse?

In the end we lost more than we thought but the journey was still completely worth while. It meant giving Steven, Wright, Fenwick, Cowans and Beardsley a game. It provided us with the sort of opposition we were going to face in Mexico, namely Morocco and, most important of all, it further cemented the growing team spirit. The trip was an education and a fascinating one. What is more we earned a morale-boosting 4–0 victory against a side that had been achieving some good results and that, soon after we left, thrashed the crack Austrian team, Rapid Vienna, 7–1.

We came straight back after the game so that the players could be with their clubs on the Thursday for training. We returned them fit and happy and I was equally pleased to see just how much strength I had in reserve. There were now exactly four months left before the World Cup began in Mexico City with the match between the holders Italy and Bulgaria. Many may have been surprised to see me so close to the big kick-off at Home Park watching Plymouth and Brentford on the first day of the month. But not all my work for the Football Association revolves around the England Football Team for I am heavily involved in coaching at the grass roots level and I was in Plymouth to open one of the new Centres of Excellence, which are my particular baby. However, it was back to the big league next day as I set off at 7.30 a.m. on Sunday morning to watch Bryan Robson continue his comeback against West Ham United at Upton Park.

Having seen him sent off eight days before, I now saw him hobble off. My last sight of England's most important player was of him disappearing down the tunnel long before everyone else. This time it was his ankle and he was clearly in a lot of pain. I sat through the match until five minutes from the end when I hurried down to the dressing room to see how bad it was before the rest of the team came in. Bryan was still in his kit, lying on the treatment table with his injured ankle immersed in ice. I felt so sorry for him as he lay there cursing his luck and asking when it was going to change.

There was precious little I could say in the circumstances other than to make the usual sympathetic noises, encouraging him to persevere. He was having a spate of bad luck, the sort that most professional sportsmen suffer at some stage in their careers. While I was talking to him I had my fingers crossed that this latest setback would be the last. Fitness was very much on my mind for that week, sandwiched between games at Arsenal and Ipswich, I was planning a trip to Loughborough College to talk to Sebastian Coe's physiologist, Professor Clyde Williams, to ask him if he could spare the time to address the squad on how they could ensure that they were in the best possible physical shape when they were in Mexico. The next day I was due back in London to discuss the possibility of England joining the No Smoking Campaign being run by the Health Council.

I was strongly in favour of it and knew that I would receive the backing of all the players for I could not think of one of my team who smoked, while among the backroom staff only the doctor, of all people, enjoyed a small cigar after his dinner now and again. It wasn't, however, as if I asked players if they smoked before I picked them but when I was at Ipswich I had actively discouraged it and would talk very seriously to any young apprentice who smoked. Youngsters look up to professional sportsmen and copy what they do and what they wear and it is important that we are seen to be doing the right thing. After all, smoking is certainly not going to help a sportsman. It damages health and my advice to any youngster is to save the money and buy a pair of football boots or a cricket bat.

I knew there would be no problem asking the players or their pool organiser, Harry Swales, to join the campaign for I was already aware that a lot of the events they were doing before Mexico were for charity and particularly for the Variety Club of Great Britain's Sunshine Homes' buses. I had heard some lurid tales about international teams and their 'perks pools' but this had never caused any difficulties for me. No player even approached me to ask 'how much?' either for the qualifying competition or for the finals themselves. They left it to me and it must be said that they were pleasantly surprised when they discovered what their rewards were for taking us to Mexico. They also knew that it was about all that could be afforded, for a great deal of the money earned from a World Cup is ploughed back into the game at its most basic level. At the same time, we live in a real world and they should receive what they deserve.

The weather was becoming worse with more and more games being called off and a huge backlog developing. This was the last thing I wanted particularly with the congestion caused by those oddities, the Full Members and the Super Cups. Instead I packed my bags and, with my wife Elsie, headed for the hills, or to be more accurate, the Alps and the French ski resort of Val d'Isère. Now it could snow all it liked! I had never been able to take a winter holiday for obvious reasons until I became England manager but it was now the fourth time we had slipped off for a quiet week in the snow and I must say that I liked it more and more each time, in fact I was quite crazy about it. As English manager I missed the day-to-day donning of a tracksuit and the exercise and this helped compensate for that. Skiing, I found, exhilarating with a hint of danger. I was up that mountain from the crack of dawn until the light went and the mountain patrol advised me to go back.

The evenings were not too bad either as Elsie and I would enjoy a warming glass of mulled wine at the end of the day and then look forward to dinner, having survived on a bar of chocolate and an apple all day. It was a wonderful break that we both enjoyed immensely, though I couldn't completely escape from football. I found myself thinking about Bryan Robson's fitness and wondering whether he would still be in the squad I had left behind with Dave Sexton for Israel. My mind also strayed ahead to the draw for the European Championships, which was to be made in Frankfurt that week.

Once again it was not the opposition that bothered me for I now knew that we possessed the ability and experience to play any team in the world, never mind Europe, without fear. But what I could not control was the hooligan problem. With friendlies we could pick our venues to minimise their threat but with the draw there was nothing either I or anyone else at the Football Association could do. There was not even any point in me being in West Germany. Instead I wondered whether we would be as lucky as we had been for the World Cup qualifying competition when we had drawn Northern Ireland, Turkey, Finland and Romania, each of which had had different reasons for deterring violence.

At first I thought it was a joke in poor taste when I heard the names of Turkey and Northern Ireland again but when I discovered that it was true I breathed a sigh of relief. I was beaming all over my face when it was further revealed that the other opponents were Yugoslavia and that we had drawn one of the four-team groups instead of five. With all due respect to the opposition, it was nigh on perfect and I finished my week's holiday a happy man.

The vacation ended on my birthday, 18 February, as I flew from France to Portugal where our World Cup rivals were to play East Germany in their last friendly of the year in Oporto. Portugal had a disastrous night, going three down before half-time and eventually losing 3–1 with only a Gomes penalty to ease the frustration of the irate 20,000 crowd. They had a good team on view with, so far as I could see, only Futre missing. But it was East Germany who were terrific on the night with their controlled play and quick forwards. Portugal could not cope and played so badly that I thought I had best ignore it completely. They were nothing like the team I had seen in Marseilles, and I just wished they had saved that performance for us. Their manager, Torres, had to do something drastic and was very upset, particularly as he was told I was there but he had the consolation of knowing that no one watched from either Poland or Morocco.

Even though I had to disregard the team as a whole I still gleaned a great deal from the individual performances and in particular from the home play-maker Pacheco who unfortunately left the pitch after little more than half an hour with an injury. How they missed him. He was their Ray Wilkins, a great architect who made the others play around him. I also liked their prolific goalscorer Gomes but I wasn't at all impressed by their captain and goalkeeper Bento, though the locals assured me that this was one of his rare off-days. I did not mind if he did not have another off-day until he played against us in Monterrey on 3 June.

There was plenty of food for thought as I flew home to frozen England to hear that Bryan Robson had returned from a clinic in Amsterdam ready to play in Israel. For once, the weather had not worked badly for me and though I knew I would have to pay the consequences later in the season, I had few injuries because no one had been playing! Indeed, when I looked at the players available I was not that far away from my projected line-up for Mexico. I wanted to look at Alvin Martin paired again with Terry Butcher and that useful-looking midfield of Robson, Wilkins and Hoddle. I also had Waddle up front and, despite Lineker being absent with a bad back and Hateley being in hospital for tonsillectomy, Dixon, who had not played since his injury against Liverpool in January, expressed a desire to take part and I had Peter Beardsley to play off him.

We ignored the usual criticism which went with our departure and confounded those who thought we would spend the whole time in our hotel as we visited all the traditional tourist spots, though I warned the players of the obvious dangers of being photographed next to the Wailing Wall! The game had been arranged a full year in advance and had been selected carefully for, while we knew from their past results that they would give us a good work-out, it was just the sort of opposition we needed to cut our teeth on before taking on the might of the Soviet Union and Scotland in the next games.

The reasons we had picked Israel were that we were sure the weather in Tel Aviv would not hinder our preparations, that our fans would not be so stupid as to cause trouble over there and that we were reasonably confident that we would win. It was the sort of game a club manager likes to undertake pre-season against teams whom he knows will provide a test but are the sort of opposition where the club can play and enjoy their football. Not quite the sort of weak rivals that the great Hungarians of the mid-1950s used to play but along those lines, after Israel had drawn with

Romania and thrashed Eire while always giving regular visitors Liverpool a game. It also kept the squad together.

I was not too worried about Dixon for it wasn't a particularly extreme case since the weather at home had been so bad that others in the squad had been kicking their heels for two and sometimes three weeks. I knew he would be rusty but I had plenty of substitutes. It was soon evident that he wasn't right but I decided to let him stretch out and have a run as he had been so keen. Our performance showed that we needed this type of work-out for, the midfield apart, we did not play to our full potential and we paid the penalty. We won an early corner and with both our central defenders forward, we were caught out when a huge punt down the middle by Mordechai Ifanir caught our full-backs Gary Stevens and Kenny Sansom dozing in the sunshine and the explosive Eli Ohana, who would hold his own in the First Division, drew Peter Shilton before slipping the ball past him.

The Press blamed our central defenders for lack of pace but they were upfield for the corner and it was two of our quickest players who were caught out. They knew whose fault it was. Martin and Butcher were playing together for the eighth time and this was only the second goal they had conceded. Now we were in a different situation with a new set of problems. Teams still love to beat England and suddenly Israel felt that they were in with a real chance.

We were in a hole, a goal down away from home. Now we had to prove how good our character and spirit was. There was no shortage of chances provided by our midfield but none was taken up with even Bryan Robson's timing askew after missing so many weeks of football. After the break I took the game Kerry Dixon off and sent on Tony Woodcock but it needed a special from Robson to put us level after 50 minutes when Hoddle picked him out with a wonderful pass and the captain hit the perfect right-foot volley into the top of the net. It was a goal that would have graced the World Cup Final itself.

What I was really pleased about was that we did not panic. Although the winning goal would not come we kept working, kept cool and waited for the winner. It came when Woodcock found the inevitable Robson on the far post and the latter's fierce header was aiming for the top corner when former Liverpool player Avi Cohen punched it over the bar. Robson accepted the responsibility of the penalty himself and with supreme confidence, considering his bad luck with the header and the importance of the kick so late in the game, banged it home. Had he knocked in one of the other chances or if anyone else had scored for a 3–1 scoreline, everyone would have been happy, but despite extending our undefeated run to seven matches, we were severely criticised by Barry Davies on television and then again in some of the papers the next day. I was particulary unhappy with the treatment I received from BBC interviewer Kevin Cosgrove three or four minutes after the end of the game. I was still on a high and should have been in the dressing room with my players rather than helping out the BBC because they were running out of satellite time. I believe that our performance was judged to be unsatisfactory because people expected us to win by three or four goals and anything else was not good enough. Football isn't like that. Ask Liverpool, for example, what happened when they went to York in successive seasons. International football is similar to cup-tie football and is about scoring one goal more than your opponents.

Cosgrove had asked me what I was going to do to put things right. What did he expect me to do? Within an hour we were heading for Luton and I would not be seeing the players again until they gathered for the game against the Soviet Union a month later. Fortunately, I had succeeded in getting what I wanted out of the game and that was what mattered. I had even managed to throw on my reserve goalkeeper, Chris Woods, at 1–1 to see how he coped in a slightly delicate situation. How many managers would have taken off the best goalkeeper in the world when their reputations were at stake? I was satisifed we had emerged with a number of positives such as the four days we had spent together to improve team spirit, which could already be compared to that of a club. It had been amply demonstrated when we went a goal behind and had kept our heads.

It was a good way to see February out with another win and if I needed any reminder that the World Cup was now only three months away, I was off again to the host's country on 2 March. I had planned to watch Luton the day before but a heavy overnight fall of snow in Ipswich put paid to that, for I could hardly reverse the car out of the drive. The snow did not last and I was able to meet my travelling companions, Alan O'Dell and Dr Edwards, on time at the airport on Sunday. It was to be a quick hectic trip with much to be done before I flew off to watch the quarter-finals of the African Championships in Cairo where I planned to have my first look at the men of Morocco.

First came Mexico City and the start of a spell of staying in six different hotels in six nights. We zipped round the capital on arrival to make a final decision on our hotel in Mexico City, eventually settling on the Holiday Inn near the airport. The double glazing shut out all the noise and the rooms and restaurants were good. It lacked the facilities of the Camino Real but if we got that far we would hardly be concerning ourselves with videos, table tennis and Monopoly. Then it was off to Saltillo that evening where we were met at the airport by the grandson of a former President of

Mexico who told me that Mexico were playing in Monterrey against Nationale of Uruguay and that the President of the World Cup Organising Committee had extended his personal invitation for me to join him at the game as he wanted to talk to me.

I was absolutely exhausted. I had been up for 22 hours and all I wanted to do was flop into bed in readiness for a busy day ahead. But duty called and while Alan O'Dell and Dr Edwards started their tour of inspection of our Saltillo hotel, I was off down the mountain to meet the very important Guillermo Canedo. He simply wanted to be polite and ask whether I was satisfied with the hotel, training facilities and the stadiums in Monterrey. He apologised that he had been unable to persuade anyone to spend any money on the local training ground near our hotel, explaining that Saltillo was a baseball town and did not qualify for any Government grants as they were not strictly a World Cup town.

The standard of football was good as Mexico continued to impress with a one-goal win in front of a huge crowd, which was still celebrating the fact that their local team had recently won the Mexican First Division Championship. I managed to stay awake and lurched back to my hotel. There was no respite for after a few hours' much-needed sleep, we met two officials from the British Embassy who suggested that it would be a diplomatic move to meet the Governor of the State. A meeting had, in fact, already been set up. I had an audience with the Governor in the palatial chambers of the town hall with a full array of Pressmen and cameras in attendance and made a speech, which seemed to be well received. Our image had been restored and we were back on the right track. There was even talk of some of the local businessmen refurbishing the local pitch for us to do some of our training and for them to enter a team into the Mexican Second Division. World Cup fever was beginning to take off.

Dr Edwards had been just as busy as me. He had been inspecting the darkest corners of the kitchens, looking at rooms and even checking water samples for viruses such as Legionnaire's disease. We also hired a jeep to go further up the mountain in search of a spot above the 7,000 feet mark where we could improve our acclimatisation. We drove 75 miles across what were little more than dirt tracks, through the woods looking at every glade and clearing. Most of the terrain consisted of rocks, rubble and cactus plants and was real John Wayne country where horses would have been a more effective means of transport than a team bus. But we did find a grassy area that had been recommended to us at around the perfect level of 7,500 feet which had barely enough room for a game of rounders, never mind football. It formed, in fact, part of the grounds of a monastery! I knew the players would find it funny when they saw it but as long as it was sufficiently large for them to have a barbecue, relax, walk about or simply sit and read a book it would mean that a sudden journey up to Mexico City would not come as a shock to their systems.

Then it was back down the mountain to Monterrey for the doctor to check both hospitals in the city, their X-ray facilities and the availability of doctors. Next we drove to the training grounds so that I could see how much the pitches had improved and the doctor could ensure that he had the space to conduct any on-the-spot treatment that might be needed. It was my third visit to the practice pitch and, though it was getting better, it was still a question of us adapting to the standard. We then gave another Press conference in Monterrey where the questions were now more on football than the administrative details, which was a good sign.

We did a little more public relations' work that night when we hosted a dinner for 14 people, who were all helping us, including the vice president of the League Champions with whom I was discussing the prospect of a warm-up game. It was another late night and an early call for, next day, we were off to Colorado Springs so that the doctor could make his checks on the Broadmoor Hotel. We met up with Keith Walker again, looked at the Academy, had lunch and were on our way to the airport to return to London and my flight out to Cairo. At least, that is what I thought. Our flight to St Louis had been cancelled because of a fractured windscreen and there was no other connection. It was back to the Broadmoor for a night's sleep and up for the 8 a.m. connection. This time the airline had gone on strike! Fortunately, we were flying Club class and we were able to change our airlines and to travel Colorado-St Louis – Philadelphia-Boston – Heathrow. We arrived mid-morning on the 8 March, after 33 hours of travelling. Cairo was forgotten and I wasn't about to chance my luck on yet another flight for the sake of one game against Algeria. I went home to Ipswich instead, had a quick cup of tea and took myself off to Portman Road where I caught sight of something as rare as an on-time flight from the United States, a Terry Butcher goal against Nottingham Forest.

I also caught up with some of the news I had missed, particularly the fact that Bryan Robson had re-dislocated his shoulder against West Ham United. It sounded bad and I started making telephone calls to find out how serious it was and what I could do about it. It was serious and I did not like what I was hearing. Everyone I spoke to confirmed my worst fears, namely that a second dislocation weakened the shoulder so much that re-dislocation was almost inevitable. It seemed as though an operation was needed but there was no sign that Bryan was going to have one, quite the reverse in fact. It was with deep foreboding that I flew off to Frankfurt to watch West Germany against Brazil.

The pulling power of the South Americans is remarkable, I bumped into Billy Bingham of Northern Ireland, Sepp Piontek (Denmark), Miguel Muñoz (Spain), former Argentina boss Cesar Menotti, Enzo Bearzot (Italy), Omar Borras (Uruguay), Gyoergy Mezey (Hungary), Guy Thys (Belgium), Andy Roxbrough (Scotland) and Anton Pzechniczek (Poland) and those were just the ones I saw. It was a match that I had to see for the draw showed that it was quite possible that we would play West Germany in the second phase in Mexico while Brazil would be likely opponents in the quarter-finals. The Brazilians had not played for some while and it showed as they slumped to a two-goal defeat. The West Germans, who had suffered some severe set-backs since we had thrashed them in the Aztec Stadium, made an electric start and thoroughly deserved their victory. While I was there I approached the South Americans to see whether they would like to play us at Wembley at the end of March. I did so with the full approval of the Football Association because, at the time, we were worried about the arrangements for our fixture against the Soviet Union in Tbilisi on the last Wednesday of the month. The Russians were making it difficult for us, refusing to allow us to fly direct to the Georgian capital and, instead, sent us an itinerary which had us travelling to Moscow on Sunday, staying the night there and going on to Tbilisi on Monday with the return trip taking two days as well. Can you imagine what the clubs would have said to that as they prepared for a heavy Easter programme? But it was no-go with Brazil for their recently reappointed manager, Tele Santana, had inherited this trip to Europe and all he wanted to do was get back home to prepare his team. He did not want to reveal his hand at this stage.

I flew back on 13 March for a coaching session at St Mary's PE College in Twickenham and then went on to Lilleshall to watch the trials for the latest intake of youngsters into the General Motors School. The entire Football Association Medical Committee were also present to give the youngsters the usual thorough going-over and, inevitably, the topic of conversation turned to Bryan Robson, his shoulder and the nationwide argument of whether he should have an operation. All of these eminent men were in agreement that if he did not have surgery there was a 30 per cent chance of the shoulder coming out again and not only during a match but in training as well. Paddy Armour, who deals with Rugby League players, told us that of the 23 dislocations he had treated, all but one had re-dislocated and the odd one player out had retired from football anyway. Imagine how I felt when someone else said he could do it again simply by putting on his jacket!

In view of the overwhelming weight of medical opinion, I made up my mind to try and persuade Bryan to think again. I telephoned Dr Edwards, who had been finding out what type of dislocation it was and, with his usual thoroughness had contacted the foremost specialist in the world, Lipman Kessel, who corroborated everything we had been told. Robson was such a priceless player that I had no hesitation in speaking to his manager, Ron Atkinson, and to Bryan himself. I waited impatiently for the usual protocol as Dr Edwards contacted both Manchester United's specialist and the surgeon who had conducted a similar operation on Liverpool's Mark Lawrenson after his shoulder had come out for the third time three minutes into the 1985 European Cup Final.

Even so, it was a tricky situation because Bryan was not my player but I wanted him in Mexico. I knew that United had flown back from a short trip to Israel and were staying in a London hotel. I phoned Ron Atkinson and put my views to him, asking him to consider changing his mind. Ron wanted Bryan back in the side as quickly as possible because he still felt that with his captain back in action, United could win the title. I asked for the ultimate sacrifice a club manager can make because an operation would have ruled Robson out for the rest of the Championship, but have guaranteed his fitness for Mexico.

'Look,' said Ron, 'I paid £1½ million for him, putting my judgement and reputation at risk, I gave him the contract that persuaded him to stay in England instead of going to Italy. He is a Manchester United player and I am Manchester United's manager and my allegiance is to the club and we want to win the Championship. We have had to play for a long time without him this season and if I can get him ready for the last few games then that is what I shall do. If the shoulder goes again it is bad luck. If he survives it is a bonus to all of us. So far as I am concerned the decision stays and I would prefer it if you left it there and did not bother the player with it for he has made up his mind as well.'

I could understand and sympathise with Ron's position but I wanted Manchester United to go further than that. I wanted the club to put the country before their own ambitions. Winning the Championship would be marvellous for half of Manchester. Winning the World Cup would be marvellous for every club in the country. But I had lost and all I could do was keep my fingers crossed that everything would be okay on the night.

Apart from the kids at Lilleshall, I still had a squad to think about for our game against the Soviet Union, which looked a remote possibility despite the fact that we had received no replies to our telex messages to Moscow. We had been in touch with Sweden, Switzerland and Greece but nothing had come of it because this was a designated international week and everyone had already made their arrangements. The one hope was that the Russians wanted this game as badly as we did but even as I thought about my squad, the Football Association were making a deadline for a decision.

The deadline imposed by Ted Croker came and went as the trip to the Soviet Union loomed. We were not bluffing and would not go if we had to abide by the travel arrangements the Russians had proposed. The first sign of a breakthrough came with a one-paragraph item from the Government news service TASS and, sure enough, a telex followed on the Thursday, three days before we were due to leave. We were to be the first football team allowed to fly their own charter directly into Georgia. It was a big relief for, after our low-key games against Egypt and Israel, it was important that we faced good-quality opposition and here was a team who had not lost a game nor conceded a goal on their home soil for some 17 matches in six years. We had built up our confidence and now we wanted a challenge.

There was a somewhat annoying problem because West Ham's Alvin Martin had been sent off for stupidly throwing a punch in the heat of the moment. It was the first time he had lapsed like that but the FA Chairman was determined that, with all the problems of the previous year, he was going to enforce the strictest code of discipline and he let it be known to me that he did not expect Martin to be selected while under suspension. As it happened I had already decided to recall Mark Wright in the centre of the defence but I took Martin along anyway, taking him to one side to tell him I didn't like what he had done and to let him know what the Chairman had said.

Central defence was not my problem on that trip as I also had the anxious Terry Fenwick demanding a return. It was up front that I faced a growing dilemma. Trevor Francis, John Barnes and Kerry Dixon were all ruled out for one reason or another while Tony Woodcock had woken the team doctor at 3 a.m. as he developed a painful infected foot during the night. That brought me down to the bare bones for, though I had asked Peter Beardsley along as cover, I had not intended to use him. Gary Lineker was with us and all I could do was keep my fingers crossed that nothing had happened to Mark Hateley in his Italian League game for AC Milan on the afternoon that we arrived in Tbilisi. We heard the result and there was no word of injuries to Hateley, Ray Wilkins or Gordon Cowans. They were on their way from Milan to Georgia via that roundabout route that we had refused to take. I decided to postpone Tuesday's training until the afternoon to give them the opportunity of joining us.

We were all ready to depart when the three arrived and the moment I saw their tired, unshaven faces I knew that they would not be training with us and that we had made the right decision in insisting that we flew direct. Worse was to follow for a shake of the head from Mark Hateley indicated that there was more than tiredness bothering him. He was injured and no one had thought of telling me. He told me he felt that he had little chance of playing and I couldn't understand why he had made such a horrendous journey when he would have been better occupied having treatment in Milan. I suppose it showed how much the lad wanted to be involved but it didn't help me as I contemplated the prospect of either plunging Peter Beardsley in alongside Lineker or whether to appear to follow public opinion and try to avoid defeat with a 4–4–2 formation.

The pressure could have been intense except that the Press had weightier matters with which to occupy themselves. When we had met at Luton it was revealed that my England assistant, Don Howe, had resigned his post as manager of Arsenal and that everyone was after the latest developments. Don had handled an awkward situation well with his usual dry humour and I even thanked him for taking the spotlight off me! I couldn't help feeling that Arsenal would regret the move in the end far more than Don Howe. He is one of the world's top coaches and would have no trouble in finding a new job.

Don and I go back a long way. I first met him 30 years ago when I was transferred from Fulham to West Bromwich Albion where Don was the young, urbane full-back with a brilliant career ahead of him. We quickly became friends as we shared the same intense, dedicated approach to the game, always wanting to discuss its finer points. Playing in front of him helped us to develop mutual understanding on the field and we progressed together into the international team and both decided to go into coaching at the same time, attending the same courses.

Even when we parted ways after six years together we stayed in touch with the odd telephone call and when we met up again in London, Don was at Highbury and I was back at Craven Cottage. We both believed in putting something back into the game and were regulars on summer coaching courses for the Football Association. You look around at some of the younger generation and wonder what they are doing for the game that gave them a livelihood. It seems more important to some of them to get their views in print rather than helping young footballers.

Don does not need me to support him, his record speaks for itself both as a player and a coach of the highest international standard. Ron Greenwood is certainly one of the most knowledgeable men in world football and he did not need to think twice and immediately enlisted the help of Don Howe when he took over as England manager from Don Revie. Ron had the pick of the Football League and chose Don, asking others like Terry Venables, Brian Clough, Dave Sexton and me to help out at various levels. Don was coach under Terry Neill at Highbury at the time and had fewer responsibilities to tie him down so I considered myself very fortunate when he agreed to continue with me even after taking on the management job at

Arsenal. His experience is invaluable. It is common knowledge that I would have liked Don with me full time but the Football Association's budget would not stretch to it at the time, so I never got around to finding out if Don would have accepted.

There are a number of people, some within the game, who have the impression that Don is a dour Midlander whose football doctrine is steeped in defensive theory. They could not be more wrong. Don is one of the funniest men in football, always looking for a laugh and is great company. Few know the game as well as he does and he is an inventive and thinking coach who retains the players' interest even when warming them up. There is always a new routine which is punctuated by Don's shrill whistle. Don is also an advocate of attacking football and when he and Ron Greenwood were discussing the squad for the World Cup Finals in Spain, it was Don who was in favour of taking a winger like Peter Barnes or Tony Morley and Ron who decided against it.

As a first-rate technician, Don is quick to spot weaknesses in opponents' armour and it was after a discussion with Don that we played 'one-in-the-hole' to beat the Hungarians twice in the 1982–84 European Championships. I would definitely rank him among the top five footballing brains in the country and my immediate reaction when he told me the background to his departure from Arsenal was that their loss would soon be some other club's gain and that the London club would not realise what they had lost until he had gone. Despite all his own personal problems, Don was as supportive as ever on the trip to the Soviet Union when I decided to go for broke and continue with my 4–3–3 line-up even though we did not have a target man to call on. Lineker had scored more goals with his head that season than ever before and we had little Peter Beardsley who could play off him. It would be a good exercise for our midfield and for winger Chris Waddle to play to feet instead of looking for the heads of Mark Hateley or Kerry Dixon when the alternatives were limited.

It is a pity that those who criticised our trips to Egypt and Israel were not in the Soviet Union to see us reap the benefits, for this particular trip demanded all the team spirit we had been building over the past two years. Although the Georgian people are very hospitable, it did not help that our quarters were distinctly spartan, that the food was moderate and that there was nothing to do. There were no complaints. The players knew they were here to do a job and were not on a tourist trip. The players trained hard, slept a lot and laughed and joked at things that would normally have brought moans. A particularly scrawny piece of chicken brought forth the observation that it would have been more filling and nutritious if it had remained as an egg while Don Howe, on being asked what was good to buy

116

in Tbilisi, responded drily, 'Airline tickets!' These may seem trivial and inconsequential matters from a distance but in circumstances like that the odd giggle is an invaluable safety valve and when someone wished me luck that afternoon I told them I thought we would win that night. I felt that the mood was exactly right and that these players were ready to win whatever the opposition even though key players were missing.

One of the most interesting confrontations of the evening was between the two goalkeepers, our own Peter Shilton and the Russian captain Rinat Dasayev. I was confident who would come out best in this clash between the two men acclaimed by most as the best in Europe and possibly the world. But even with Peter in my side I told the team that they would have to defend a great deal better than they had done in Israel, especially as we were going to take on this supposedly unbeatable Soviet team on their own soil with three forwards. I was not only putting myself on the line but the system that had evolved over the previous two years – and so close to Mexico! My main concern was over Ray Wilkins and Gordon Cowans in midfield after their tortuous trip from Italy. I felt fairly confident that the strong-minded Wilkins would cope and after bringing Cowans all this way I was not going to let him down. But I had made up my mind that, at some stage, I was going to have a hard look at Aston Villa's Steve Hodge.

English clubs, like Liverpool and West Ham, had played in the Georgian capital before and everyone had spoken of the intimidating crowd that had enthusiastically backed their local team Dynamo. We were ready for that as well – but it never happened. Whether it was politics or football I still don't know but that capacity crowd was as silent as the grave, generating an eerie atmosphere that could have done nothing to help the Russian team. It certainly did us no harm and we went for the throat right from the start. When Lineker was brought tumbling down by the home captain I thought that we were going to get the reward our bright start had warranted.

Bulgarian referee, Velichko Tsonchev, not only ignored our demands but almost immediately gave the Soviet team a penalty. Mark Wright made two mistakes that night and one of them was to dive in and leave Viv Anderson exposed to the wide player cutting in. It was probably a penalty but it was harsh coming so soon after our good appeal and, of all people, it was the local man Chivadze who was to take it. Had that one gone in who knows what the result might have been but the Dynamo sweeper missed his chance. Maybe it was poetic justice, it was certainly our one piece of luck and how well we capitalised on it. It was never easy but we stuck to our task in the best possible manner. They had some very talented, dangerous players with Sergei Gotsmanov and Oleg Protasov in particular giving us problems. 'Get hold of that number eight and stay with his runs,' I told Ray Wilkins at half-time.

'Give me a motorbike and I'll do it,' the breathless Wilkins responded.

It was obvious then that I could not risk both Ray and Gordon for the entire 90 minutes and, as I had planned two days earlier, I soon had Steve Hodge on in place of the Bari player. No one let me down and, in fact, our performance had an immediate and far-reaching effect on my plans for Mexico. I had selected Mark Wright for his pace and touch and he had not disappointed me at all. He had taken on the best and come through like the international player I knew he would be. I decided that night that Terry Butcher and Mark Wright would be my two central defenders in the match against Portugal in Monterrey on 3 June. Steve Hodge also confirmed that he could be the cover I had been seeking for Bryan Robson and this was further endorsed when I played him against Scotland. But by far and away the biggest bonus was the 90-minute performance of Newcastle's Peter Beardsley, the stopgap who had won his place because of the lengthy injury list. He had been given an unexpected opportunity, knew it and grasped it with both hands. If he could play like that in those circumstances surely he could do so in Mexico as well. Suddenly I had an extra choice. He owed a lot that night to those round him who adjusted to the lack of inches of the front two who, in turn, responded by working like Trojans. Both were quick and difficult to pin down and forced sweeper Chivadze further and further back.

Beardsley's biggest contribution came with the goal, of a sort developed in the north east of England when both he and Chris Waddle were Newcastle players. Waddle's long ball into the corner saw Beardsley chasing as hard as ever and, though the giant Bubnov was always favourite, Beardsley slid into the tackle, sending the defender tumbling head over heels while our striker bounced up. It was a trick he had used to great effect before but the real skill was to remain calm once he had done it and that is where his understanding of Waddle came in. He knew his former club-mate would continue his run after the pass and where he would find him. Beardsley drifted the ball to the far post where Waddle had some space because of Lineker's unselfish run and Waddle with great touch turned it into a good ball and thumped in his shot. A great goal.

The crowd loved the goal and seemed to love us. You could feel that they would almost have liked to cheer us. We put on a good display for them, always prepared to take our share of the attacking and not just defending our lead. When Steve Hodge went on I told him to play his natural attacking game, get a good first touch and he would be on a flier. As it was, his first two touches were horrible but he settled down quickly as did

Trevor Steven whom I brought on for goalscorer Waddle to counter the Russians' introduction of the 100-times capped Oleg Blokhin. It was not a strictly defensive move for I told Trevor: 'We are an attacking side and I want you to get forward as often as you can. Give it all you have got, blow yourself out in the 20 minutes you have left.' He did that and looked after Blokhin as well but then I never had any doubts about the qualities or the place on the plane to Mexico for this young man.

When you consider both teams' preparations for the game, with Eduard Malofeyev's team having been together well before the fixture and their superb home record, it was quite a feat to win that night in Tbilisi. I felt that it could eventually prove to be a huge psychological boost for us. Not only had we extended our undefeated run but we had also won well without Bryan Robson. I was having to face up to the harsh reality that there was a real chance that our skipper could miss the World Cup and, at one stage, it looked as though we might suffer the same complex that afflicted Manchester United when they were without him. Now we had proved that we could beat the best when he was not around.

We celebrated after the game with some help from Tbilisi's Georgian coach, who threw a party for the officials at the hotel, while the players had a deserved drink in the hard currency bar in the hotel where they met Soviet citizens who had travelled from Moscow and other places to support England! They had books and pictures of our players and knew everyone by name. Football is full of surprises.

Predictably, we had a long delay at Tbilisi Airport on the way home next morning but it hardly mattered. Going back via Moscow would have been far more tedious. I hoped we were setting a precedent in flying direct. It would certainly do the Soviets no harm if that were the case for it would considerably enhance their chances of staging a major competition like the European Championships or even the World Cup if there was easier access for the teams who would have to travel and play all over that vast country.

I had planned to fly straight on to Switzerland on Good Friday for a youth tournament but I was so tired I could hardly remember which country I was in. I settled for Ipswich and home instead where I caught up with the football news and in particular with that about our biggest rivals in Monterrey, seeded Poland, who had gone down 3–0 to Spain while we were winning in Russia. I would soon hear all about it from my 'spy' Joe Mallett but I took immediate satisfaction from the knowledge that had I been in the place of Polish manager, Anton Pzechniczek, I would have been none too happy when the two results were put side by side.

I certainly went into the European Championships fixtures' meeting at Lancaster Gate in a very relaxed frame of mind. My contract with the

Football Association would run for a year after the 1986 World Cup Finals so, whatever the result, I was deeply concerned about the Championships. Having become used to the job and having got to know the capabilities of the players at my disposal, I knew most of the pitfalls and I had become increasingly philosophical about such things as fixtures. They had worked out more or less as I wanted but, in the end, you must play everyone at home and away sometime. We were to begin with our old rivals Northern Ireland away and Yugoslavia at home and we would be looking for another good start. But all that seemed a long way off and I was much more concerned with the events of June than those of next season. I was back at Lilleshall that first weekend in April and it gave Don Howe and me the chance of going to Villa Park to watch the FA Cup semi-final between Sheffield Wednesday and Everton.

It was a useful visit for, apart from the obvious Everton players, I was interested to look at their former goalkeeper Martin Hodge and full-back Mel Sterland. I was enjoying the game until half-time when, in the Villa Board Room, I heard the awful news from the other semi-final at White Hart Lane that Mark Wright had broken his leg against Liverpool. It was a terrible blow for the youngster whom I believed was going to emerge from Mexico as one of the new stars. It was not helped by the fact that Mark had sustained his injury in a clash with his fellow Southampton and England goalkeeper, Peter Shilton. I sat there thinking about it for the rest of the game.

Mark's absence left a gap in the squad for the game against Scotland, which was to be named in a week's time. I arranged to watch Dave Watson against Sunderland but, before I could check him out, I went to Birmingham for their Sunday game against Luton, attended an FA Dinner for the Monterrey Organising Committee in England on a goodwill visit and took an England team to Luton to play in a well-deserved testimonial for Ricky Hill. I also watched Spurs at Luton on the following Saturday, contemplating Gary Stevens and his possible role in the World Cup squad now things had changed so much. Did I want an orthodox centre-half to replace Wright or did I need that little bit more in view of the question marks over the fitness of Peter Reid and Bryan Robson? It was easily solved when I announced my squad for Scotland – I named both Watson and Stevens even though there wouldn't be two places available for Mexico.

Before we met there was an important engagement in Zurich where FIFA had organised a seminar for the 24 competing nations. I went to Switzerland with Bert Millichip and Ted Croker. FIFA made it clear that they intended to clean up the game's image for the emphasis was heavily on behaviour. Foul play and gamesmanship would be stamped on; there would be drug tests; and even minor details such as shirts tucked into shorts and socks rolled up were to be observed by all players. I was also delighted to hear that players would be able to take in fluids during a game, something which had been banned in Spain.

There was an equally important meeting back at the Football Association on our return when Ted Croker, Bert Millichip, Dave Sexton, Charles Hughes, the assistant National Coach, and I talked about the future of England at youth level. The problem was the ever present one of being unable to gain the release of the youngsters from their clubs so that, often, Dave Sexton was having to make do with third and fourth choices. To be blunt it meant that a great deal of the Football Association's resources were being wasted on the wrong people. Dave Sexton is a craftsman who deserves the best tools to work with. It was bad enough at Under 21 level where players were wanted for their club first teams. He had managed to win the European title twice in succession under these unbelievable conditions but then, this time, he had come up against an Italian side that were much better prepared for the semi-final clash. They had even cancelled their First Division programme to let them train for the first leg at Pisa, which was watched by a capacity 25,000 crowd and televised live throughout Italy.

We decided that the Under 21s must continue because it gave such valuable experience to the young, future internationals. Somehow, we had to explain how important it was for clubs to release the cream of their youth and, in return, we would send them back better players, if only by giving them that international experience they cannot obtain anywhere else. As for the younger teams, we decided that we must sort out a system of dates where we could gain proper use of the most talented when they weren't required for such important games as the South East Counties' League or some junior cup. I recorded *Desert Island Discs* that night with Michael Parkinson, which was to be broadcast when we were in Monterrey. Sometimes, I felt as though I could do with a desert island.

The England party gathered at the Crest Hotel in High Wycombe on Sunday evening. I felt I had too much to do to attend the Milk Cup Final between the unfancied winners Oxford United and Queen's Park Rangers, a decision that proved to be the right one judging by the time the journalists arrived from the game for my Press conference. I had hoped to play something like my definitive team against Scotland for this last game before naming my Mexico squad and departing for our Rocky Mountain retreat. There was no chance. Because of the winter freeze-up there were fixtures that still had to be played with poor West Ham United having to

121

chase the Championship with a whole backlog of games to be taken up. That denied me the services of Alvin Martin, Peter Beardsley and John Barnes, who would have been required to play three games in five days if I had picked them, while Bryan Robson and Gary Lineker, two certain starters in Monterrey if fit, were with us but unavailable because of injury. Tony Woodcock was injured yet again and I was prevented from using Terry Fenwick by our own strict disciplinary code because he was serving a one-match suspension for QPR, having reached 41 points.

We lost Manchester United goalkeeper, Gary Bailey, in the most unfortunate of circumstances on Monday morning when, in torrential rain, he caught his foot in what must have the only hole on the entire pitch and went down in agony. His knee was locked and the immediate diagnosis was a problem with the cartilage. Gary was stretchered off to the warm of the dressing room. My heart went out to the lad who was going through a dreadful time, having lost his Manchester United place to Chris Turner after injury and, according to reports, his long-term relationship with his girlfriend Kate having finished. But such is the irrepressible spirit of the young man that even while he was being carried away in pain he was laughing and joking, saying it was the third unlucky incident that season and he was now looking forward to some breaks.

I hoped he was right and, until there was a full examination, I was prepared to wait for him. So far as I was concerned, he was still one of my three goalkeepers for Mexico and until someone told me otherwise I refused to discuss the alternatives, though I was obviously running through them in my mind with Martin Hodge of Sheffield Wednesday the most likely candidate. I hoped I would not need him especially when Gary told me had had had problems like it before with his knee unlocking in a hot bath. I wished him well.

It was a question of making the best use of the situation and, with the impending squad uppermost in my mind, I decided to have a long, hard look at Steve Hodge, give Dave Watson a fling at the back and have one last appraisal of Trevor Francis. He was playing in Italy that day in only his ninth full League game of the season, and they and five substitutes' appearances had reaped but a single goal. Any other player would have been out of the reckoning but this was a special character for whom I had a great deal of respect. He had been outstanding for me in Mexico the previous summer and I was loath to rule him out. One more chance, one more look ... then I heard that he had fractured his cheekbone.

I received a message that Trevor was to have an X-ray in Genoa on Monday morning and was then to fly into London, determined to play. When he arrived you could see the depression in his cheekbone and I was most reluctant to select him, remembering a year earlier when he had nearly died after colliding with another player in Italy. Dr Edwards arranged for him to see a top specialist in London next morning and, though an operation was deemed necessary, he was told that if the match was so vital to him he could play. It was a major dilemma. I was afraid that more damage might be done playing against the likes of Souness, Miller and McLeish, who were hardly likely to hold back and say: 'After you, Claude'.

I could see how important it was to Trevor to play for he was a thoroughbred who would not even train with injury, yet here he was prepared to risk all in a last bid for a ticket to Mexico. Selection was by no means cut and dried at that stage for there were two strikers' positions open with three players, Francis, Peter Beardsley and Kerry Dixon, challenging for them and Luton's Mick Harford waiting in the wings. I felt obliged to give Trevor a chance provided he took the responsibility and satisfied me in a training session. I noticed him pull back from a Ray Wilkins' cross in our practice game and so, afterwards, I had Dave Watson pumping the ball up for him to head until he had satisified both himself and me. Trevor asked me what was required for a guaranteed place in the squad and I told him it needed a dazzling performance, maybe with a goal or two thrown in. It was a huge task but he deserved the chance.

Francis and Bailey apart, the build-up to our annual battle with the Scots was smooth and relaxed. We hardly talked about Alex Ferguson and his team as we went through our preparations for Mexico with a lecture on physiology from Professor Clyde Williams, medical tests, plus fittings for our Mexican wardrobe. We broke up the routine with a splendid meal at the ancient Bull at Bisham opposite the Abbey gates and a special luncheon in our honour at the Hilton given by the Variety Club of Great Britain.

I was asked to speak in front of this glittering audience and seemed to hit on the right note by promising that we would do well in Mexico and finished with a joke against myself. I told them that when I took over the England job, former manager Ron Greenwood had handed me three envelopes telling me to open the first one if things became difficult. I explained that I remembered Ron's words after our Wembley defeat to the Danes, opened the top envelope and inside it simply read, 'Blame me!' I called a Press conference and said that it was all Ron's fault for leaving me a squad with all the top players having retired and no new blood. This excuse was fully accepted.

The next time I needed the envelopes was after that dreadful result against Wales at Wrexham. I hastily tore open the second and inside it said 'Blame the Football League!'. I did exactly that, telling the media how impossible it was to run a national team when I could never get my best players together, when the League refused to let me have a clear Saturday before big games and that the number of fixtures meant the players were always tired when they were fit to report. Again, I told the audience, my excuses were accepted and on we went until the moment arrived in Mexico in 1985 when, after successive defeats by Scotland, Italy and Mexico, a friendly journalist stuck his tape recorder in front of my nose and asked, 'Did you realise, Bobby, that no England manager in history has ever lost four games in succession?' I hadn't and as we were due to play World Cup runners-up West Germany in our next game at the Aztec Stadium I couldn't wait for the advice contained in that third envelope. I opened it in the privacy of my hotel room, pulled out the note and read, 'Write three envelopes'.

It was the sort of joke you could only tell when on a winning sequence and I sat down to a good round of applause hoping that no one had taken it seriously. But it put us all in good humour for the journey back to the Thames Valley and a late afternoon training session. As we arrived at Bisham Abbey a glorious, clear rainbow seemed to spring right out of the Abbey grounds. Was it an omen? Was there a pot of gold at the end of it? Only time would tell.

The prize the next night was not quite the Jules Rimet trophy but then we never needed an excuse to play the Scots and, anyway, there was the Sir Stanley Rous Cup that the Scots had won at Hampden in its first year. They were on a run as we were with no defeats and no goals against them since Alex Ferguson had stepped into that enormous void left by the sad death of Jock Stein and, just as we had done in the Soviet Union a month earlier, they came at us with all guns firing. The World Cup was the furthest thing from most people's minds as both teams thundered into the challenge, playing the game for all it was worth, providing a great spectacle for the fans.

Obviously the first goal was going to be critical and, fortunately, it was us who scored it. We came up for air and won a set piece in a good position. Watson's challenge for Glenn Hoddle's free kick hindered the clearance and young Hodge was well placed to get in a Bryan Robson type header back across the goal for Terry Butcher to score from close range. The goal settled us down though it needed a super save from Shilton to stop the Scots' skipper, Graeme Souness, scoring. We went on to get a second goal as Kenny Sansom took a cross-field pass from Hoddle, cut inside and hit a fierce shot which Alan Rough could only parry for Hoddle, who had continued his run, to head home. I was delighted for that was exactly the sort of position I had asked Glenn to look for, not only in this game but all the time. I felt sure he could score more goals for England.

We lost Ray Wilkins at half-time after a challenge from Steve Nicol and I sent on Reid, telling him to harry and hustle Souness who had been pulling the strings and making Scotland tick. But Alex had thought ahead and pushed Richard Gough into midfield behind the front two. I had warned the players that the Scots would come out an angry side after the break but I had not counted on this tactical switch and it took us some time to sort it out. We might have killed it with a third goal had Mark Hateley accepted one of the chances that came his way but, instead, the Scots scored from a penalty by Souness after Butcher had upended Charlie Nicholas. That fired up the Scots even more and they threw everything at us. We showed our character again and hung in, playing some quality football when the chance presented itself. There were no cowards on that pitch, though in the fierceness of the struggle we lost Hodge with an injury and finished with Reid and Watson limping heavily.

Everyone gave their all. I was impressed by the courage and character shown by Francis as he suffered from awful cramps after his thin season, while Hodge had done enough before he went off to convince me he was, indeed, the cover I required. Ironically, he was replaced by Spurs' Gary Stevens who dealt with Gough and showed me that his versatility was something I needed. That was sad for Dave Watson who, after a shaky start, had done everything I could have asked. I was going to have some difficult telephone calls to make the following week.

One of the reasons I was so pleased for my team was because of the continued undermining of their confidence, not so much by journalists, who were being supportive, but by people who should have known better. The day before we played Scotland, former England manager Sir Alf Ramsey attacked my players through a newspaper article, saying that neither Gary Bailey nor Chris Woods were good enough; that he would not give Ray Wilkins a game and that he also questioned my use of Glenn Hoddle and Peter Reid. He went on to say that Chris Waddle and John Barnes promised more than they produced. He ruled out Trevor Francis and Tony Woodcock while adding that Kerry Dixon was not sufficiently good because his control let him down and that Mark Hateley did not score enough goals.

Imagine how the players felt reading that from a successful ex-England manager and then, on the very morning of the game, seeing Brian Clough dismissing Glenn Hoddle, Mark Hateley, Kerry Dixon and Chris Waddle. I did not read anywhere of bad Scottish players or that Alex Ferguson had it wrong. On the day I was to name my 22 for Mexico, Sir Alf was at it again in a different paper with headlines that screamed, 'You're wrong Robson,' and then went on to contradict his first piece by naming Hoddle, Reid, Wilkins and Barnes in his side for the Mexico World Cup. It saddens me that a former England manager should take players to task like this on the eve of a World Cup. I wonder how he would have felt if Walter Winterbottom had done the same to him before 1966? The attack upset me coming so near to a game and then marring what should have been a special day for the players selected to go to Mexico.

Everyone is entitled to an opinion, Sir Alf Ramsey more than most having won the World Cup for England 20 years ago, but unconstructive criticism cannot possibly be good for the game and surely everyone who loves football should be working for it right now. We have done our best to raise hopes after the dramatic and damaging events of 1985 and it is painful that personalities who have the ear of the public should dent the confidence of our top players.

It seems to be a growing trend for football people to knock their sport and it has become such a critical business that it breeds unpleasantness, aggression and jealousy. I must admit that I was surprised when Sir Alf Ramsey began to travel the country with a journalist commenting on England players. I have tried to accept it with dignity, learning to take the punches that seem to go with my job. But if you keep punching someone on the nose then one day that person is going to punch back. I should have got the message when I bumped into Sir Alf in the guest room at Stamford Bridge after a Chelsea game. I said hello and asked him how he had travelled to London from Ipswich. When he told me he had come by train, I said that I had my car at the ground and would be delighted to drop him off at his door, thinking it would be an ideal opportunity to talk about Mexico. I was amazed when he coldly replied, 'I came by train – I will go back by train.'

I had still intended to talk to him about Mexico despite that apparent snub until I read in the newspaper that he was surprised I had taken so long to ask his advice, adding, 'Three times he said he'd love to meet up for a chat. Three times he couldn't make it!' For the record I telephoned Sir Alf once and requested a meeting the next week. He said he was too busy. My own programme is scarcely littered with blank days and I was going to ring him again until I read his newspaper articles. After that I wrote to him at his Ipswich home, thanking him for his interest and left it at that. He had passed on his recommendations in public.

Since Sir Alf took his squad to Mexico 16 years ago medical science has progressed and we have sought out the top experts in their fields to give us the benefit of their advice. I have read what Sir Alf has had to say in various newspapers and I have listened to as many people as I could, including Carlos Alberto, the coach and trainer of the Brazilian side that beat England in 1970 and went on to win the World Cup in Mexico that year. I sincerely believed that the 1986 England side left as the best prepared ever and I only wish that we had gone with the backing of everyone in the game.

10. The Die is Cast

The moment of decision had come. The deliberations were over. I had promised the media that I would name my final squad of 22 players for Mexico at a Press conference in the Football Association's headquarters at Lancaster Gate at 11 a.m. on Monday, 28 April. I could have made it easy for myself by doing what Sir Alf Ramsey had done 16 years earlier and taken an extra five or six to our training camp in the Rocky Mountains but I thought that would have been even more disruptive with players wondering which of them were going to be sent home. In any case sentimentality has been the downfall of more than one manager over the years and with a competition as important as the World Cup, there was no way that the heart could rule the head. However, that didn't make it any easier when I telephoned Trevor Francis and Dave Watson on Sunday, 27 April to tell them their services would not be required when the rest of the squad left for Colorado on Wednesday, 7 May. The best I could offer was my personal thanks and the request for them and four others to remain in training in case we suffered any injuries before FIFA's deadline for the final nominations on 23 May.

It had been a long, hard road following that first, controversial selection for my opening game against Denmark in September 1982 when Trevor Francis had scored both our goals in an undeserved 2–2 draw. Now I was casting him to one side along with the Norwich centre-half, Dave Watson, who had done a sterling job for me at a time of dire need in South America. But such is football. It is not a game that stands still and new players are constantly emerging while others take a pace backwards.

Over four years I had come to appreciate the need for me as manager to be flexible and to adapt to changes. To many onlookers, international football looks slow and ponderous compared to the fast action stuff that dominates our bread and butter game on a typical Saturday afternoon. Nothing could be further from the truth and I vividly remember asking the great Tom Finney before my début as a player against France to tell me what it was like to play in an international. His response is still valid today. 'You will find it the hardest game you have ever played in.' Tom had said to me on the team coach: 'It is not only physically but also mentally

128

demanding. The pace is difficult to cope with because your opponents think so much more quickly. Remember, however, that though they are the best from their country in that position you too are now considered the best in your country in your position and you will find you are being backed up by better, faster-thinking players than you are used to. The more you play the easier it becomes.'

Tom was absolutely right. I never dreamed that it would be so hard. It was a battle of wits between sharp players of the highest technical level. From a managerial point of view, I remember my predecessor, Ron Greenwood, saying that a good international footballer is quickly able to adapt to other players. I have come to realise the significance of his remarks, watching how a player improvises with strangers and you just do not know how that will work until you plunge a player in at the deep end. After four years I get an instinctive feeling but you still cannot be sure until the player performs at top level and, even then, you cannot always judge from those first few appearances. To play international football at a consistently high level a player needs technical excellence in the major skills of heading, passing, tackling, shooting, control and running with the ball. There are also the mental factors such as the importance of keeping his nerve on a big day, how he reacts to being two goals down in an intimidating stadium on the other side of the world and, with something like the World Cup, how he copes with being away from his family for a couple of months, how well he travels and how he gets on with his team-mates so that there is harmony on and off the field. In other words, an international not only needs to be talented but has to be strong minded as well and, in that direction, I had no worries about the cream of our players and the first names on my list: Peter Shilton, Ray Wilkins, Bryan Robson, Terry Butcher and Kenny Sansom.

They were top of the 22 not only because each and every one of them is a genuine, world-class professional footballer but because their commitment and behaviour is an example to the rest. They have come through our desperate days and emerged as stronger individuals. They are the backbone of my squad. There is no greater example of professionalism and dedication than that displayed by our goalkeeper, Peter Shilton. Some consider him to be among the best in the world, though personally, I have no doubts at all on the subject. He has been safe during all the years that he has kept goal for England. He was born in September 1949 and yet in all the time that he has been playing football he has lost none of his enthusiasm for the game, his fitness, his agility nor his ability. He has kept his weight and he has remained internationally motivated. Ron Greenwood believed in alternating between Shilton and Ray Clemence but I know that Shilton was never happy about that. I picked him because I thought him the best.

When our goalkeeping coach Mike Kelly is not about, I know that I can trust Shilton to look after the other goalkeepers, to take them through his own special training routine, working not only for their future but for the future of the country as well. His exercise routine is so good that one Australian coach pleaded with me to let him have a video and would not believe it when I told him we did not have one. I am certain that when Shilton does eventually quit he will have a huge part to play in the game as a coach of future generations of goalkeepers. That could be a while off and the way he is going, we will still be talking about him for the next World Cup in four years' time.

Circumstances have meant that there has been a change in the pecking order behind Shilton, with Chris Woods leapfrogging over Gary Bailey to claim the number-two seat. It just goes to show how dramatically matters can alter in football for, less than 12 months ago, Chris Woods came to me on our tour of Mexico to ask whether it would make any difference because his club, Norwich City, had been relegated. Then Gary was our undisputed number two but I told Chris that I was not too concerned providing he kept his form and that he should stay loyal to his club. Now he was returning to Mexico knowing that he would be back in the First Division for the start of the next season and, if anything happened to Shilton, he would be playing in the World Cup Finals. He has advanced steadily since learning his trade as understudy to Shilton at Nottingham Forest. I like Chris because he is tall and strong yet still manages to get down to the low shots. He coped well when I threw him in as a substitute against Israel in Tel Aviv. The score was 1–1 at the time and I wanted to see how he reacted in that type of tight situation. He confirmed that he has an even temperament.

Providing Chris takes a lead from Peter Shilton and works at his game, he can continue to improve. He will need to because there is a lot of young talent around and he will not have things all his own way. Gary Bailey, for one, will see to that. He is athletic and a good shot stopper and at the start of the 1985–86 season I considered him second to Shilton rather than the older, more experienced Ray Clemence of Spurs and Phil Parkes of West Ham. But then came a series of problems which, even as I selected the squad, had him marked down as a serious doubt. The season began brilliantly for Manchester United and for him but an injury caused him to lose his place and he was unable to regain it from the talented Chris Turner. I was ready to keep faith in him because he had done exceptionally well for me as an over-age player in the Under 21s and he had the invaluable experience of training and playing in Mexico a year before the World Cup

Finals. Then came his knee injury on the eve of the Scotland game and I found myself looking around for goalkeeping cover after all.

There was no immediate alternative. The best of the rest were still the vastly-experienced Clemence and Parkes and, though both had let it be known that they were prepared to go to Mexico, I could not forget that they had previously stated that they did not want to play for their country again. Clemence, in particular, had made some very hurtful comments when he had bowed out and I felt that recalling him could cause unrest among the other players and that would have been sad after the team spirit we had built up. Why, after all, should a player decide when he should play for his country, coming in to take the glory of the World Cup Finals after all the hard work has been done by others? In any case, I trusted Woods as a number two and felt that it was important that I should look around for a younger man to build on for the future.

The Under 21 goalkeepers, Bobby Mimms of Everton and David Seaman of relegated Birmingham City, were outstanding prospects but too young. Goalkeepers tend to mature late in life and there were a lot of saves and caught crosses between Mimms and Clemence. To add to the difficulties, Tony Coton of Watford had emerged as a contender in the second half of the season but I found myself having to rule him out because of some off-the-field difficulties he had had while with his previous club Birmingham. Since the Football Association Chairman had laid down a strict code of conduct that prevented players from representing their country while serving a domestic suspension or when in dispute with their club managers, I could hardly select a young man with a suspended sentence hanging over his head. But once he has paid his debt then I will consider him again if his form warrants it. In the end I was prepared to surprise a few by going for Sheffield Wednesday's 27-year-old Martin Hodge. I wanted someone with experience and he fitted the bill having been at Plymouth, Everton, Preston, Oldham and Gillingham before spending three years in the First Division with Sheffield Wednesday. I knew from his manager, Howard Wilkinson, that he would be as keen as mustard and prepared to blow up the balls, change the studs and carry the bags in order to go and be a part of it. I always thought of him as safe and solid rather than spectacular, though he is very brave. I marked him down as my number-four choice, still hoping that Gary Bailey would recover from his cartilage operation.

Selecting my full-backs was positively easy in comparison. They picked themselves. Take Everton's Gary Stevens, for example, who is a natural athlete and has grown up with Everton's tremendous success. Gary has the stamina to get up and back along his line as well as the pace to get round on cover. He is meaty in the tackle and well equipped in the air. Normally, he serves the ball very well, though this part of his game had slipped at the time I picked the 22. However, I am not overly concerned for it is something that will return as he has all the basics. Gary can't afford to be complacent, though, for he has an outstanding challenger in Viv Anderson. In fact, the Arsenal full-back has never had a bad game for me in an England shirt. He is a better attacker than a defender, is very quick and delivers a good final ball. He also gets up well. Viv is blessed with a lovely personality and has become more outgoing since his move from Nottingham to London.

Viv and Gary are so close that they should be able to encourage one another to great heights but, at left-back, Kenny Sansom is out on his own with no competitor in sight, the only player in my squad for whom there is no cover. He is also one of the smallest. For a while I was concerned that Kenny might lose that critical edge to his game because he had no immediate rival. I even brought in Alan Kennedy when he was at Liverpool but, apart from one dodgy match against Mexico in the Aztec Stadium last summer, when Kenny allowed himself to be pulled about, he has never shown any lack of commitment. I am delighted with him for he is quick on the turn and is blessed with explosive pace, a devastating sliding tackle and springs in his heels. He is world class.

Apart from Sansom the best left-footed full-back is Derek Statham of West Bromwich Albion but injuries and inconsistencies have denied him the chances his early potential demanded. In fact, there is not a natural replacement for Kenny and it has become a matter of increasing concern that he should stay fit. Alan Kennedy had now gone beyond international football while Mitchell Thomas at Luton was still a little young and inexperienced. Gary Mabbutt of Spurs would have been a candidate but I was happy with the cover that Terry Fenwick offered. There was not the same problem at right-back with the likes of Mel Sterland of Sheffield Wednesday, Paul Allen of Spurs who had impressed since dropping back from midfield and, indeed, his White Hart Lane club-mates Danny Thomas and the versatile Gary Stevens.

I have known Terry Butcher for a long time and respect him greatly as a player and as a person. I always used to recommend him to Ron Greenwood and he emerged from the last World Cup in Spain as a very promising young player. Since then he has served his time at Ipswich and has made great strides every season to become the world-class defender he is now. We saw what a fighter he was when he battled for his life after being kicked in the head at Luton. He is a born winner who transmits his enthusiasm to others. His team-mates like him as much as I do. He is a tall man who is not beaten in the air too often and those long legs of his often get him out of trouble when all looks lost. He also has a superb left foot and, because of his other qualities, his distribution tends to be overlooked.

Terry Fenwick is another winner and a great competitor who, like Butcher, desperately wants England to win everything. His big advantage is that while he is a central defender he can also play right- or left-back or do a marking job in midfield. He is a lad who always thinks he should be in the team, which is an attitude I like, but he will have to learn to control himself in Mexico and to temper his natural aggressiveness with cool judgement. In the thin air of Mexico City we would not be able to give away free kicks anywhere near the penalty area because of over-enthusiasm.

Alvin Martin is something of a mystery, for he is truly outstanding at West Ham where he has been a hero for years but he has still to transfer that form to the international arena. I have no doubts that Alvin is one of the best centre-backs in the English game. He is so comfortable on the ball, which he uses to great advantage. As a defender he reads situations accurately, is a good tackler and intercepts well. He can attack too, just ask Newcastle United! Alvin scored a hat-trick against them. I originally left him out because I was looking for more pace in defence but his performances for John Lyall's West Ham put him back into contention. At worst he is not going to make many mistakes and at best he may reproduce his club form for his country.

There were a few raised eyebrows when I named Spurs' Gary Stevens as the extra central defender to replace Mark Wright instead of going for the more obvious selecton of Dave Watson. After all, the Norwich defender had played well against the Scots despite a rather shaky start while Gary came on only as a substitute in the game which was his first international appearance in more than 18 months having spent much of that time on crutches as he overcame a serious ligament injury. To be honest I had written him off for I did not think that he could regain his full form and fitness so quickly after such a long absence. He was lucky. I chanced to watch Birmingham City play Spurs at St Andrews one Saturday simply because it was the nearest game to Lilleshall where I was helping Dave Sexton with the selection for the next intake of our youngsters at the General Motors School. Gary looked his former self that day and scored a goal to cap a good display. To be fair he had been in my thoughts since South America when he had looked to be a good prospect in international terms. Spurs had bought him from Brighton as a central defender but wherever he plays he looks good as he burns up the ground. He is strong in the air and hard to knock off the ball and, with both Bryan Robson and Peter Reid suffering excessively from injuries in World Cup year, he offered cover in those positions as well as anywhere in the back-four. Gary also happens to be a superb character who fits easily into the squad.

It is said that you don't appreciate something until you don't have it any more. That was certainly true about the injured Southampton centre-half Mark Wright. When he broke his leg in two places in a collision with his own goalkeeper Peter Shilton it was a great blow. Make no mistake, if Mark had been fit he would not only have gone to Mexico he would have been my first choice to partner Terry Butcher in the heart of our defence. I have a strong feeling that if he had been able to play he would have come back a hero because the football would have suited him. He reminds me of a young but more elegant Terry Butcher. However, it was no use crying over spilt milk and Mark would be back to make his name in the European Championships and the next World Cup. His time would come.

When Mark was injured everyone assumed that Dave Watson would be the natural replacement, especially as he was picked to play against Scotland while Fenwick was suspended and Martin was on club duty. He produced a typical display and I must admit that he made me ponder long and hard before making up my mind to go for the versatility of Stevens. It was difficult telling him he had not made it because he is such a great character, tough and uncompromising, a man who wants to play for his country very badly. He is a good defender who showed his courage against the Scots when he played the last quarter of an hour limping heavily on a bad ankle but refusing to give anything away. If I had wanted an out-and-out centre-half he would have been my choice, but I needed that added cover. Gary Mabbutt of Spurs is another character I like very much and I still had him in mind right until the last moment. Derek Mountfield of Everton also came in for late consideration but both were behind Dave Watson in the end.

The first choice in any England midfield has to be the skipper, Bryan Robson. The only problem is that I have not been able to include that name as often as I would have liked because of his injury misfortunes. Quite simply, Bryan Robson is a world-class player to be considered alongside Platini and Maradona. Bryan is an inspired leader and a match winner. Midfield players tend to be able to win the ball, pass it or score goals. Average players can perform one of these, a good one two and a great one like Robson all three. What is more he is a big match player who rises to the occasion. He is brave, mobile and tackles anything that moves. He is fearless and sees nothing but the ball when it is in the air. Some critics say that he is too brave for his own good, which is just as ridiculous as suggesting that he should be playing as a sweeper. It is goals that win matches and he scores goals. Bryan is the sort who captains the team by example. He can always go to one of his team-mates and demand more from them because no one could ever turn round and accuse him of not giving everything. Captaining England is a big responsibility, which he enjoys and responds to. He is the sort of player that opposition coaches and managers have to take into consideration when they are planning to meet England. I have watched the determination in his bid to overcome his problems and disappointments. He deserves to succeed and if he does come through it will be as an even better player.

We are lucky to have two natural captains in midfield for next to Bryan we have his great friend and former Manchester United club-mate Ray Wilkins, who was my original choice as captain until he shattered his cheekbone. Other players look up to him for he has a commanding personality and a good knowledge of the game. He always wants the ball and is a collector and despatcher who likes to set goals up. He has taken some criticism over the years mainly because he does not get into the opposition penalty area enough to contribute goals on a regular basis while he also plays a little square at times if you do not get on to him. I confess that I have harboured doubts because of these faults but I have missed him when he has not been there and I have always gone back to him. When he is in the team he sparks them off, keeps them flowing and never goes out of the game. When I have left him out he has taken my decisions without a complaint, more often than not performing brilliantly in the next practice session and making me wonder whether I did the right thing. Italy has not changed him. He was a good player when he went – which is why Milan paid a £1 million for him – and he is a good player now. When he persistently hits forward balls instead of square ones he is without question one of the team's world-class members.

Glenn Hoddle may be regarded in the same light after Mexico. It is entirely up to him. There has never been any doubt about his enormous potential and his grievance was that he had never been given a good run in international football. It was no one's fault but his own. He was unlucky to suffer injuries at critical moments but he also lacked consistency. He has come to grips with the latter and has been rewarded with a regular place. His admirers thought that the demands were to increase his work rate but that is not strictly true. When he is allowed to play he destroys teams single handed but, in the past, he has too often been put under wraps. I, and others, thought that he needed to be a little more competitive when in a one-against-one situation so that he could display his full range of skills. That is what he did in the run-up to the World Cup despite a troublesome knee injury. When Glenn is on form he is majestic, blessed with talent, vision and the full range of passes. He is, without question, one of our most skilful players. In Mexico he could be in his element. Because of the heat and altitude the game will have to be played in bursts making accurate distribution essential. That is his game. He sees in a split second at ground level what we see with an overall view from the stands. He will also be important with his free kicks and his long-range shooting. I am delighted with his progress. Blessed with a few more goals and a realisation that talent alone is not sufficient, the world is at the feet of this young man.

I like Peter Reid. He is a fighting, tenacious player who probes, prompts and is prepared to work for others. He is fearsome in the tackle. Like Wilkins he is not a prolific goalscorer. He has been a huge influence on the dramatic rise of Everton and I am sure that, but for his transfer deadlock and injuries, he would have had many more international appearances behind him. Peter is more than making up for lost time now. Reid's Everton colleague, Trevor Steven, has not made many England appearances over the past year but he has been an automatic choice in the squad. He is a naturally right-sided player who enjoys the wide berth on that side of midfield. Much of his play reminds me of Steve Coppell and I have high hopes he will become as good as that very talented England winger. Like Coppell, he can pinch the odd important goal and offers the full-back behind the chance to play off him while giving protection. He has good feet and good technique and if we do need to change from our 4–3–3 formation to 4–4–2 then he is the obvious choice to come in. I woud have no hesitation in playing him. For a young player he has played an awful lot of football in the last two years and sometimes this has slightly blunted the fine edge. But Trevor is in the England squad to stay and is one of the rocks on which future teams will be built.

The same could be said of Steve Hodge who saw an opening and went for it despite not having played in a full senior international. He came on as a substitute against the Soviet Union in Tbilisi and failed to finish the game against Scotland because of injury. But, while a World Cup manager needs four years to build a squad, he is the exception that proves the rule. Important changes occur in the final few weeks. To the public it seemed as if Steve had come from nowhere to snatch his place but we have known all about him for some time as he has come through the Under 21 scene where Dave Sexton liked and backed him. He has also managed to catch the eye playing for Aston Villa even though the team have not enjoyed the best of seasons. He is quick and neat and where he triumphed over other contenders for the vacant place was because he gets forward and scores goals. I wanted cover for Bryan Robson and he has displayed the same sort of instincts.

His joy at his late arrival inevitably brought disappointment for others like Paul Bracewell who was another that did well for the Under 21s, but suffered because there were more experienced players ahead of him in his best role. Then there was Gordon Cowans who had done the hard bit by establishing himself as an international only to suffer two broken legs. Although he is back playing for Bari in Italy and scored on his England return in Egypt, the injuries had taken their toll and he was not quite ready. But, unluckiest of all the contenders, was Arsenal's Stewart Robson. He would have been in the squad had he been fit. He is a non-stop player, good in the air, a fierce challenger, capable of scoring goals and unwilling to accept defeat – he sounds like his namesake, Bryan, doesn't he? Unfortunately, a persistent groin strain ruined his season at Highbury and eventually cost him dearly. He is another one for the future.

I like wingers but they do need to be effective to warrant their continued inclusion. Many have suggested that I abandon my policy in favour of a more circumspect 4–4–2 but I was trying to keep faith and retain a system that had given us only three defeats in two years and an unbeaten run of nine games behind us going into the World Cup. I was in the same position as Alf Ramsey in 1966 when he decided that his flank men were not good enough and so did not play them. I was going the other way and taking both Chris Waddle and John Barnes with me. The way football is played now it needs someone to get round the outside and that, for me, is what a winger is for but if they do not get past their defender they are no use to me or anyone else. Both Chris and John had been short on consistency but I was hoping that we would reap the benefit from their talents in Mexico where they could have proved to be at their most effective. At their best both are scorers of goals as well as architects of them and both give me two edges with Waddle looking just as comfortable on the right while Barnes plays well down the middle.

I like Chris Waddle. He is quick, beats people, is good in the air and scores goals but sometimes he is his own worst enemy. He gives the wrong impression when he loses the ball, makes a mistake or sees a move break down for it looks as though his head drops. With those rounded shoulders and that natural stoop he looks anything but an international footballer at times. He would need to be on his mettle, for Mexico could just provide his great rival John Barnes with the sort of platform he has been looking for. Being Jamaican born, John would not only cope with the heat, he would relish it. Watch him play in England in the depths of winter and you can see how much he hates the cold, often wearing gloves and always looking unhappy. In Brazil when he scored that wonder goal in the Maracana Stadium he was happy and in full control. That's what I will expect of him in Mexico. We had obtained results with our system so it would have been foolish to change it at the last minute but who fulfils that role will depend on who produces the goods.

However, wingers are still in short supply and, apart from Alan Devonshire, there were no other real contenders. That is certainly not the case for the strikers where I wrestled with the choice right up to the last moment before reluctantly deciding to omit the luckless Trevor Francis, Tony Woodcock and Mick Harford. The last-named gave me a jolt on that final weekend with a hat-trick against Watford to take his haul for the season to 25. In the final reckoning I went for Mark Hateley and Gary Lineker as my number-one choices, backed up by Kerry Dixon and latecomer Peter Beardsley with Trevor Francis and Mick Harford standing by in case of difficulties. But it was touch and go and was not quite as straightforward as some thought it.

Two years earlier I had taken Mark Hateley from Second Division Portsmouth and the successful Under 21 side and had played him against Brazil in the Maracana Stadium. He responded with a fine performance and a well-taken headed goal. It won him a big money move to Italy and a chance to earn himself a regular place in the England side. He was hailed as a hero when he scored two goals against Finland at Wembley, and was seen as some fearsome mixture of Lawton and Lofthouse. But one swallow doesn't make a summer just as two goals against a second division soccer nation don't make an international footballer. I knew that Mark needed to pack in as much international football as he could before the World Cup to realise his potential and all too often he was unavailable through illness or injury.

There was also a theory about how he would come back from Italy with vastly-improved touch and highly-developed technique. Because of the games he has missed he would go to Mexico still with much to learn. But I was hoping that he would adapt to how we play and would hold the ball, knock it back into midfield and go. He has a lot going for him. He is willing, arrogant, aggressive, a good target man and very quick for such a big fellow. He looks as though his pre-match diet is raw meat and as if he is capable of frightening opponents in Mexico. He is young and if he listens and learns he will be around with England for a long time.

Hateley's partner, Gary Lineker, is a fast learner and a good listener who is improving all the time. He has come on a great deal since I first brought him in for that disastrous night in Wales. He did well enough for Leicester but he has taken great strides since moving on to Everton where he has benefited from having quality players all around him. He is one of the quickest in the game in the box and is an outstanding finisher who is always in for the kill, happy to knock them in with feet, head or any part of his body that he can get in the way. His technique and first touch are getting better and better and I could see him not only scoring goals in this World Cup Final but in the next as well!

Kerry Dixon managed to prove his fitness and that he had not lost that special goal touch just in time when he scored two goals against Manchester United at Old Trafford shortly before I named my Scotland squad. In the end I decided to stick with Kerry because he is a proven goalscorer with that important element of luck about him. He is not a great leader of the line and, to be honest, 18 months before I did not think he would make an international footballer and, though he needs to be more confident when playing balls back into midfield, he is improving all the time. He is useful in the air but his greatest asset is his pace. He wants the ball over the top and once you get him into position in the box he is quite prolific. He is a happy character who wants to do well for England.

Newcastle United striker Peter Beardsley was the one who came in at the end forcing me to pick him with that outstanding performance against the USSR in Tbilisi. He has been playing for some time, doing well in North America and then coming within a whisker of joining Manchester United. Instead he went to Newcastle and made his contribution in the shadow of first Kevin Keegan and then Chris Waddle. When they left, Peter came into his own proving his considerable ability and particularly his sharpness around the penalty area. He is quick in short bursts, has a cool head and is quite a good finisher. Peter is modest and likeable and was instantly accepted by the rest of the squad, which was an important consideration in his selection for his presence so late in the day could have been disruptive. People would see him as an alternative to Lineker if the Everton striker is injured but Peter showed in Georgia that he can play with him and provide us with another option.

It was hard on Trevor Francis to miss out and he came desperately close. It was the culmination to a miserable, depressing year for one of the nicest young men I have ever met. The sad thing about it was that it was not Trevor's fault. For much of the season he was fit and raring to go but fell victim to the politics of his Italian club Sampdoria. A year ago Trevor had been my best player in the Aztec Stadium against Mexico and Italy. He is an instinctive player with tremendous pace and a good right foot. He is also a gentleman and it was an awful job telling him no, especially after he had put himself on the line by playing against Scotland with a double fracture of the cheekbone. I gave him a glimmer of hope but had Lineker been fit I would have wanted to give him another run out with Hateley while Beardsley would have been hard to drop had he not played for Newcastle twice in three days before joining us. It was still worth a gamble for Trevor because I had not made up my mind.

Tony Woodcock's chances were wrecked by illness and injury and, but for an infected foot, he would have played against the Soviet Union instead of Beardsley. That is how the ball breaks. I have always rated Tony because he is such a good selfish finisher and he was another contender until the last though Mick Harford, perhaps, came even close. He was unlucky he did not gain a chance during the season. Not only did he score a lot of goals but he is also an excellent hold-up player who has the ability of bringing other players into the game. He is difficult to handle in the air and had he pace he would be truly outstanding. Peter Davenport, after creating that opportunity for Lineker against Eire, was an obvious candidate while little Tony Cottee enjoyed a wonderful season for West Ham. The World Cup probably came a year too soon for him and his ambitions should be channelled towards the next one and the European Championships in between. The odd thing was that in view of all his goals for West Ham he did not score once for the Under 21 side.

So, after 42 games in charge of England's international fortunes and having used a total of 61 players, I had finally come up with my definitive list of 22 as well as a back-up of half-a-dozen others to give me cover in case of injuries or other eventualities before the deadline day. These were the names I presented to the Football Association and then to the media on Monday, 28 April: Peter Shilton (Southampton); Chris Woods (Norwich City); Gary Bailey (Manchester United); Gary Stevens (Everton); Viv Anderson (Arsenal); Kenny Sansom (Arsenal); Terry Butcher (Ipswich); Terry Fenwick (Queen's Park Rangers); Alvin Martin (West Ham United); Gary Stevens (Tottenham Hotspur); Bryan Robson (Manchester United); Ray Wilkins (AC Milan); Glenn Hoddle (Tottenham Hotspur); Peter Reid (Everton); Trevor Steven (Everton); Stephen Hodge (Aston Villa); Chris Waddle (Tottenham Hotspur); John Barnes (Watford); Mark Hateley (AC Milan); Gary Lineker (Everton); Peter Beardsley (Newcastle United); Kerry Dixon (Chelsea). The back-up group were: Martin Hodge (Sheffield Wednesday); Dave Watson (Norwich City;); Paul Bracewell (Everton); Stewart Robson (Arsenal); Trevor Francis (Sampdoria); and Mick Harford (Luton Town).

11. Colorado Springs

Here begins the diary that I kept during the immediate build-up to the World Cup and throughout the Finals themselves.

TUESDAY 6 MAY: The great feeling of excitement was tempered by a certain sadness as I made my way to the team's meeting point at the Post Hotel, Heathrow. My companion from Ipswich to London was Terry Butcher who, the night before, had learned that Ipswich Town would start the next season in Division Two. Terry had taken it badly because he had spent a long time chasing honours with my former club – and I knew exactly how he felt. It was ironic that I should be heading out to the World Cup Finals on the very day the club I had quit for England should find themselves relegated. We did not talk about it a great deal but I could sense he was angry and upset. I think he knew how I felt, too. It was almost the end of an era for me as I doubted whether I would visit the ground very much with Ipswich playing in the Second Division. I wondered, too, whether Terry would still be there next season.

Fortunately, for both of us, we had plenty to occupy us. My first concern was that I should have a reasonably fit squad to take out to the United States the next day. There were the usual bumps and bruises at the end of a long, hard English season and if we had had a game the next day instead of an aeroplane flight, I would have been without Peter Shilton, Ray Wilkins, Bryan Robson, Steve Hodge and Alvin Martin. There were also problems with my back-up players for Luton striker Mick Harford had gone into hospital for a knee operation while Trevor Francis was still recovering from the operation on his fractured cheekbone. I was worried enough to have checked out Peter Davenport on the previous Saturday but I decided that I did not want too many on stand-by and that I could always call up Davenport at a later date as he would be keeping fit and in match practice on a tour of the Far East with Manchester United.

David Pleat was keeping me well informed on the progress of Harford while I decided to stick with Francis despite his outburst to the Press when I left him out of the squad. I could understand his disappointment but not his reaction. I had thought we were better friends than that and if he had

141

wanted to say something he could have said it to my face. I even telephoned him to tell him so.

A major problem was Alvin Martin who had been hugely disappointed when West Ham came tantalisingly close to winning their first Championship. West Ham's respected manager, John Lyall, had telephoned me to say that Alvin was physically and mentally exhausted and to ask whether he could be temporarily withdrawn and fly out with the Everton players after the Cup Final. I knew that John would not make such a request without good cause but my first reaction was to say no though I promised to consider it carefully. I spoke to our team physician and we determined that Alvin should report with the others and that we would make a decision when we saw him. The doctor felt that the change of scenery, the new company and the excitement of the World Cup would be the best way to revitalise him. I also pointed out that Alvin would find himself the subject of considerable Press attention if he stayed behind. However, in the end, I left the decision to the lad and he was happy to travel with us. Alvin, like me, could sense the feeling among the squad. There was an air of excitement at the challenge that was now so near.

That night we were given a send-off by the Minister of Sport, Dick Tracey, and other ministers at Government House. There were the usual speeches with Bert Millichip responding on our behalf and echoing my sentiments when he told the gathering what an outstanding group of professionals we had at our disposal. It could have been added what an outstandingly professional Chairman we had as well. As I listened to his speech I reflected that no Chairman in the history of the Football Association had had to deal with the kind of problems that had confronted Bert. Discipline on and off the pitch had fallen to a new low with action being taken not only against players but against clubs as well after riots at grounds like Luton and Birmingham. There was also the European ban which had followed the tragedy in Brussels. Bert had needed all his skills as a lawyer to keep England involved in international football and he had worked at the job full time.

WEDNESDAY 7 MAY: We were certainly given the star treatment when we set out on our great adventure. Security in the wake of the Libyan bombing was intense as we were flying TWA to Colorado Springs and our training centre. At Heathrow our coach was directed straight to the plane without our having to go via the terminal and the normal formalities. Our security check was completed on board the coach and then there was a brief delay while the officials collected autographs. Security was not at all lax, however, for the doctor had his medical bag studied and it needed the captain of the jumbo to clear his bottle of local anaesthetic.

The long flight was made very comfortable for us but when we arrived at Colorado Springs Airport the players were exhausted. I took them off to the Broadmoor Hotel in the Rockies while the rest of the staff, including Don Howe, Mike Kelly, Fred Street and Norman Medhurst, stayed behind to look after our 174 pieces of luggage. There was so much that they filled a coach and a van and even then the bus had to make a second trip! It made me realise once more what a superb back-room staff we had. They were every bit as tired as the players and yet they cheerfully undertook these extra duties without complaint. The marvellous spirit was evident not only among the players but the whole group.

THURSDAY 8 MAY: Throughout the journey I had told the players and the staff about the hotel's wonderful setting and how beautiful the weather would be. We had discussed the amount of sunbathing that would be allowed, the walks in the sun and how we would use the swimming pool for some of our exercise programmes. We woke on the morning of the 8th from our disturbed, jet-lagged sleep to snow and temperatures barely reaching 50°F. The blizzard was so heavy that you couldn't see the mountains from the hotel. It snowed for seven hours and, to start our acclimatisation programme, we went to the steam rooms at the United States Airforce Academy, rounding the day off with a swim. As we arrived at the indoor pool there was a test in progress for the cadets and one of the youngsters was having difficulty in jumping off the 10-metre diving board, which was supposed to simulate a burning aircraft carrier. It demanded a lot of courage and the lad, try as he might, could not bring himself to make the leap and he gave up. When I returned to the pool a little later it was to discover that half of my valuable World Cup squad had been happily leaping out of the sky under the appreciative eye of one of the American instructors. Had I been there I would never have allowed it and it did my nerves no good when I learned of the dangers involved. The biggest of these was the terrific upsurge of water between the legs as they hit the surface, but, fortunately, the experience of standing in defensive walls had shown them how to prevent injuries in that department! I was relieved that no one had been injured and secretly pleased at the players' courage.

I also confirmed during the day that we would have a practice game with fellow World Cup finalists, South Korea, the next week, which was just the sort of fixture I wanted to keep the players sharp before we tackled Mexico.

FRIDAY 9 MAY: Our acclimatisation programme began in real earnest today.

The Americans had plotted a hiking route for us that would take us high into the Rockies from our 7,000-feet training centre to 10,000 feet. It was a strenuous, five-mile-round trip but everyone loved it, or at least seemed to, and admired the breathtaking scenery. Television reporter Martin Bell had flown in from New York and, though the camera crew gave up, Martin stuck at it, completing the climb in his jacket and tie. The upward trip took around 75 minutes but some of the boys came back in half an hour – it was that steep.

SATURDAY 10 MAY: We trained for the first time as the weather began to change. It was good enough for the monitored sunbathing to begin and sufficiently warm for a dip in the hotel pool before we headed up the mountain for a two-hour session. It was still too early to train very hard but we used the time to warm up and become used to the flight of the ball in the thin air. Although Robson and Wilkins still could not train because of their injuries, they were up before breakfast running round the lake outside the hotel while Mike Kelly worked Gary Bailey as he continued his remarkable recovery from his cartilage operation. It further showed the value of having this specialist coach along with us for he was able to devote the time to our goalkeepers that neither Don nor I could afford.

I was worried about both Shilton and Robson, who were struggling with their fitness. Shilton suffered a reaction to his injured wrist after training. It was swollen and hot and looked quite serious to me while Robson seemed to have jarred his injured Achilles tendon with his voluntary running.

SUNDAY 11 MAY: No one could believe this weather, which was more unpredictable than that at home! The temperatures soared into the middle eighties but I was not complaining for this was what we were going to have to get used to in Monterrey. We had arranged a 3 p.m. kick-off against the United States Airforce Academy on their grounds. They were a keen young side who had lost 1–0 to Canada in a similar warm-up match. This was a good public relations exercise and better than training. The young, fit Americans made it as difficult as they could for us with a squad of 22 which their coach used like an ice hockey or basketball team, constantly swapping groups of three and four players to try and keep them fresh. There were no such luxuries for us as I had only 14 healthy players available to me. Woods, Anderson, Butcher, Fenwick, Hoddle, Stevens, Hodge and Beardsley all played the full match under the blazing sun and at 7,500 feet altitude.

Almost 4,000 people turned up at the Academy for the game and they were genuinely thrilled with what they saw, telling us afterwards that they had never seen football of that quality. Glenn Hoddle is some player when he gets everything right and he gave a supreme demonstration of passing. He also scored a couple of goals, including one from the penalty spot, while Mark Hateley and Kerry Dixon played a half each and scored a hat-trick apiece. Those three from Kerry also provided a boost for Hateley as it kept the pressure on him to play well and retain that number-one position. Steve Hodge, who continues to impress me, scored a couple and Terry Butcher added the other. Beardsley did not score but played well as did John Barnes. I sometimes wonder about this relaxed young man's attitude but there was nothing wrong with it then.

We enjoyed the run-out and I was pleased with the passing, which was going to be so important. We did not allow the thin air to affect us because we retained possession and dictated the pace of the game. All of the players were shattered afterwards but they had shown their commitment to the cause by refusing to ease off. It would have been so easy for them to have sat back and relaxed in the second half but instead they came out to score another seven goals and keep it going right to the end. While we were playing, Peter Shilton was nursing his injured wrist. Nursing did I say? He worked so hard at his body exercises and agility training that he lost five pounds! Mike Kelly shook his head and muttered in awe: 'The man must be mad.'

MONDAY 12 MAY: After winning 11–0 the players had earned the right to rest their legs and recuperate so, after a compulsory swim in the morning, there was a day off with 13 of them making use of one of the two golf courses owned by the hotel. Hoddle, the star of the day before, did it again by winning the competition. Bailey, Robson and Wilkins were up at 8 a.m. training. Mike Kelly continued to work with Bailey while Robson and Wilkins hired some bikes and went off on a ten-mile ride into the mountains, the idea being to give them plenty of exercise without jarring their legs by running. Despite having a day off there was still not a drink in sight. The players had been warned by Professor Williams and Dr Edwards how alcohol hindered the acclimatisation process and the players had responded by agreeing that beer, wine and spirits were definitely out. It was a sensible decision and once again showed their absolute dedication to the task ahead. The four Everton players arrived this evening and we were at last up to full strength.

TUESDAY 13 MAY: The Everton players were a little tired and depressed after their defeat at Wembley and the long flight. I had not bothered them when they arrived but talked to them by the side of the pool this morning. I told them that, despite losing out on both the Championship and the Cup, they still had had a wonderful season but that was behind them and now they were playing for the biggest prize of all. We left them to relax by the pool and breathe the air while we went training. It was good to see Robson and Wilkins exercising with the others and, though Bryan began sluggishly and tentatively, he gradually loosened up. Wilkins also looked a lot better but young Hodge, stiff and sore, was struggling badly and, clearly, his ankles, injured against Scotland, had not fully healed. The sessions were improving day by day and we took the opportunity to put the boys through the 660-yard physiological tests, with even Robson and Wilkins having a go. Although the tests were done a day sooner than they had been in Mexico, the graphs showed an improvement on last year. The doctor reckoned that one reason was the banning of all drink and I thought the other was because the element of fear had been removed and the players were fitter, more confident and happier.

We ended the session in the Academy's steam room with the thermostat turned up to 110 degrees so that the players could get used to the sort of heat they were due to face in Monterrey in just three weeks' time. That made the training match against South Korea at a local school's ground important, especially as Shilton, Robson and Wilkins all expressed desire to take part in the game. I wanted them because I needed to play as close to my World Cup starting line-up as I could. I told them to have a crack at it and if there were problems I would pull them out. I required them to play matches but I did not want to force things and let the team peak too early.

The trick was to combine all those factors to achieve the peak at exactly the right time. That was my job, to get 22 players fit, ready and eager to play on 3 June. Tomorrow would be a good test of how that theory was going in practice for the Koreans who, though not a world power, had been together for over a year and had obtained some interesting results. On a tour of Mexico they had lost 2–1 twice to their hosts, 1–0 to Hungary and I had watched them beat Algeria 2–0. In Europe they had had even better results, having fought back from two goals down against the crack Belgian side, Anderlecht, to beat them 3–2 in Brussels.

WEDNESDAY 14 MAY: Arriving by bus at the Fountain Valley High School was like taking a step back in time. There was not a hooligan in sight, just a couple of thousand people, mainly families, out to enjoy the afternoon. Many were waving flags and banners making the carnival atmosphere delightful with the aroma of beefburgers and sausages wafting across the pitch. It quickly became evident that the South Koreans were taking the match very seriously. They saw the prospect of England's scalp as a World

Cup booster and they came at us with skill and pace. They had some talented players and we began a little slowly. For the first ten minutes they were undoubtedly the best side and our marking was slack. But, as Robson and Wilkins began to feel their fitness, we became more assertive, though our touch and our crossing still left a little to be desired.

Then our game began to come together. Waddle switched to the right to counter the threat of their attacking left-back and suddenly the ball flashed around as though it were on a piece of elastic. Mark Hateley scored the first goal, taking it in exactly the same way that he had done in our qualifying campaign against Northern Ireland and Finland. Bryan Robson heralded his return with a brilliant volley. He pots them like Steve Davis pots the reds. It was with some relief that I took him off at half-time because I wanted him to have a nice, steady run at it without provoking a recurrence of his injuries. I must admit that Bryan's shoulder was still causing me concern. I kept thinking back to the medical advice and wondering if it was going to go again. I closed my eyes every time he went rushing in for one of those crosses and willed to see him on his feet when I reopened them. But he seemed confident enough about playing and he went on with his usual lack of fear. His timing was not quite there but it was coming back.

I asked Ray Wilkins to stay on for the whole 90 minutes while sending on Steve Hodge for Robson. I also put on Alvin Martin and switched Terry Fenwick to left-back as I had done for the match against the Academy. This served a double purpose as it kept Kenny fit and fresh while giving Terry a run at left-back in case we ever needed him to play there. Up front I had Kerry Dixon on for Hateley, who had tweaked a hamstring, and John Barnes for Waddle. It went well as Kerry followed up his hat-trick of three days earlier with two more goals, John Barnes having a hand in both. However, there were the usual injury problems with Hodge not lasting the half and being replaced by Spurs' Gary Stevens and Beardsley limping off with a bad ankle after a nasty tackle. That was a result of a bit of nonsense from Terry Fenwick who elbowed one of the Korean players in the face. It was unnecessary and made the Koreans, who had played the game in the right spirit until then, a lot more fierce.

If Italy, Argentina and Bulgaria thought South Korea were going to be a pushover, they had a surprise in store. Although their goal in the second half looked well off-side, they had created chances and looked an accomplished side in a 4–1 decfeat. So far as I was concerned, it was a good result and another step in the right direction.

THURSDAY 15 MAY: The players had complained of being stiff and sore after the first game against the Academy in Colorado Springs so we introduced a compulsory morning swimming session, which was designed to relax and loosen the muscles without putting any undue strain on them. It was not something I had done before with the players but I was well aware of the therapeutic value of swimming and it was also of value in promoting the still-growing team spirit. Players pretend that they do not like to be organised but they do. Any sign of lax organisation and they soon start to moan.

It was a short, 30-minute session as they went through exercises, diving and relay races for competitiveness. Naturally, I was soaked standing on the edge of the pool, mainly from Kenny Sansom's antics, but at least the players had the decency to warn me that I was about to be thrown in when I heard Ray Wilkins ask Bryan Robson: 'Is the gaffer's watch waterproof?' I got my own back that afternoon. I think the players had expected a nice, quiet day lounging by the pool but, after some consideration, I decided we needed an extra session, partly because we would be travelling on Friday. Sometimes they need a little extra push and this was one of those days. We trooped off to the Academy where we reduced the pitch to 40×40 yards and had an hour of explosive work, increasing the pace with lots of crossing and shooting. It was short, sharp technical stuff and they put their backs into it. The four Everton boys worked with us for the first time, Robson trained without his yellow shoulder harness and goalkeepers Woods and Shilton were outstanding.

Absent from the session were Hoddle, Hateley, Hodge and Beardsley. All four were doubtful for the game against Mexico but I was especially anxious about Steve Hodge. I had a word with him, the doctor and Fred Street. We were all concerned. The lad was suffering intense pain around the ankle bone and up towards the shin but there were no visible signs of injury, with no swelling or even bruising. We were baffled and Steve was pessimistic. He had not been right since the Scotland match and, though he had run like a stag on Tuesday, the game on Wednesday had found him out and time was beginning to run out. I was already gambling on Bryan Robson's fitness and I simply could not afford to take risks with his cover. I was seriously considering sending Steve home and calling up a replacement and I was sure it was in his thoughts as well.

FRIDAY 16 MAY: The injury problems had receded considerably by the morning. Hoddle had iced his leg to bring down the swelling around his knee and Beardsley, though still badly bruised, had made a remarkable recovery. Hateley, due to have a fitness test at 10 a.m., was so eager to play that he was up and out with Fred Street and on his way back as I went to check how he was, telling me he was fine, fit and available for selection. It meant that, with the exception of Trevor Steven, I could leave the Everton players behind to continue their delayed acclimatisation, and field an almost full-strength side against quality opponents in Mexico. Not only were they the last side to have beaten us 12 months earlier but they had built up an undefeated record in Los Angeles' Olympic Stadium in a 17-match sequence including a recent victory over the South American Champions, Uruguay. It wouldn't have been a disaster to have lost to them, but I did not want to. I wanted to keep our own unbeaten spell going. It was a good fixture for many countries were struggling to find top-quality opposition so near to the World Cup and it also gave us a game in high temperatures.

We could not have picked a better day to leave Colorado Springs. It was cold and wet with a hint of more snow in the air. What happened to those glorious sunny days I had been promised? At least it was localised for, as we flew out to Phoenix, we crossed the Arizona Desert, which was shimmering under the noonday sun. It was also hot in Los Angeles and the players had an early night to conserve their energy while we officials did our duty with a visit to the British Consulate. It turned out to be a pleasant one as the Consul had his family home in Suffolk, not far from my own in Ipswich.

SATURDAY 17 MAY: What a day! We recorded another victory by beating the fancied Mexicans 3–0 but I was heavy-hearted as I put on a brave face to the media, hiding the fact that the thing I feared most of all had happened. My skipper, Bryan Robson, had dislocated his shoulder for the third time. He did it in front of 63,000 spectators, including some of the sharpest photographers in the business, and the television cameras, which were relaying the game live back to millions at home. Yet only Fred Street, who quietly and professionally slipped it back, Bryan himself, Dr Edwards and I knew and we were not about to tell anyone.

The day had started well enough. We had played at the Coliseum the year before and we knew roughly what to expect. I was a little concerned at the width of the pitch but when the promoter suggested we widen it with Astroturf I quickly told him to forget it, for we would have needed two pairs of boots. We had a team talk before the game when I stressed the importance of the result and how difficult it could be against a side who considered the Olympic Stadium their second home, hardly surprising in view of the huge Mexican population in Los Angeles which had played its part in that unbeaten run of some 17 games. I also emphasised the need to take our unbeaten run into the World Cup but, even more important, was the need to play well and to give it everything we had. This match would be a good pointer and if we won the message would be flashed around the world, confirming our result in the Soviet Union.

I addressed individual players as well. Although Peter Beardsley, for example, had performed very creditably he had not had a shot at goal against the Academy in an 11–0 win and he had not scored against the Koreans in 85 minutes. If a striker is playing well then his game should be about shots at goal in addition to setting up other people. I wanted Peter to show more thrust and not to play in front of the centre-half all the time. I also told Glenn Hoddle not to abuse his talents. There is nothing you can't do, I informed this talented player. I asked him not to waste energy on impracticable attempts and said that realism was to be the key that afternoon.

We made another bad beginning. For the first ten minutes we gave the ball away far too much and, but for a bad miss and a wonderful save, we could have been two down very early on. Carlos Hermosillo was guilty of missing the target while Peter Shilton showed his class when he kept out a goal-bound shot from Luis Flores. Shilton continued to perform heroics, particularly in the second half when we tired, and I abandoned my plans to give Chris Woods a run-out. I was enjoying watching Shilton demonstrate why he was the world's number one, not to mention the 63,000 crowd.

I was pleased with the response from Glenn and the rest of the midfield as they gradually took a firm hold. Everyone seemed to come to terms with what was going on around them at the same time and we swept Mexico away in 15 scintillating minutes. I had been worried about both Chris Waddle and Mark Hateley. Sometimes Waddle's crosses were poor and Hateley was not always as fearless as he had been when he first came into the side. They relieved all concern in a split second when Chris whipped in a centre and Mark dived full length among the boots to head a great goal. The team were instantly transformed and we were in the driving seat. We were soon two ahead as Wilkins held up the ball to bring Beardsley in on the right and Peter showed good touch before floating a searching cross towards the far post out of the reach of goalkeeper Larios. I thought it was too high for Mark as well but he made an explosive leap to head a picture goal.

When Ipswich were at their best I had always felt that once we went a goal up, we were invincible. That is the hallmark of a great team. I was beginning to feel the same way about England.

The third goal was the icing on the cake. Kenny Sansom rolled a quick free kick to Glenn Hoddle whose broad vision enabled him to spot Beardsley in a good position. The Newcastle striker had found a hole and took total advantage of it, controlling the ball beautifully, holding off a challenge and scoring his first-ever international goal. I was delighted for this likeable young man.

We tired in the second half but it was understandable with the temperatures in the middle eighties. We had a commanding lead and Mexico were only going to get back into the game if we did something stupid. The talent of Manuel Negrete was the one way the Mexicans were going to stage a revival and we had Ray Wilkins sitting on him and Peter Shilton always in the way when they did get through. We showed no real signs of cracks.

Bryan Robson was doing his captain's job and urging his team-mates to lift themselves to another great effort. He had told me before the game that he felt far better than he expected and was keen to last a full 90 minutes. My original plans were to play him for an hour but I thought I would give him a chance and look for the signs when he began to wilt. I was just about ready to bring him off when he chased back to make a sliding tackle only to end up underneath the attacker clutching his shoulder. I knew from the way he knelt on the ground that the suspect right shoulder had gone again.

This time it was for real and Fred leapt up from the bench so quickly that he pulled a hamstring, while the doctor was right beside him. Whatever the injury, there was no question of Bryan carrying on and I started setting up substitutes ready to go on. Fred, the doctor and Bryan came back with Fred saying out loud that the fall had just shaken up the shoulder but from the nods and winks I knew it was much worse and Fred whispered that he and the doctor had put the shoulder back into place while they treated Bryan on the pitch. It slipped back in that easily, which showed how loose it was. It was no consolation being proved right.

A fit Bryan Robson is truly world class, full of controlled aggression, always hard, never dirty, brilliant in the air, brave in the box. But to be all of that he needs to be 100 per cent fit, for when he is not he cannot give it. He is going to protect himself, even if it is only in his subconscious, and who can blame him. It was a great blow for if I was going to risk Robson it would effectively reduce my player availability from 13 to 12. One of the substitutes would have to be on permament stand-by for the skipper as the shoulder was as likely to go after 5 or 85 minutes. Out of courtesy we extended the circle of those who needed to know about the problem to six when Dr Edwards telephoned the Manchester United specialist, Mr Noble, with the news. He was not surprised. If that was the case, then why in the name of football, hadn't Bryan had his shoulder pinned?

I could not let this latest anxiety show if we were to keep the injury under wraps. As I went through the dressing rooms I noticed that Kenny Sansom had lost eight pounds during the game and Ray Wilkins five. When I returned after speaking to the Press I was told that most of the players had shed between five and six pounds and I felt that it was somehow appropriate that we flew back via Salt Lake City arriving in Colorado Springs around midnight.

The players' wives were waiting when we returned. They had arrived on Friday evening and, though they were tired, most of them were there to greet us as we joined them for a club sandwich and a cup of coffee. I had not been at all sure about allowing the wives to come out but, after hearing the players' view as put forward by their spokesman, Bryan Robson, I gave in to my better judgement. The Football Association picked it up from there and funded the entire trip, which was a magnificent gesture even though the players had offered to finance it themselves. I was keeping my fingers crossed that it would be money well spent. It certainly began well enough for my wife Elsie had gone into our room to discover a large bouquet of flowers with a message that read: 'We are pleased the Governor picked us. Thanks for lending us your husband for seven weeks,' and signed from the players. A number of them had also put flowers in their own rooms to greet their wives.

SUNDAY **18** MAY: The snow that had welcomed the wives on Friday night and turned to rain over Saturday had cleared up sufficiently to permit the ladies to parade the latest fashions in swimwear around the pool. We had lunch together so that everyone could get to know each other and the Chairman of the International Committee, Dick Wragg, made a short, sincere welcoming speech to the newcomers, telling them that they would be asked to come back if we were in a position to win the World Cup. I had my fingers crossed while he said that.

I kept them crossed as I faced some searching questions from the Press at our evening conference about the fitness of the skipper. I have never felt happy telling even white lies. Bryan and his wife had gone up into the hills on hired bikes with Bryan pushing Denise up the steep inclines. I wondered whether the shoulder was now so loose that it could be put back and he could continue playing? However, I was informed that the more it came out the worse it was going to become.

MONDAY **19** MAY: I actively encouraged the players to join their wives by the swimming pool and to soak up the sun so that it would not come as a shock when we arrived in Monterrey. After the worry over Bryan Robson it was good news indeed to hear that Steve Hodge had been out at 9.30 a.m. with Fred Street to test his ankle. He worked for half an hour and I knew before I asked it, from the happy smile on his face, what the answer was to my question. He hadn't felt a thing and he joined us for our altitude training session at the Academy that afternoon. Only Gary Bailey was missing and even Bryan Robson came with us and trained. We worked hard for we had a game looming against Canada at the weekend and I felt that I would rather tail off to leave them fresh than have an easy beginning to the week.

It backfired. After 70 minutes Bryan Robson limped off and he came over to tell me quietly that he was feeling his old hamstring injury. I could not believe it. We lied to the watching Press that he had felt a twinge in his Achilles and had come off as a precaution but he quickly disappeared with the doctor to have the injury iced, strapped up tightly and hidden with a pair of borrowed tracksuit bottoms. He went and sat on the coach out of everyone's way until we were ready to leave.

Bryan had to put on a brave face and use his acting talents at the Broadmoor Hotel that night when he held a Press conference to announce that he had just signed a million-dollar contract for seven years with the American shoe company, New Balance. He talked about playing the full 90 minutes against Canada and how well his shoulder felt. I bet he would willingly have given up that money for a fit and healthy body. The Press went from his conference to mine and again I found myself covering up for my injured skipper, concealing my gloom.

At that precise moment I was convinced that we would have to start our World Cup campaign without Bryan Robson. A hamstring takes anything up to three weeks to heal and our game against Portugal was now just two weeks away. I felt desperately sorry for the lad. He deserved some luck after such a rotten season. If it had been any other player I would have patted him on the back and sent him home to receive treatment in readiness for the new season. But this was Bryan Robson, who was so special and so important to the squad. I needed him for his contribution to the team's morale and for his stature even though I had originally vowed that I would not take injured players with me to Mexico after what had happened to Ron Greenwood with Kevin Keegan. But, at least, I knew that Bryan was a different type of person from Kevin and that it would do the squad good to keep him with us, even if it meant we were reduced to 21 players.

I could not concentrate on dinner at the magnificent hotel restaurant and as I write these notes I find it hard to imagine Bryan playing in the World Cup at all, never mind against Portugal in two weeks' time. He can't even train to keep his muscle tone going. I desperately hope I am wrong.

TUESDAY **20** MAY: The day started considerably better than the last one had ended for the first person I bumped into on my way to breakfast was Gary Bailey. He greeted me by holding up both thumbs and showed me how the swelling had completely vanished from his injured knee. I had put Sheffield Wednesday's Martin Hodge on official alert but it now looked as though neither he nor Stewart Robson would make a dramatic late entry into the World Cup arena. Gary would still have to undergo a strenuous fitness test but both he and Steve Hodge now seemed very confident.

After the usual routine around the swimming pool with the wives we had a good 45-minute training session followed by another set of physiological tests. The responses were good over the tough 660-yard course with everyone except the absent Robson giving it a go. The pulse rates were coming down nicely and, clearly, the boys were acclimatising a lot more quickly than they had in Mexico the year before. They are undoubtedly a very fit set of players. There are always surprises and one of them was Chris Waddle. The lad often looks as though he is on his heels with those stooped shoulders and his hanging head but when I spoke to Peter Shreeves a few days before we left he had told me that Chris was one of the fittest on his books. He did really well today leaving Hateley, Dixon, Lineker and Barnes trailing in his wake. All his tests are good, whether blood, urine or weight. He is really trying hard.

The same can be said of Everton's Gary Stevens who had arrived in the United States out of form and not having trained very much because of a bad knee. He was now training well and showing his fitness. He had a chat with me after training, explaining how he had been hounded by the Press over the break-up of his marriage, but he was looking more relaxed and happy and I was ready to give him a game against Canada on Saturday. Alvin Martin was also a lot perkier and was looking for a game as well.

That night the Football Association entertained the players and their wives to dinner in the impressive Penrose Restaurant overlooking the man-made lake and the Rocky Mountains. The decision to bring them out was already paying handsome dividends. They were all perfect ambassadors for their country just like their husbands. The spirit was better than ever and everyone was very relaxed.

WEDNESDAY 21 MAY: The players deserved a day off. The hard ground had left them with sore feet and blisters. Terry Fenwick had a niggling groin injury, Chris Waddle a slight tightening of the hamstring and Peter Reid's ankle was in trouble. With Bailey and Robson also sitting out training, I thought that a day spent sightseeing, shopping, playing golf or just sunbathing would be a sound investment for everyone. Elsie and I went off to see some of the tourist attractions, taking in the Indian Reservation at the Garden of the Gods, a spectacular place bristling with fingers of bright red stone which, incredibly, are supposed to be between 150 and 250 million years old. It is an old Indian prayer ground and I said one or two myself that morning. We followed this with a visit to the cowboy town of

154

Manitou Springs and then returned to our training base at the US Airforce Academy to look at their famous church that caters for all denominations. Back at the Broadmoor I checked out Gary Bailey who had been put through a tough 45-minute session by Mike Kelly to test his injured knee and spoke to Bryan Robson, who still claimed that he was going to be ready for the game against Portugal. Perhaps he overheard those prayers of mine but, before he can think of playing, he has to stand up to full training without any of his three injuries recurring.

THURSDAY 22 MAY: We tried hard to arrange a game for next week as I particularly wanted everyone who was fit and able in the squad to have at least one full game to sharpen them up for some had not played since their last club fixture three weeks ago. I spoke to our liaison officer, Brian Gay, in Monterrey who was checking with the local League Champions and nearby Tampico. I had also arranged a morning Press conference to convey the good news on Gary Bailey and I thought that while I was doing that we would let the photographers take pictures of a smiling manager and captain to prove that there were no problems. It almost backfired for, when the written Press saw me emerge with Bryan, neither of us was smiling, and they thought the worst, namely that I was sending Robson home 24 hours before the deadline for the 22.

You could feel the tension in the air and then the relief when I explained what we were doing. They didn't know how close to the truth their first impressions were! Bailey, too, was a close-run thing. This was the absolute deadline and the knee was still puffy but I decided to take the risk when Gary assured me that if there were a game tomorrow he could play. It was worth the risk to nurse him through the next few days as he had two more years' experience than his nearest rival.

I spent an hour by the pool before being interrupted with the news from home that Sir Alf Ramsey was continuing his campaign against me in one of the tabloids by publishing the private letter I had written to him thanking him, tongue in cheek, for the offer of help. I suppose nothing should surprise me anymore, but it does. I hope my response to these continual assaults was a little more dignified. The training session restored my confidence as we enjoyed a strenuous work-out in the heat of the day. Yesterday was the hottest day in the Springs for eight months and yet snow had been forecast for today. Happily, there was no sign of it and we made full use of the glorious sunshine and the thin air. I named the team for Canada, bringing back Everton's Gary Stevens and Gary Lineker for Anderson and Beardsley while Alvin Martin stood in for the injured

Fenwick (I would have given him a game anyway) and Steve Hodge did what he came for, replacing the injured skipper.

We trooped back to the dressing room only to discover it had been cordoned off by police cars. Bryan Robson, Terry Fenwick, Fred Street and Norman Medhurst had been hastily ushered out and men in spaceman-like breathing suits were going through the place. My first thoughts were of the recent nuclear accident in the Soviet Union, though it turned out to be a dangerous spillage of mercury, which was still bad enough for us to decide not to mention it back at the hotel, especially as we had our farewell dinner that night. We made use of the resulting free half an hour or so spent waiting for the all-clear talking about our arrangements for the next few days.

The evening went off without incident. It was a superb finale to a very successful week. Dick Wragg bought all of the wives and girlfriends a present, the food was good and everyone seemed to be relaxed and happy. The wives thanked the FA for their hospitality and promised they would see us in Mexico City for the semi-finals, which was not an unpleasant thought at all.

FRIDAY 23 MAY: It was a tearful, emotional farewell when we left the magnificent Broadmoor Hotel for Canada as all the wives and girlfriends came to the door to wave goodbye and wish us luck. I owed those girls a vote of thanks, for they had helped the squad unwind. There was not a word out of place in the entire week and the squad were, simply, a pleasure to be with. What is more, our regular group of travelling journalists and one or two fresh faces also responded to the atmosphere, leaving the players alone when they were with their wives. A member of the senior hotel staff told one of the journalists how much the English party would be missed and added: 'They are world-class sportsmen – and first-class people.'

The first major logistical problem we encountered was on our flight out of Denver on our way to Vancouver when, as is usual with internal American airlines, there was a severe case of overbooking. I thought that we would be all right because we had confirmed our seats but so had a lot of other people and 12 volunteers were asked to give up their seats in return for an overnight stay, a flight out the next day and a free round trip on any of the airline's routes. They had no trouble finding the dozen they needed with one girl happily claiming that it was worth 600 dollars to her to get off. But imagine my surprise when the seats were filled up and one of the lucky passengers was our own John Barnes! He had lingered on the way to the gate and was lucky that he had the experienced Thomas Cook's representative, Cyril Broderick, to fight his case for him.

I was welcomed back to Vancouver, where I had been player-manager, by messages, telephone calls and letters plus visits from a number of old friends including one of my former players, Bobby Cram, the uncle of my favourite runner Steve Cram. It was a pleasant return but I still managed an early night.

SATURDAY 24 MAY: It was on odd day, not least of all because our kick-off against Canada was scheduled for 11 a.m. It meant a compulsory 8 a.m. breakfast followed by a team meeting with Ted Croker, who was to leave us for FIFA meetings in Mexico City while we travelled to Monterrey. It was the last chance we would have before the tournament began of informing the players what bonus they were on. No one had asked and I had told Bryan Robson to leave it to me. Ted and I explained the structure. The money seemed quite generous to me and there were no comments at all from the players. I had the distinct impression that they were concerned with more important matters than the money but I still wanted to make sure that they were given what they deserved. We knew from a few enquiries that our offer compared favourably with those of West Germany and Scotland and, just as we had increased the qualifying bonus, I knew we would do the same if we managed to go all the way. We followed this with a team talk, which received far more attention, as I demanded that we gave the Canadians a pasting. I said that if Wales could beat them while their star players, like Ian Rush, were missing surely we could do as much and once we had scored three we should go for four, five, six and seven. I asked for a good attitude and reminded them that they were playing for their World Cup places.

But football is the game it is because it is so unpredictable. You know in your heart of hearts that you cannot keep on winning indefinitely. You don't look for or foresee it. More often than not it is the game you least expect to lose against the most unlikely of opponents that ends the run. This time we did not lose but, after so many good performances, it was disappointing not only in the 1–0 scoreline but even more so in the way we played and, to cap everything, our 40-goal Footballer of the Year, Gary Lineker, looked as though he had written himself out of the World Cup with a suspected broken wrist.

The goalless first half was desperate. Centre-half Alvin Martin had clearly not recovered from his stressful season while Everton's Gary Stevens needed that first 45 minutes to settle down. Glenn Hoddle and Ray Wilkins, who had been playing so well, hardly functioned at all and never

157

got to the front two, who had to battle it alone against some very tough defenders as well as some weak officiating by the local Vancouver referee. The exception was young Steve Hodge who was the pick of the midfield and might have had a hat-trick as he hit a post in the first half, had a perfectly good effort disallowed and was in there scrapping when goalkeeper Paul Dolan failed to hold a free kick from Hoddle. It was, however, Mark Hateley who pounced to score our only goal, showing how he had recovered his appetite for goals since leaving England. Certainly, we did enough to have won by four or five while the Canadians did not test Peter Shilton in the first half nor his second-half substitute Chris Woods. But we could not escape the fact that we were half a yard short and were unable to step up the pace. Good players looked ordinary with only Sansom, Butcher, Hodge, Lineker, before his injury, and Hateley up to scratch.

Hodge pleased me, especially as Bryan Robson was still struggling and looking unlikely to make the game against Portugal. He is a good player but a funny lad. When everyone wears a cardigan and slacks Steve will appear in a tracksuit; when we were queuing up at gate 30 he was at gate 28 on his way to Acapulco instead of Vancouver; he frequently loses his boots half an hour before the kick-off; and forgets which room we are eating in. On the very first day in Colorado we issued the players with really smart wet tops because it was so cold. I warned everyone to look after them as they would become collectors' items. There are no prizes for guessing who left his behind. He admitted: 'I'm like that boss, I forget things you know.' However, most importantly, he does not forget his instructions on the pitch for he is a good player and a lovely kid.

So is Gary Lineker. Playing his first game since the Cup Final, he looked sharp and dangerous despite the buffeting he was receiving from Randy Samuel and Terry Moore and he and Hateley were looking a good pair in a poor game. He suffered yet another crashing fall 20 minutes from the end of the game but instead of jumping up as he normally does he lay on the pitch in obvious pain clutching, I thought, his ribs. Fred Street could see he was in trouble and almost as soon as he reached him he called for Dr Edwards. Fred is a cool, calculating man who never panics. He is also tremendously experienced and when he did this I knew it was something serious. As they pulled Lineker to his feet and brought him off with his arm held to his side, I feared another dislocated shoulder. My priority, however, was to look after the team and I already had Peter Beardsley warming up to replace Chris Waddle. I sent him on for Lineker instead.

That accomplished, I turned to Fred and the doctor who were steering the white-faced player through the horde of photographers. Fred did what he had done in Los Angeles, winked at me and said quietly that they were taking Lineker off to a local hospital for X-rays. The lad was in awful pain, distressed and perspiring heavily. At that point I was convinced that there was a break. I was sure that I had lost the second of two of the world's best goalscorers, this latest one a day after the deadline for selecting the World Cup squad. It looked as though we could be down to 20 players before we had even kicked a ball in earnest.

I had to try and forget about it and concentrate on the game where I was making further substitutions. As we finished I walked off to be met by a grim-faced Alan Bass, England's physician in 1966 who had emigrated to Canada. He told me: 'I fear the worst.' There was some mumbling about protective covers but we all knew that if there was a break that was it. That was certainly the thought I took with me to the reception after I had showered and changed. We were just preparing to leave the subdued party when Dr Edwards came up to me and said: 'We have got away with it, you won't believe it, he has a bad sprain.' The news was a huge relief and when I returned to the hotel later that night Gary confirmed that he was still in there shouting. He is a good lad and was putting on a brave face, well aware of everyone's concern. He could not have had a better room-mate, under the circumstances, than Peter Shilton who looked after him. But the one incident I will always remember was when Peter Beardsley came up to me after the game and asked if he could miss out on the reception because he wanted to visit Gary in hospital. This was the lad who stood to benefit most from Lineker's injury yet here he was more concerned with his team-mate's welfare than his own place. It was typical of this tremendous little chap and I liked him more and more.

SUNDAY 25 MAY: If anyone thought I would wake up deeply regretting the fixture against Canada they could not have been more mistaken. You can just as easily sustain a serious injury in training. We needed that game before going into the World Cup and the travelling, the morning kick-off and the other obstacles made it that much tougher a test. We had come out of it with our unbeaten record intact and our confidence unblemished. We had now won six successive games, which was just one short of the post-war record gained in 1966 immediately before England won the World Cup, and it was our seventh consecutive win away from England.

It was raining heavily in Vancouver when we were called at 5 a.m. for our departure to the airport. Lineker and everyone else was chirpy despite the ungodly hour and, indeed, the trip from Vancouver to Los Angeles was uneventful apart from a chuckle on landing when Peter Beardsley turned to me and said: 'He's wrong you know.'

'Who?' I asked.

'The captain,' replied Beardsley.

'Bryan Robson?' I asked, becoming more perplexed by the minute.

'No,' said Beardsley, 'The pilot, he said the flight would take 2 hours 23 minutes and it has taken 2 hours 25 minutes.'

That's the sort of precise mind he has. For example, when I was taking the pulse rates he was working them out quicker than me even after a fast 660-yard run.

I needed a laugh for it turned out to be a frustrating journey. We had left Vancouver expecting an 11.40 a.m. connection to Monterrey but not only did we discover that the flight was scheduled for two hours later but also that we were not registered on it despite having confirmed and reconfirmed our group booking. We somehow managed to get everyone seats but as we were about to take off an American shouted out in anger when he saw his bag sitting on the runway along with a great deal of our baggage. The furious American said that if his case wasn't going with him it wasn't worth him going and demanded to be taken back. That meant an hour sitting on the aircraft and when we did get under way it was only as far as Chihuahua where we landed on an unscheduled stop that made us even later and kept our hosts cooling their heels in Monterrey for three hours.

But what a welcome we received when we did eventually turn up with speeches by officials from FIFA, the state and the local Organising Committee, a warm Press conference and a tumultuous ovation from the locals. Liaison officer Alan O'Dell, who has been on a great many more of these trips than most, reckoned it was the best by far in his long memory. The level of security was even more impressive as we were ushered out of the newly-built terminal into our official coach. The calvacade of twelve police cars, six motorcycle outriders and other armed escorts, including a helicopter, was awesome to say the least. Such elaborate precautions meant that the players were a bit subdued at first but we gradually unwound and enjoyed the thrill of it for, after all, this was where it was all going to happen.

Even the locals who were waiting for us at our hotel, the Camino Real, had never seen anything like it. They said it was very exciting for them after they had applauded us and presented us with red roses and carnations. What is more, every country received the same treatment. I can only say that there must be a lot of police in Mexico.

No sooner had I settled into the suite that the Mexican President, Señor de la Madrid, had occupied a couple of nights earlier, than I took an urgent telephone call from Mexico City telling me that I had made a dreadful mistake in my squad of 22. Yugoslavian, Ivan Toplak, of the Organising

Committee was most concerned because I had named Gary Stevens twice. He couldn't believe they were different players and when I mentioned it at dinner it transpired that Walter Sieber, the FIFA representative in Monterrey, had raised the same query with Alan O'Dell at the airport. At least it was nice to know that someone cared!

12. Monterrey

MONDAY 26 MAY: It was our third country in four days and in the morning the sun streamed down on our delightful hotel, which was swarming with security guards. After breakfast the local police chief talked to us, telling the players that they wanted them to be happy and relaxed, that the guards were there for their protection and that they would do everything they could to help them. He assured us that England were not being given any special treatment and that they were doing this for every one of the 24 competing countries. He added that anyone leaving the hotel must tell him or one of his men so that they could maintain constant surveillance while I chipped in at that point to say that I also wanted to know of anyone leaving the hotel.

Despite the guards, the players quickly adapted to their new environment, appreciating the pool, the putting green, tennis courts and games rooms. They had what they wanted. Training at the well-equipped Cima Club was the next item. Again we were given a massive escort with the police blocking off every crossroad to give us a clear run, which took us exactly 67 minutes. The Press seemed more concerned about this daily trip than the players who were prepared for it. When I had been considering the problems of living at altitude and training in the heat, I had asked our local man Brian Gay to see if it was possible to have card tables installed on the coach. The Mexicans eventually had acceded and given us the only coach with card tables and our eight Cincinnati kids were well catered for. The others had their tapes and I quickly learned the lyrics of every Whitney Houston song. With the slick police escort the journey was little different from the trip to the Airforce Academy in Colorado or the Reforma Club in Mexico City 12 months earlier.

Tales of the heat of Monterrey were not exaggerated with Dr Edwards recording temperatures of 97°F at the training ground and everyone lost between five and eight pounds during the course of our 100-minute session. Even Bryan Robson lost three pounds in his much gentler work-out. It was tough in view of the game on Saturday and the long, tiring trip on Sunday but everyone stuck to it, even the incapacitated Lineker who trained, ran, shot and headed despite having his arm strapped to his chest.

He had to have a chance of playing against Portugal and I would not have to make up my mind until the following Monday but Bryan Robson still posed a major problem. If he was to make our opening game he really should play for half an hour against Monterrey on Wednesday.

I was still contemplating these problems on the way back to the dressing room when I was suddenly assailed by a long-haired drunk sticking a tape recorder under my nose and demanding to know why I had kept him waiting for the Press conference. It was suggested afterwards that it was an Argentine journalist deliberately trying to wind me up. It was something I shall have to watch for. Words can easily become twisted and public relations are so important when you are abroad. No sooner had I got rid of him than one of the guards mentioned to me that two of my players had been quenching their thirst at the drinking fountain against every piece of advice. Dr Edwards can be very loyal, and if he knew who the culprits were he was not about to tell me.

TUESDAY 27 MAY: Training in the oppressive heat was taking a great deal out of the players and it was decided at a staff meeting that we would have to cut down on the sunbathing. We did not want to stop it completely but to ensure that it was more closely monitored. Circumstances had changed since Colorado and the heat was different. Everyone knows from their own experience that lying in the sun on holiday leaves you feeling lethargic and tired and we had never intended the players to be out in it for three hours or more. Instead we banned all sunbathing after 11.15 a.m. when the sun was at its strongest. I also told them that whoever it was who had drunk water from the fountain the previous day was very stupid while the doctor admonished them all to go back and reread the booklet he had specially produced on the subject of caring for health in Mexico. It had been a good moment to impose some discipline, before it had a chance to slip.

The cloud cover reduced the temperatures for our training session today. Robson and Lineker trained well and the doctor's prognosis that we would feel better every day was being confirmed. My only disappointment was that afterwards Bryan Robson told me he was not ready to play against Monterrey the next day. He said he was only three-quarters fit and did not feel it was the right moment to test the hamstring under match conditions. There were also other problems as Peter Reid hurt his ankle and his Everton colleague, Trevor Steven, developed a fever. I had announced my team for the friendly against the Mexican League Champions and decided to wait to see what the morning would bring.

We met the FIFA representative, Walter Sieber, in the evening and, somewhat apologetically, he informed us that FIFA had, at the last moment, decidèd to go against their original recommendation and allow only two substitutes from five even though they were allowing all of those not playing to sit on the bench. I told him that I would be one of 24 surprised managers and, for the life of me, I could not understand the reasoning behind the decision. They are all on the bench and all have a number. Why not involve them fully?

WEDNESDAY **28** MAY: Public attention in an event like the World Cup is inevitably centred on the men who play the games in front of the television cameras and the manager who does most of the talking. But, as I tried to emphasise earlier in the book, the squad embraces a much wider circle with key figures like physiotherapists Fred Street and Norman Medhurst; liaison officer Alan O'Dell; my invaluable coach Don Howe; our goalkeeping specialist Mike Kelly; Press Officer and translator Glen Kirton and the members of the International Committee. However, the most important person in our preparations for Mexico was undoubtedly the team physician Vernon Edwards. He has been with the Football Association in one capacity or another for 15 years and this was to be his final fling for he planned to retire after the World Cup. For two years he had put his heart and soul into the job. He had set up meetings and interviews, supervised a variety of tests and had loved every minute of it.

His self-prescribed duties did not end with the medical care of the players for he kept a close watch on the food the players ate as well as everything else that anyone asked him to do. I never once heard him say 'no' or that he was too busy whether it was a player, an official or one of the media. We often told him he worked too hard and on this particular morning he was his usual busy self, checking some food that had arrived from England.

It was the start of a day that was to see this popular man suffer a massive heart attack that sadly and prematurely led to the end of his World Cup involvement and his splendid career with the Football Association. There was no indication of the traumas that were to follow when I sat down at breakfast with the doctor to talk over the busy day we had ahead, starting with a visit to a monastery some 2,000 feet up the Sierra Madres, at the same height as the Aztec Stadium. It had been found for us by Hernan Garza, head of the local Organising Committee, with whom I had become quite friendly on my visits to Mexico. He was pro-English and when I had mentioned that I needed somewhere higher than Saltillo for the odd day's acclimatisation he had recommended Los Pinos. It took us around half an hour to reach the Catholic Sanctuary and after we had parked I walked about 10 yards with the doctor before he turned and said: 'Sorry, I am going to have to go back to the car.' When I showed concern, he shrugged it off and put it down to altitude. I made a joke about it and caught up Hernan and Brian to look over the facilities. It was perfect, having a number of areas for the players to relax, play and have a barbecue. We had already made a donation to help with the upkeep and to make the slight improvements we needed.

We went back to the car before going to look at the eating area and the doctor decided to come with us. We lagged behind the others as I urged him to take his time and he confided: 'Don't say anything to the rest of the staff but I have a touch of angina. I'm all right but if you could keep it between you and me.' I was shocked and when we returned to the Camino Real I asked him whether it was advisable to undertake any of his plans for the rest of day, which included taking Gary Lineker to hospital in Monterrey to be measured for his lightweight cast. He said he would take advantage of the visit to the hospital to see a doctor he knew and to have an ECG. I said that sounded a good idea and told him to go straight back to the hotel afterwards without bothering to come to the game.

Fred Street commented on how ill the doctor looked and we combined forces to persuade Vernon to have a good breather. He insisted that he would join us after the hospital visit and I reluctantly agreed provided he promised not to carry kit or chase footballs in the way he normally did. With the game to occupy my mind, I thought little more about it until midway through the first half when the doctor reappeared on the line. He had sent Gary on to the Cima Club while he underwent his promised check-up. The specialist had told him that something had happened that morning and that he should be careful. But, having dosed himself with tablets, he came on to the match instead of returning to the hotel. I thought he looked an odd colour and my concern was confirmed when Alan O'Dell called me to one side to say that Vernon was ill. I decided we should get him away as quickly as possible but the doctor was just as obstinate as he had been before lunch.

Fred Street, with his medical knowledge, was most alarmed and when he checked Vernon's pulse it was immediately evident that he would be better off in a hospital than at a football match and this time Vernon agreed to return to the hotel. As I watched him being helped away, I realised that if we did not take him straight to hospital we would be guilty of neglect. Glen ran after them but Fred had already reached the same conclusion. He asked the doctor what he would do if the roles were reversed and that clinched it. Fred and Brian Gay took him to the hospital he had visited that morning and he was promptly put into intensive care. He was a very sick man who had suffered a huge heart attack.

It was a terrific shock and we could not keep it from the players as they had already missed him. I told them the full story after dinner but asked them to say nothing to the Press, whom we had informed that Vernon had suffered heat stroke, until we could get in touch with Jean Edwards. We decided to wait until midnight (7 a.m. London time) before we rang her. When we did get through Jean was not at all surprised and explained that he had suffered chest pains while they were together in Colorado. We told her to fly out at our expense as soon as she wished.

It was quite clear at that moment that we would not be seeing the doctor back in Saltillo again and that, as soon as we he was well enough, he would be flown home. So the next call was to Arsenal's doctor, John Crane, who had often worked for the Football Association, to see whether he could come out to relieve Vernon. But, obviously, he needed to arrange matters at his own practice before he could travel to Mexico for up to five weeks. Fortunately, London Weekend Television had their staff doctor, Lesley Young, in Mexico and one telephone call brought her back from Mexico City to Monterrey to fill those vital few days for us. But losing Vernon like that was as bad as losing one of my best players. He was an expert, a terrific fellow and I was going to miss him.

Needless to say, this overshadowed the rest of the day but I know that Vernon would have enjoyed the result and the game against the local champions. Although we had lost Peter Reid and Trevor Steven on the morning of the match, it was another good day. More than 4,000 people crowded around the touchline with hundreds more on roofs of houses around the ground. It was a throwback to the old days, we had turned back the clock as people lined the streets on our journey to the ground and there was a real family atmosphere, just as there had been in Colorado. What is more, Monterrey were a good side. Certainly better man-for-man than World Cup qualifiers Canada whom we had struggled to beat 1-0 on the previous Saturday. I used 15 players and, considering that half of them had not played a full match for a month, no one looked out of place. We didn't just beat Monterrey, we steamrollered them. We won 4-1 and it could have been 8-1. Terry Fenwick had a penalty saved; unlucky Steve Hodge had yet another good goal disallowed; and several good opportunities were missed. There were a lot of pleasing performances. Ray Wilkins, who played for one half, was back to his commanding best while Spurs' Gary Stevens, after playing himself in at centre-back, proved to be a great stand-in for Glenn Hoddle in the second half, who was feeling that old knee injury.

Viv Anderson played well until a leg injury forced him off while Peter Beardsley came within a whisker of scoring one of the best goals I have ever seen when he beat four men on a sixpence and chipped the goalkeeper with his left foot only to see the ball pass the wrong side of the upright. I replaced him with Waddle to keep him fresh and Waddle looked every bit as sharp as his former Newcastle United team-mate. Bryan Robson watched from the bench and when I discussed his progress with him he felt he would be ready to be involved by the weekend. I had still to be convinced. Hodge had again played well and I thought that a fully-fit Hodge might be of more use to us than a half-fit Bryan Robson. I still had a few days to make up my mind but I was not going to let my heart rule my head. Kerry Dixon again showed his talent for scoring goals with two more to add to his collection and only the width of a post robbed him of another hat-trick. John Barnes and Spurs' Gary Stevens added the others and our warm-up games were completed without mishap. We had maintained our unbeaten record in all matches and that could do us no harm at all.

THURSDAY 29 MAY: Everyone in the hotel noticed the doctor's absence. You couldn't help be aware of it because he was larger than life, and equally popular with those who were not part of the inner-circle of the football entourage. We telephoned the hospital to get an update on our doctor's condition and, though the news was good in that he had had a comfortable night, I did not relish having to tell the Press and apologise for misleading them. They were as low as we were and there was a genuine sadness around the hotel that morning.

Dr Lesley Young arrived that morning, back from Mexico City where she had gone just hours before we needed her. She was quickly into the swing of things as she diagnosed tonsilitis for Trevor Steven and gave him an injection in the backside. The cameramen and news reporters soon realised how attractive she was, and swooped. It must have been difficult for her but she remained above it.

At least, some of the attention was diverted away from Bryan Robson. He had not touched a ball for nine days and his technique looked rusty. He worked with Fred Street for a while and then joined in a seven-a-side but stayed shy of the action. I was certainly not going to push him and said so at our evening Press conference. I was still sceptical about him playing against Portugal. As part of our intensive public relations' campaign I was scheduled to speak to local coaches and students in Monterrey that evening. It had been a long day and it turned into an ordeal as it lasted for a solid two hours with Glen Kirton interpreting as we told them about our League set-up, the residential school at Lilleshall and the 85 Centres of Excellence around England. We finished with a lively question and answer session.

From there our twin police-car escort took us to the hospital to see Dr Edwards, who was still in the intensive care ward. I was delighted to see him but he was emotional and it upset me. Whether it was the long day without food or simply seeing my friend lying there wired up to drips and machines, I don't know, but I started perspiring and felt so faint that I had to sit down. I was deeply affected when the doctor began to apologise, saying: 'I'm sorry I let you and my 22 adopted sons down. They are grand chaps and I should be with them at such a crucial time. Tell them if they want to do anything for me to go out and win that World Cup for me and everyone back home.'

Vernon was so poorly that they allowed us to stay for less than 10 minutes. It was enough and I was ready for the dinner that had been laid on at the magnificent, luxurious home of an ex-Monterrey Football Club President. It was, perhaps, the nicest house I had ever been in and in startling contrast to some of the hovels around the outskirts of this industrial town. The brick-built gazebo where we and a dozen more guests enjoyed a barbecue was bigger than most of those family homes. Even so, it was what I needed.

That should have been the end of the day but it was not to be. The police car which was escorting us home suddenly suffered a puncture on the remote mountain road. The rain was torrential and our driver had only a small torch and an even smaller idea of what to do with the jack. I resisted the impulse to tell him as Glen and I got out in the rain to show him what to do. It took him 45 minutes and meant that it was 2 a.m. before I climbed into bed.

FRIDAY 30 MAY: Because of the storm I had witnessed on my journey home there had to be a hasty rearrangement of our training venue as the Cima Club was under water. I telephoned a local ground in Saltillo that I had looked at on a previous visit. It meant an hour or so extra at the hotel with no 55-mile journey in front of us and as I collected my thoughts after my long night, Bobby Charlton, who was with the BBC team, asked if he could have a word with me in private. It was in his role as a Manchester United director that he wanted an update on Bryan Robson and he did not seem surprised when I told him about Los Angeles and the shoulder coming out for a third time. He wanted to know what would happen if it came out again and, should it do so, asked could we send Bryan home to have it pinned so that he could be ready for the start of the season? How the boot was now on the other foot! I had to restrain myself as I thought of how I had pleaded with the club to have exactly that done so many weeks ago.

Ironically, Bryan showed vast improvement that day. After his stamina and endurance session with Fred, he played in a 30-minute eight-a-side game and for the first time was involved competitively. He began to look like the player he is, fetching, carrying, pressing players and making runs. To my delight, and his, he was freer and felt more comfortable. He had taken a big step forward and was thinking positively.

In the evening we went back into Monterrey for an official FIFA function for the four competing teams in the group. The Portuguese did themselves no favours by not turning up, the Moroccans arrived in tracksuits and the Poles kept themselves to themselves. Our lads were terrific, circulating and chatting with everyone. Everything centred on our smartly-dressed players and when the Moroccans began to relax, they made a bee-line for Robson, Shilton, Wilkins and our other top players, posing for pictures and asking for autographs.

SATURDAY 31 MAY: The World Cup had started at last. The long weeks of preparation and waiting were over and, even though we were not involved ourselves, we could still feel the excitement 600 miles away from Mexico City where holders Italy were to play Bulgaria in the Aztec Stadium. With the kick-off scheduled for midday, it meant that we could watch at least part of it and Ray Wilkins and I commentated for the BBC, who showed the match live, while others watched on video or in the BBC's television annexe. I had to call it a day at the break for I received a call from Brian Gay to tell me that our training ground was again in a bad condition and it would make it worse if we trained on it. It was a pity as we had arranged with Hernan Garza to entertain 22 local boys from Monterrey for the day and expected a lot of people and another gala occasion at the Cima Club. I asked the Portuguese if we could borrow their training pitch but was told that manager José Torres was at lunch and would call me back. I telephoned the owners instead and they immediately said that it was their decision and that we were welcome to use it. Out of courtesy we informed the Portuguese and made certain our training times did not clash.

That done we then arranged to have the Monterrey kids and their friends brought up the mountain by bus. The television companies and photographers had a field day as we played for half an hour against the youngsters. I was referee and not only did I award five penalties but I also sent off Terry Butcher, Gary Stevens of Spurs and Ray Wilkins, not to mention booking one of their players to the delight of his mates. It was 5-5 with seconds to go when I awarded the Mexican boys another penalty and told Shilton he had to save it to maintain our unbeaten record. He did and honour was satisfied as the kids chanted 'England, England' and we exchanged our big shirts for their little ones.

However, it was not all play as we enjoyed a good training session and for the second day running pinched the good weather, for while it was still dull and unseasonal down in Monterrey it was hot in Saltillo. Bryan Robson's shoulder harness, which I had come to hate, suddenly became a symbol of hope as my skipper pulled it on. It was like a soldier fixing his bayonet ready to go over the top. As Bobby Charlton had said the previous morning, Bryan is tough and brave and he had improved his chances by 20 per cent by the end of the session. That was still not enough for me for I wanted him much closer to 100 per cent before I picked him. I didn't want him to play to be subbed, I wanted him ready to play for 90 minutes. He still had to satisfy me that I could get the best out of him for there was no point his playing in the opening game to miss the rest of the World Cup and I have always been very wary of hamstring injuries. But, at least, now there was hope where previously there had been none.

The football between Italy and Bulgaria that we had watched earlier had done little to dampen our enthusiasm. Although we all hold the reigning Champions in the highest possible esteem, these two countries were hardly the two you would have picked out to live up to the expectations of the first day with its world-wide audience of two billion. Neither are ever going to be full of imaginative attacking football. The Italians had started slowly in 1982 and were again sterile and cautious, though clearly the better team. They were a goal up through Altobelli (the last man to score in the 1982 World Cup and the first to score in this one) but then let it slip when Nasko Sirakov equalised four minutes from the end. Both goals came in the last five minutes of each half and emphasised the importance of fitness and concentration under these conditions.

Dr John Crane was due to arrive that evening and we said thank you and farewell to Lesley Young for her efforts, presenting her with a carriage clock and other gifts. She had made a valuable contribution in a time of need.

SUNDAY 1 JUNE: We turned the lounge of my suite into a classroom and had an hour-long teach-in on the blackboard for all our set-plays. You need good weather to do it outside for it is a slow, drawn-out process involving only a few people at a time and our weather in Saltillo and Monterrey was about as predictable as an English summer. We took the short circuit on the blackboard. To accomplish this I had to tell the players the team even though I was not going to announce it officially until the next day when I would be sure of Robson one way or another.

It was·a useful session with a good response as we went through free kicks, throw-ins and corners. Mark Hateley was nominated for the penalties and the free kicks were to be shared between Hoddle, Waddle, Fenwick and Wilkins. We then watched a little of Spain and Brazil on television before heading off for the Technological Stadium for our first and only session on the pitch before the game against Portugal. When we arrived we found the doors to the dressing room locked and bolted and when we did gain admittance we discovered that there were no lines marked out and no nets on the goals. I was furious. Sometimes administrators do not understand the importance of seemingly small things like this for the whole idea was for us to get used to the pitch width, be able to judge distances and put into practice our theories in dead-ball situations. How can you do that when there is no penalty area marked out? It is like asking a top golfer to play a course the day before a tournament without knowing where the pin is going to be placed on the green. I asked Alan O'Dell to make the strongest possible complaint to FIFA and when Walter Sieber arrived he was clearly distressed about the situation. However, I was able to turn it to our advantage. Although we were scheduled to use the ground for only 45 minutes, we stretched our session to 75 minutes.

I also told Walter that the grass was half an inch too long and this came after complaints by the Poles that the grass at the University Ground was also too long. Even so we had a good session and our numbers were boosted to 21 out of 22 with Trevor Steven climbing out of his sick bed to take part in the exercise. This boy is going to be a very good player and will be one of England's major assets in the next World Cup. He might even have a role in this one. He is intelligent and hard working and he is able to sense danger behind him as well as anticpating what is going on in front of him. We certainly began well enough with both Hoddle and Fenwick scoring from their first free kicks. I told them to make sure they saved something for the Portuguese! Robson also did everything I could have asked of him and subject to there being no reaction he would play, which was remarkable considering he had suffered a third dislocated shoulder and a pulled hamstring so recently. I was glad to have been proved wrong.

When the team left I went off to a meeting with the Yugoslavian, Ivan Toplak, and I again was made to feel like the President of the United States with a police car in front and behind and every intersection blocked off on the way. It took me eight minutes to make a journey I had allowed an hour for but I was brought down to earth when my car to take me back up the hill to Saltillo failed to arrive at the appointed time. Eventually, thanks to a man from the Embassy and our own security man Les Walker, it arrived an hour and twenty minutes late. It was their first slip-up.

MONDAY 2 JUNE: It rained so hard during the night that I leapt out of bed

171

thinking I had left the shower running. I went back to sleep knowing that I would have to change our practice pitch yet again for the ground we were due to use had left the lads heavy-legged and feeling their hamstrings and this time it would surely be worse. With the Portuguese due to use the stadium, we again switched to their ground and afterwards I was able to confirm to the media that I would be fielding my strongest team, even though it would be the first time they had played together as a full unit. It had developed piecemeal throughout the previous two years. To my great surprise and delight Bryan Robson would be leading out the side and Gary Lineker had improved so much that a boxer-type of strapping ensured that he would play and no referee approval was needed. He was comfortable and confident.

In the afternoon Don Howe and I set off for Monterrey to watch the opening game of our group between the seeded team Poland and the outsiders Morocco. We both thought that the Poles would win easily, even though African football was improving so quickly, but after a goalless draw, I thought that the skilful Moroccans more than held their own and were, in fact, the better side. Admittedly, they faded towards the end when Poland could and should have snatched a winner but it would have been more than they deserved. The Poles were sluggish and did not push anyone forward from midfield, not even the talented Boniek who looked less effective than Abdel Aziz who was doing the same job for Morocco. The only players who looked likely to swing it for the Poles were the experienced Smolarek and Dziekanowski, who was surprisingly replaced early in the second half by Urban who missed a hat-trick. There were weaknesses I could see that we could exploit when our turn came, though we would have to treat Aziz and goalkeeper Zaki with the utmost respect on Friday.

However you looked at it, it was a good result for us and it meant that if we could beat Portugal tomorrow we would be in the driving seat in the group. Not only that but if we could do it with a bit of style and excitement we would undoubtedly draw the locals to our side for there had been little to thrill the Monterrey inhabitants in this first match. The Soviet Union apart, who had thrashed a poor Hungarian side 6–0 in the morning, sides generally seemed to be frightened to play in case they made mistakes. I wanted us to set a new pattern and have a go from the start. I wanted us to be brisk, aggressive and to play bright, attacking football. Why not? We were not playing at altitude, the weather was still dull, cool and wet and we were in good shape.

As I sat there on the eve of our first game, I was praying everything would go right. The past four years and, in particular, the last six months,

Top: The Rocky Mountains formed the attractive backdrop to our important acclimatisation programme in Colorado Springs. Here, I am taking the pulse of goalkeeper Peter Shilton at the extensive sports complex in the United States Airforce Academy

Above: One of our lighter training sessions. In the pool at the luxurious Broadmoor Hotel in Colorado Springs. It was not only relaxing for the players but it was very therapeutic

Top: The moment I thought we had lost Gary Lineker for the World Cup during our match against Canada in May 1986. The immediate diagnosis was a broken wrist but he survived to score six goals while Dr Vernon Edwards had to sit it out after a heart attack

Above: Will Lineker make it? That is all that matters in the after-match Press conference following our 1-0 victory over Canada in Vancouver in May 1986

Right: The lull before the storm. My wife, Elsie, along with the players' wives and girlfriends, flew out to the United States to help us relax before getting down to the serious business of challenging the world on the football pitches of Mexico

Below: It was all a bit of fun when I showed Ray Wilkins the red card in our public relations' exercise against the kids of Monterrey. A few days later it was a bit more serious when a Paraguayan referee did it for real in our game against Morocco

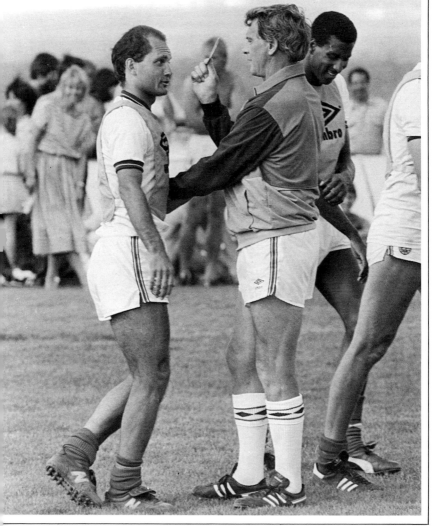

Above: The Portuguese goalscorer, Carlos Manuel, seems to be rubbing in the point that Portugal were one goal ahead by sticking his tongue out at a surprised Ray Wilkins

Left: Trevor Steven, one of the great successes of our World Cup campaign, seen here during his outstanding performance against Poland

Right: Me looking very happy after defying our critics and humbling Poland 3-0

Centre: Gary Lineker, the 1986 World Cup leading goalscorer. How many would he have scored if England had stayed in the competition?

Bottom: Lineker in the wars again. This time being treated after an off-the-ball incident when he was punched in the throat during our match against Paraguay. While he was off the pitch Peter Beardsley scored our second goal and Gary went back to add a third

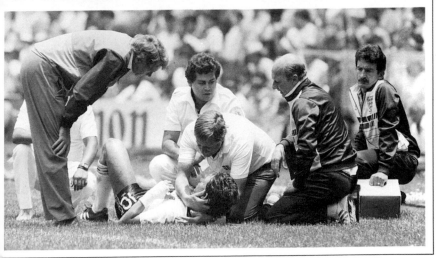

Left: Steve Hodge emerged at the last moment as cover for Bryan Robson and did enough to suggest that he will be around the international scene for a long time

Below: A place had to be found for Peter Beardsley, who entered the World Cup arena unknown but who finished as one of England's brightest young prospects

Top left: Peter Reid, a determined player and a likeable character

Top right: Glenn Hoddle, who took on added responsibility when Robson and Wilkins left the field, worked harder than I have ever seen him do before

Above: The sad sight of England's most influential player, Bryan Robson, missing England's most important game against Argentina. But for his desperate misfortune with injuries, Robson would have been playing instead of taking pictures

Top: This time the world's greatest player, Diego Maradona, could not escape the challenge of England's most consistent defender, Terry Butcher

Above: A hand for the losers. Diego Maradona knocks in the crucial first goal in our quarter-final as seen by the photographer and everyone else in the stadium apart from the most important men of all, the referee and the linesman

have sped by and here we were on the verge of the great adventure. I had felt excited before the opening game of the tournament but now it was our turn and that was something different. The excitement was tinged with just a little anxiety. I knew the best players were with us and that the preparations had been ideal. I had done all I could and now it was up to them. We have the talent and we are fit, strong and determined. Great individual skill is important but sometimes it can come down to a group of fellows looking round and saying to each other that they can go all the way and win. That was the feeling I had from my squad of 22 players. The next day we would get on with the game and see how real our chances were.

TUESDAY 3 JUNE: Rain and more rain, it was more like a February day in Birmingham than a sunny one in Mexico. The rain was so bad that I thought there was a real danger that our long-awaited first match against Portugal might be called off, though in retrospect that might not have been a bad thing.

We had a meeting in the morning when I talked for 50 minutes about the importance of this first game, emphasising that if we won it we were halfway to the second phase. We watched a little of the Mexico-Belgium game before setting off from Saltillo for Monterrey. As we boarded the coach, Dr Crane told me that Gary Lineker felt queasy and was suffering from stomach pains – he had given him some tablets and he would see how Gary felt by the time we arrived at the ground. It was a bad start to an important day and, to make matters worse, the heavy cloud cover began to clear and the temperature started to rise. I gave Lineker half an hour to decide whether he was well enough to play and he finally declared himself fit an hour before the kick-off.

They were all in a confident mood in the dressing room before the game and that was how the match started. No one went wild in the high temperatures as the ball was knocked around. We were comfortably the best team in the first half with the only apparent danger coming from Carlos Manuel, who was making forward runs from the midfield pack without being picked up. Lineker, despite his problems, looked sharp; Hateley had gone close and Waddle was also doing well. We were not being outgunned in the midfield despite Portugal's five against our three. At that stage I believed we would win and if we scored once we would get more. In the first nine minutes of the second half we had three good chances, twice through Lineker and once through Robson, and I knew that if we maintained our concentration we would be fine because Portugal were not in the game at all.

But, the first time they entered our 18-yard box, they scored. It was as unbelievable as it was shattering. Kenny Sansom, of all people, made a stumbling tackle on Diamantino who had been complete nonentity. Then Terry Butcher backed off instead of closing down and when Diamantino crossed neither Gary Stevens nor Terry Fenwick picked up Carlos Manuel, who was left free to hit the ball past Shilton from close range. Even then he almost put it over the bar. All of our back-four were equally at fault. If any one of them had played it correctly we would not have conceded that first goal.

To be fair, we could have lost further goals after that one. From where I sat, Terry Fenwick looked to have conceded a penalty when he challenged substitute Futre who then left him for dead with a run that was only ended by a brilliant save from Shilton. The West German referee, Volker Roth, gave us little apart from two bookings for our centre-backs Fenwick and Butcher – Fenwick was unlucky but Butcher had stupidly lost his head.

I was annoyed at losing an international match we should have won but it was only much later that night, sitting on my patio, that the thought struck me that I had just lost my first-ever World Cup match. It was still hard to take, though, from a side who had not played to win, so much as to defend. The only consolation was that we had not played badly and had deserved victory. I was still optimistic and certain that we would qualify. Even at this early stage I decided to stay with what I had for the second and now crucial game against Morocco on Friday. If we were considered good enough to challenge for the World Cup we hadn't suddenly become a poor team because of one result. I had watched a lot of the World Cup action on television and I had still not seen anything to frighten me. Of course, we had put ourselves under pressure but I hoped it would put the players on their toes. I knew that we still had considerably more chance of winning the World Cup than the team who had just beaten us. As for our supporters, from what I saw and heard, our large following were well behaved, gave us a good reception and were respectful during the anthems. It was a pity we didn't give them a result to match their behaviour.

WEDNESDAY 4 JUNE: I woke up at 5 a.m. with the game still weighing heavily on my mind and I didn't get back to sleep. We had an early start anyway for, thanks to modern technology, we had been invited to watch the Derby with ITV. My choice was 'Wise Counsellor', which never got a mention. Ironically, the race was won by 'Sharastani', clearly second best to the favourite, 'Dancing Brave', whose jockey mistimed his finish. It was rather like us and the owner of the second-placed horse must have felt exactly as I had done the previous evening.

This was supposed to be my day off. I gave a Press conference, an interview with Ian Wooldridge of the *Daily Mail*, a live television link-up with Jimmy Greaves and Ian St John, an interview with Jimmy Hill for BBC and another interview for BBC News. While I was doing all I could to help the media, however, they were not doing the same for me. Jimmy Hill told me that Emlyn Hughes had ripped into us again and had been highly critical of Butcher and Sansom, but what did he want me to do? Leave them out? Even Jimmy was cross because the comments had not been balanced by anyone in the studio. The best way to get back was to make them eat their words by qualifying.

With this firmly in mind, we had a training session for those who had not played, plus Beardsley and Hodge who came on as substitutes and Bryan Robson who volunteered for the session after playing for 75 minutes against the Portuguese. Not all went well, for Viv Anderson tweaked a hamstring and Peter Reid again hurt his ankle.

It is not often that as an international manager I have the opportunity to debrief my team. This time I did and we talked for a full 90 minutes with the players having their say after I had spoken my mind. But that result was history and the only thing that concerned us now was beating Morocco on Friday. There were no drooping heads. We all felt the same way. We wanted to put things right as soon as possible.

THURSDAY 5 JUNE: At last I had a day away from it all. There is no better place for me to escape to than a golf course. It was too hot for Don Howe but I played threeball with Ted Croker and Jim Bisset, the Managing Director of our kit suppliers, Umbro. I did not play badly, only losing on the 18th to Jim. I finished in plenty of time to make it to the Tecnological Stadium for training where the surface had not improved. How can they play World Cup matches on grounds like these? If the long grass were to be cut the surface would break up. As we had not trained the day before we had a good, long warm-up followed by our set-plays and a ten-minute game across the pitch. Two of my key players, Bryan Robson and Ray Wilkins, hardly got involved and I remarked to them, 'If I were picking the team from training, you two would be out. I hope you play better tomorrow'. It was all said tongue in cheek and as a form of motivation but I didn't blame them for conserving their energy the day before a game.

After training I went to visit the doctor and was delighted to see how much better he was and what a good mood he was in. I called a staff meeting after dinner to discuss the programme for the next five days. I also contemplated making changes on the substitutes' bench. Heaven forbid it, but if things were to go wrong against Morocco and we needed a goal in the last 20 minutes I thought of playing two wingers, John Barnes and Chris

175

Waddle. I knew I had to have Steve Hodge to cover Robson in case of that feared mishap, which was never far from my mind, and Gary Stevens as the utility substitute, but I still needed Peter Beardsley and I would have liked Kerry Dixon as well. Yet again I asked myself why they had changed their minds over the number of substitutes. Sometimes, I feel that the legislators have no real feel for the game – I even thought of leaving reserve goalkeeper, Chris Woods, off the bench. After all, you do not have a substitute goalkeeper on the bench at home so why one now? In the end discretion proved the better part of valour and I stuck with the original five.

FRIDAY 6 JUNE: I confirmed that it was to be the same 16 at a meeting with the players this morning. I told them that there was nothing to panic about and that I had kept faith with them because they had let no one down, they had lost to Portugal but had not deserved to. If we played the same way against Morocco that afternoon we would win by two or three goals. The players' attitude was still superb. Their pride had been wounded and they had been put on their toes. I knew how crucial it was to win and I was still mindful of the possible need to play with two wingers and two in midfield with Barnes coming on for whichever midfield player was not having a good time.

Before we left I had time to watch most of Algeria's narrow defeat by the tournament favourites, Brazil. I knew most of the players would have watched it as well but I did not say what was on my mind. If this was the quality of African football, then we could have problems. Algeria were terrific and lost only because of a dreadful blunder. It became hotter as we neared Monterrey and by the time we arrived at the ground it was a staggering 100°F in the shade and, though it dropped into double figures by the time we kicked off, it was hotter than it had been on any of our training days. It undoubtedly affected us and our mood. We were tentative and Morocco were the better side in the first half and as half-time approached I readied myself to do something about Abdel Aziz. But I wasn't too concerned as I thought that it would begin to cool off and we would have a slight advantage from the breeze that was blowing up.

Then, in the space of five minutes, my world collapsed. Had our World Cup hopes gone the same way? My injured captain Bryan Robson was helped off and my vice-captain Ray Wilkins was sent off. You would not expect that sort of thing to happen in an entire World Cup campaign, never mind in five minutes of one half.

I had been thinking about my half-time talk when I saw Bryan Robson going for a ball in their penalty area. Suddenly he was hit and went bowling over, landing badly on his elbow just as he had done against Mexico in Los

Angeles. Fred Street and Norman Medhurst were up and off even before the Paraguayan referee had brought play to a halt. I feared the worst but sent Mike Kelly racing round the pitch to confirm the extent of the damage while I shouted for Chris Waddle to pull back into the left-half role as Steve Hodge began to warm up. Mike came haring back to tell me that Fred had put the shoulder back but Robbo could not possibly play on. I immediately sent on Steve Hodge.

I was still trying to adjust to this dramatic change of events when I noticed Ray Wilkins being fouled in the far corner of the field. I remember being surprised at the offside decision given against Ray and at seeing him toss the ball in the direction of the referee but when I saw the red card appear I was shocked. This couldn't be happening. The rights and wrongs of the situation were hardly important at that moment. I was only aware that our backs were against the wall and that we could well lose and go out of the World Cup.

Morocco had shown in that first half that they were no mugs against eleven men and I knew our remaining ten would have to compete with both them and the searing heat. I was thinking of how we could salvage a point from this incredible nightmare situation. As I reached the dressing room, I asked Ray what on earth he had thought he was doing to get sent off and then saw Bryan Robson slumped on a seat, drowsy from the pain-killing drugs. I asked Fred to take him away because, to put it bluntly, he was a distraction and my concern was with the ten healthy players I had left. I had decided we should hold on to what we had and try and retain a point which, at least, would keep us in the competition with a chance.

I told Gary Stevens that I would be using him in the second half to replace Chris Waddle after 15 minutes. I told them I wanted a point and that if they played with the spirit and character I knew they had they could even be heroes and win it. As it happened, Waddle played so well for me that I couldn't take him off and, instead, I sent on Stevens for Mark Hateley, for my big centre-forward was not doing well and had been booked for a foot-up offence. He was charging about risking a second caution and the chance we could be reduced to nine men. Gary came on and did his usual fine job burning up the ground and running with the ball in the way I had asked Ray to do.

The strange thing was that my heart was beating less quickly in the second half than it had in the first. The back-four had come to terms with the situation and played really well while Glenn Hoddle relished his move into central midfield. He took on the responsibility in the absence of Bryan and Ray and gave me food for thought. In fact, after the disappointing first half, we outplayed the Moroccans. They became timid, passed the ball around their back-four and would not come out at us even from free kicks and corners. We might so easily have won against the odds but I told them at the end of the game that it was a priceless point we had gained. They were shattered, physically and mentally, and I had to lift them even though my mind was racing, wondering if we had blown two years of hard work and preparation in two games. Now we had to beat the seeded team, Poland, even to stand a chance of qualifying.

As soon as the players had eaten, I called a meeting in my room to impress on them that we were still well in the hunt and that a win on Wednesday would see us through and it would then be a different game completely in the knock-out stage. I was adamant that spirits should not flag during the next five days and that we should proceed with every hope and intent.

Ray Wilkins, refusing to be downcast by the sad events of his first sending off, said he did not know if he had the right to say it under the circumstances but suggested that the players were tired, had trained well and that he thought rest was the most important thing. I was open to sensible suggestions and agreed that we would switch training to the morning when legs and minds were fresher and then rest in the afternoons. I also thought rest and solitude would do no harm and told them we would head for the monastery at Los Pinos at 9.30 the next morning and be back in time to watch Poland play Portugal on television while Don and I would carry on down to Monterrey to watch our next opponents.

Bryan Robson not only wanted to stay but had already declared himself fit and ready to play on Wednesday. I was not sure about that but I would chat to him first and see what he had to say for himself. There was no rush to make an instant decision on that any more than there was to name my side for Wednesday, though I had already decided that Peter Beardsley would replace Mark Hateley and that Kerry Dixon would be on the bench. I also knew that everyone would expect me to play four in midfield. I was going to upset them again. Chris Waddle's legs might have gone in the second half but he had done enough to satisfy me and keep his place.

SATURDAY 7 JUNE: The game had exhausted me and by the time I went to bed at around 1.30 a.m. I needed no rocking but, by 5 a.m., I was wide awake, thinking of the events of the night before and hoping that all we had worked for had not gone up in smoke. It really was a case of the morning after the night before and I couldn't get back to sleep, but I had to appear bright-eyed and bushy-tailed for if I was not, how could I expect the players to be and for that same reason I had decided that we should proceed just as if we had qualified.

This was to be our first day at 7,260 feet at the monastery Los Pinos and if I had changed it, it would have looked like chucking in the towel. In the event I suppose it was suitable, for this was where people went for solitude and to pray. When we arrived we sat down on the grass and talked. It was supposed to be for half an hour but by the time the senior professionals had had their say it went on for an hour with the recurring theme being that we were far from out of it and that we needed flexibility in our pressing game. The players were responsive and there was a mixture of opinion. I listened and told them what I thought they must do. The meeting was steaming up and I was quite pleased by the time I cut it off, wanting to save some of this discussion for nearer the day. I also wanted them to enjoy the facilities, which included tennis, volley ball, head tennis and the small football pitch which we had helped fund.

I had a couple of chats with Bryan Robson about his shoulder, fitness and how he was feeling generally. I had already spoken to our consultant surgeon from Mexico, Louis Castanada, who had offered to pin the shoulder there and then and he had warned me that my captain was now a bigger risk than ever with the shoulder likely to go at any time. He also said that Bryan would, albeit subconsciously, be playing more cautiously. For the second time I was close to sending him home but here he was doing press-ups and telling me how how much he wanted to play. I decided to keep him. We were playing on Wednesday and, if things continued to go wrong, we might all be going home the next day.

There was certainly little sign of an improvement in our luck that afternoon. When Don and I left for Monterrey to watch Portugal play Poland, we were both hoping that the Portuguese would win so that the Poles would have to come out and attack us, but this was not to be. Portugal dominated for most of the game before the talented Smolarek scored the only goal towards the end to give Poland a 1–0 victory. This was probably the worst scoreline we could have had for, on the face of it, it looked as though we would have to beat them 2–0 to qualify. That was going to be hard for the Poles were strong, tough and not afraid to be aggressive. But I was relieved when I discovered that a 1–0 score might be enough. I took Bryan to one side to ask him about morale among the players in view of this but he was quickly able to reassure me that they not only wanted to beat Poland but wanted to go all the way.

SUNDAY 8 JUNE: I should have learnt my lesson by now. I had allowed myself to be pictured with my hands over my ears while listening to my Walkman by a photographer and a television crew, who inevitably portrayed it as, 'Robson in despair'. There must be miles and miles of film on Bobby Robson in Mexico for I couldn't scratch my head without a camera clicking. I don't know what they expected me to be doing but when I walked out of my room this morning there was a camera set up ready. It was just the start for Ron Greenwood had watched us train and he came over to ask me if I knew of the uproar back at home, explaining that Bryan Robson had been interviewed on television and had said that the players didn't know what they were supposed to be doing or how to interpret my instructions.

Bryan came over to say that he had given a television interview but denied saying any such thing. Ron quietly advised me to rise above it and wished me good luck. He had already supported me against a lot of criticism.

When we returned from training, Ted Croker, who was waiting to tell me the further bad news that Ray Wilkins had been suspended for two matches instead of one, Bryan, Ray Wilkins, Glen Kirton and I went to watch the tape of the controversial televised interview and I couldn't fault what Bryan had said. Unfortunately, however, not everyone else had seen it that way and back home Bryan's words had been translated as a split in the camp and evidence of rows between the captain and the manager. It was scandalous for I had never been closer to Bryan.

We watched unlucky Scotland lose to West Germany and then went back up to Los Pinos for a barbecue and a game of hit-and-run cricket. In typically English fashion, we played in the pouring rain until it drove us back to Saltillo in time to watch the scintillating Danes play some of the best football of the tournament in beating the Uruguayans 6–1 after the South Americans had had a player sent off in the first half. At least we were better off than the second favourites. I finished the day with a couple of Press conferences; one for international Press and another to put the British boys in the picture over what was happening in the England camp. I assured them, as they could see for themselves, that the English spirit was as good as ever. What I didn't tell them was that I was going to disappoint them again by playing three in the midfield with Peter Reid replacing Ray Wilkins and Steve Hodge for skipper Bryan Robson.

MONDAY 9 JUNE: Today I had to tell my best player, Bryan Robson, that he would not be playing against Poland in two days' time. It was not an easy moment for either of us. It took a lot of soul-searching on my part and it was a hell of a blow to him. He had set his heart on it but how could I pick him for such a critical game in the knowledge that his now four-times dislocated shoulder could go again at any moment? Substitutes were too valuable to keep one on permanent stand-by for Bryan and even to use him on the bench was a gamble that could leave me playing out time with ten men. It left both of us feeling very depressed.

The temperature was way over 100°F again when we went to Monterrey for our first look at the University Stadium where we were due to meet the Poles on Wednesday. It was a better arena but another very poor pitch. Chris Waddle will bear witness to that for even as we warmed up he put his foot in a pot hole and turned his ankle. It looked bad enough to consider having to replace him and it was more and more tempting to play Trevor Steven.

It was amazing the way everything had changed after our first two games. Some of the stories were extraordinary such as the ludicrous tale of former England manager Ron Greenwood having to separate Bobby Charlton and me in a row over Bryan Robson. On one occasion BBC television man Mike Blakey approached me at the ground to ask for my comments on the fact that my wife Elsie had been receiving obscene telephone calls. The Charlton story had started in Italy, would you believe, and the heavy breathing story originated in a newspaper in Oslo, which I knew to be untrue as Elsie had not been at home at the time.

TUESDAY 10 JUNE: The messages of goodwill were pouring in by post and telephone and the attitude of some of the televisions panellists back home did not seem to be reflective of the supportive attitude of the English public. The strange thing was that I felt fine. Remarkably calm. I suppose I had come to accept the situation even though it was the most important game of my entire life.

Looking back critically on our preparations, I could honestly say that there was nothing I would have changed. Nevertheless here we were in a situation where if we lost we would be out of the World Cup and all those fine hopes and ambitions would have come to nothing. I was still confident.

Overnight I had come to a firm decision on Trevor Steven and I was going to play him. It was sad for Chris Waddle, who had not let me down but this was a one-off team selected to pull us through to the next round and I would have both Chris and John Barnes on the substitutes' bench along with Kerry Dixon. Trevor can score goals, he is lucky and those were the qualities I was looking for tomorrow. One of the reasons I chose Trevor, a fine player in his own right, was that I feel that Glenn Hoddle is always more comfortable playing with someone outside him and Glenn could prove a critical figure in the absence of both Robson and Wilkins.

It was another boiling hot day and, rather than making the long journey to and from Monterrey, we trained locally. It proved a quick, sharp, bright session. We deliberately kept it lighthearted and cut the session short just as we would have done on a Friday back in England. Everyone enjoyed it except Kenny Sansom who suffered an over-the-top tackle that gashed his ankle. Normally, I would have been furious on the day before a match but as I was the culprit there was not a lot I could say. The diet I am on must have made me quicker than either Kenny or I thought.

We went back for lunch with the Minister for Sport, Dick Tracey, and the British Ambassador. Curiously, the latter's previous assignment had been in Poland and he knew all of our opponents. But then our game is full of such ironies for, 13 years ago, Alf Ramsey lost his job as England manager as a direct result of failing to beat Poland at Wembley in a World Cup qualifying match. This time the stakes were even greater.

The mood was still good and in the evening the Camino Real at Saltillo resembled the Crucible at Sheffield as we all packed into our games room for the final of the Pool Tournament between snooker expert Gary Lineker, a 100 break man and the gritty Terry Fenwick, who does not like losing at anything. At first Fenwick led 2–1 but then, in front of a full house, Lineker came storming back to win 3–2 with a scoreline that would suit us very nicely tomorrow. It left everyone in good spirits and I took a sleeping tablet before I went to bed knowing that there was nothing more I could do until I told the players what the line-up would be at 11.30 next morning.

WEDNESDAY 11 JUNE: Before a game I always instruct the hotel switchboard to stop all calls between 10 p.m. and 10 a.m. to give everyone an uninterrupted night's sleep. However, last night, despite my anxiety, I was sleeping like a baby when I was awakened at 6.45 a.m. by the bedside telephone. I had forgotten to include myself in the list of rooms I gave to the switchboard. The caller introduced himself as Mr Venables – not Terry, I asked, knowing from the accent that it was not – and he explained he was telephoning from Devon to wish the team and me luck. He went on to say that he just had to tell me that the whole country was behind us and that I should ignore the television panellists. I dozed off only for the telephone to go again. This time it was a Mrs Porter ringing from Newcastle. She was an old age pensioner and the first thing she said to me was that the call was costing her a fortune but she couldn't let the day go by without wishing me, the players and especially her local boy, Peter Beardsley, good luck.

By this time I was wide awake and I leafed through the numerous messages of goodwill, many of them from ordinary people. When you are down there are always a lot of good people ready to rally around. These are the people who give you inner strength. The messages came not just from England but from all over the world, including some from our friends in

Mexico. A typical one was the telegram from Sigurt Burmester, the President of the Reforma Club in Mexico City, which read: 'All your friends in the Reforma Club are with you at this difficult moment – history is full of fantastic recuperations carried out by the spirit of human beings with the absolute will to triumph. We will be with you once again and wish you good luck in the match against Poland.'

By the time the 11.30 a.m. team meeting was due to start I was uplifted and ready to motivate the team. I had already quietly told Trevor Steven, Steve Hodge and Peter Beardsley that they would be playing to give them time to get used to the idea. I informed the rest of the squad of the line-up and said that we were going out with two results in mind: a draw might see us through depending on the other result but a win would definitely do the job. If we were defeated then we were on our way home. Such was the state of the group that we could either win it or finish last. I told them, however, to forget all the possibilities other than winning.

There were other points I wanted to raise. I told the players to acknowledge the fans both before and after the game whether we won, lost or drew. I wanted them to be aware of their attire on the pitch. I was unhappy at the way we had finished against Morocco with shirts not tucked into shorts and socks around ankles. Sometimes there is a good reason for socks to fall down, but nobody has won a match or controlled the ball better because their shirt was worn outside their shorts. I reminded them that they were professionals, that they should be aware of their image and that kids back home would identify with them. I also pointed out some more materialistic factors and while I knew they were not overly concerned about the financial rewards of the World Cup, money was still a motivating force along with pride and ambition. Finally, I remembered those telephone calls and messages and reminded them that they were playing above all for the fans back home.

Because of the changes in personnel and formation we also had to change some of our set-plays. We were no longer as big a side as we had been and we needed to make some adjustments to our defence as well as to our attack. I also talked about pressing and whereabouts on the pitch we wanted to win the ball – there would be no misunderstandings this time. I spoke individually to both Chris Waddle and Mark Hateley, telling them that I had picked a team to win a particular game and that it was no reflection on Chris's form, which had been superb, and that he could still come on towards the end and be a hero. I also talked privately to Bryan Robson and Ray Wilkins, telling them how important it was for them to stay in the dressing room for as long as they could to help rally the spirit and atmosphere. They might not be playing but they still had their part to play.

183

It all went well on the 55-mile trip down to Monterrey with Gary Bailey playing his usual awful music and the intermittent cries of the card players. The players were under tremendous strain but you would never have known it. On the face of it everything appeared normal.

The nerves were there, however, and we scarcely made an auspicious start to our bid to reach the last 16 as we gave the ball away several times in the opening minute. Peter Reid was guilty twice but the greatest scare came when Terry Fenwick made a suicidal pass that let in, of all people, Boniek. It needed a wonderful save from Peter Shilton and a typical Terry Butcher lunge to stop him scoring. As we regrouped, Reid ran up to Fenwick, and shouted in his face: 'What are you doing? Trying to lose this game!', forgetting he had just done the same thing twice.

But, by the time we walked into the dressing room at half-time, we were three goals up with all of them scored by Gary Lineker. Each was a beauty, too. The first, after only seven minutes, was critical in settling our nerves and the second was a classic with Beardsley and Hodge delivering perfect first-time passes. But there were still 45 minutes remaining and a job to be done. It may have looked a formality after our superb ground football of the first half but what the supporters, television viewers and media could not know was that Fenwick needed ice on a torn groin muscle and that Fred Street had also whispered in my ear that Butcher had opened his knee joint in that early incident and that it could go at any moment, either in this game or at anytime. That was why it was important to keep it tight in the second half. The last thing we wanted to do was to let the Poles back into the game.

Peter Reid lightened the atmosphere as he remarked: 'We must be playing well, it's all too fast for me.' Peter then took his ice-cold, wet towel from Norman Medhurst. It almost sizzled as he covered his torso with it, saying: 'I am so hot, even the towel feels warm.' It was funny and just what we needed. Fenwick volunteered to struggle on and we went out to defy our critics and clinch our place in the second phase. There was no way that the Poles were ever going to get back into the game with Peter Shilton in the mood he was in. It was as if he had said to himself that we would qualify if he kept a clean sheet. He made two great saves from Boniek and came for crosses that he had no right to reach, never mind catch. He was unbeatable.

I was not at all nervous. I had given the selection of the team careful consideration and knew that all we needed was the bounce of the ball and a decent referee. We had both. Trevor Steven and Steve Hodge gave us width and pace while Peter Beardsley was exceptional. He ran himself into the ground until I had to replace him with his former club-mate Chris Waddle. Chris ran on with half-a-dozen plastic bags of water but was so quickly into the action that he was still carrying them as he went for the ball. He even put them down, challenged a defender and then picked them up again to hand round.

The atmosphere on the coach back to Saltillo was terrific and it was even better when we arrived for we were given a wonderful reception as all the hotel staff and many of the guests turned out to cheer while a mariachi band serenaded us as we ate dinner. I called a brief meeting to tell the players how magnificently they had played, how proud of them I was and that they must handle success without letting it go to their heads, particularly as we had a little Champagne reception given by Umbro afterwards. I reminded them what alcohol did at altitude. I need not have worried. They were as responsible as ever.

THURSDAY 12 JUNE: Gary Lineker was everyone's hero and while the rest of the team headed up to Los Pinos for the extra altitude, he, Peter Reid and I went on television with Jimmy Greaves and Ian St John. We also did interviews for BBC and, though I wanted my players to have as much time as possible at altitude, I felt it important that we kept in touch with the people back home. There was a pleasant surprise in store for me, however, as the BBC had arranged for my father Philip to be in a Newcastle studio to talk to me.

Don Howe, Mike Kelly and I then went into Monterrey to watch Spain and Algeria as we could be facing Spain in the semi-finals and the boys knew Los Pinos well enough to look after themselves. I was impressed by the Spaniards as they won 3–0. They played a flat back-four with no sweeper, four across midfield and two lively strikers, very much in the way we had done the day before. The difference was that in our front two, Beardsley and Lineker, we had the best.

We now knew that our next opponents would be Paraguay in Mexico City and I already had had a broad picture of them painted by my 'spies', Howard Wilkinson and Dave Sexton, who were both convinced that we could beat them to go into the quarter-finals. The next problem was to find a suitable hotel and Ted Croker had already left for Mexico City to confirm our booking.

FRIDAY 13 JUNE: We made an early start for Monterrey Airport in the morning as we flew into Mexico City at exactly the time Scotland were drawing with ten-man Uruguay to leave us as the only British representatives. The tournament proper was now about to start.

13. Mexico City

Our arrival in Mexico City was something of a culture shock after the luxury of Colorado Springs and Saltillo. The traffic was heavy, the sky overcast and there was smog. We had decided not to stay at my original choice of hotel, the Holiday Inn, after all for the players were anxious this time to be close to our training ground. However, the Vallé de Mexico, which was in the middle of an industrial estate, was in stark contrast to our previous surroundings. But it was little different from the sort of hotels English teams stay in every week at home and it would have probably passed without problems but for some television, radio and newspaper reporters who immediately saw a story and started to tell the players what a dump it was, looking for a reaction. It was nothing to do with them and if they did not like it they should have looked for somewhere else.

A couple of days earlier the players would have agreed to sleep in tents for the chance of playing in the second round against Paraguay in Mexico City. I talked to the players and told them that they would soon settle in once the video room, table tennis, pool and other diversions were organised.

I was far more concerned about the continuing saga of Bryan Robson. The same risks were still there. He had shown his character by volunteering for extra training and by not letting his team-mates see how upset he was. He told me he was around if I wanted him and I appreciated that. He would love to play in the back-four against Paraguay but it was going to be between Alvin, who was rediscovering his zest for the game, and the versatile Gary Stevens. I would not finally make up my mind, however, until I had spoken to Dave Sexton and Howard Wilkinson.

Don Howe, Mike Kelly and I were invited to a buffet for former players here in Mexico but it turned out to be another round of television interviews as I did my bit for Dutch, West German, Moroccan and Mexican television. This intense media exposure would get worse the further we went but it gave me the opportunity to project England's image and to some extent to shield the players. One compensating factor was that I met both Sir Stanley Matthews and that great French goalscorer, Just Fontaine, who had scored 13 goals in the 1958 competition. Afterwards we visited Dr Edwards, who was now in Mexico City. He looked well but I had a go at him, telling him to make full use of the ameneties of the Camino Real Hotel and to rest before flying home in ten days' time.

SATURDAY **14** JUNE: The first thing I heard on wakening was that Kerry Dixon had injured himself playing tennis the previous evening. He had followed through on a shot and opened up a gash on the bridge of his nose that needed four stitches and would cost him his place on the bench on Wednesday. I was upset rather than annoyed for tennis was not banned and it was a good way to supplement training. It was a freak accident. We were certainly having our share of mishaps but we were surviving.

I was irritated at some of the Press reports on our hotel and the effect they could have on our players. I called a meeting that morning to hear the players' views. Only a couple complained of not sleeping and one of those was Peter Shilton, who was sharing a room with Gary Lineker who had slept well. The main problem seemed to be the noise from the busy roads and the hotel plumbing but I suspected that the travel, change in altitude and new beds had all played a part and I still felt I should give it a little longer.

We then went off to the Reforma Club and it was like returning home. The new boys like Hodge, Beardsley and Martin could believe neither the set-up nor the welcome we received. The ground was soft and springy from the daily rain and the players enjoyed their training even though it was a bit of a carnival as just about every club member plus their children had turned out to watch. Shilton put on an exhibition for them and Chris Woods again worked like a Trojan. He had to, mind you, for we were still nursing Gary Bailey. If we lost one of our goalkeepers we would be in trouble for Gary was a gamble that had failed. His knee was far from right, but to be fair, no one could have known especially after he had come through that tough session in Colorado.

I spoke at great length to Dave Sexton and Howard Wilkinson about the Paraguayans when they handed over their comprehensive report. It sounded encouraging though both agreed they were a good side. It was evident that they are a better attacking side than they are a defending one with a big sweeper in a naive defensive system. They play two wingers wide and come through the middle from midfield with Romero being their main protagonist. My old Ipswich captain, Mick Mills, always said that he had more opportunities to attack when there was a winger up against him because he could catch them asleep and get in behind them. I must say that if Bryan Robson was fit I would play him in the back-four and, if Terry Butcher should fail to reach necessary fitness, I would definitely play

Robson because the percentages would have changed. As it was I had more or less decided on Alvin Martin.

That night we gathered together in our recreation room with some playing table tennis, others pool and the rest of us watching a Burt Reynolds movie called *Stick*. It was a good night but we still had some reservations about the standard of the hotel.

SUNDAY 15 JUNE: The first thing I did was ask the players how they had slept. I had lain in bed on the eleventh floor listening to a spectacular concert from the hotel's plumbing and felt sure that the players, after their previous complaints, would be up in arms. No one mentioned it. We brought training forward by an hour to give those players who wanted to the opportunity of watching Mexico play Bulgaria. They trained hard and, as I expected, were gasping for air at the end of it. We always knew it was going to be hard coming up from Monterrey and even the 2,000 feet difference from Saltillo had a significant effect. We still had a fair bit to do before we would be ready for Wednesday. We were going to have to grit our teeth and show our character. Apart from the difficulty of breathing, we were having to learn to cope with the effect the thin air has on the football, which really flies. Nothing was going to get easier. We were now in a different tournament as was shown when the much-favoured Russians surprisingly went down 4-3 to Belgium in extra time. That in itself should have served as a warning for the Belgians had finished third in the same group as Paraguay with whom they had drawn 2-2. There were no easy matches for anyone now.

MONDAY 16 JUNE: Enough was enough. The Vallé de Mexico had tried their best but one thing they could not help was the noise. I was woken up just before 6 a.m. by the traffic from one of the two trunk roads that passed our hotel. I thought to myself that if the players were suffering the same problems then it was no way to prepare them for one of the biggest games of their careers. I sought out Dr Crane, who checks the players first thing every morning for sore throats and the like. He confirmed that while a lot had slept much better there were others like Bryan Robson, Ray Wilkins, Peter Reid, Peter Shilton and my coach Don Howe who had hardly slept at all. The final straw came when Mike Kelly, along with Robson and Wilkins, had no water for a shower, shave or even to flush the toilet.

I spoke to the International Committee and then telephoned Ted Croker to tell him to move us out of the Vallé de Mexico and into my original choice, the Holiday Inn. It was now more than a matter of money. It was rather about preparation for a place in the World Cup quarter-finals. I left it to Ted and, to his credit, he turned up at the Aztec Stadium to tell us that all the arrangements had been made. What a stadium the Aztec is, probably the finest in the world, but sadly the pitch itself was not. We were forewarned because every team who had played there had complained about the surface. But that scarcely made up for the shock of arriving to see 400, or maybe more, divots being replaced back into the ground. They looked like an army of hedgehogs. We waited for an hour before enough of them had been put back for us to have our allotted time. The problem soon became obvious for, within minutes, we were taking off the top layer of the pitch with almost every kick. Even so we had a good session with shooting, penalties and a bit of a match practice where we used our wingers John Barnes and Chris Waddle and striker Mark Hateley like the Paraguayan forward line. Bryan Robson played in midfield when Glenn Hoddle pulled out with a slight strain. He looked good. He looked fit and I decided that, with Wilkins suspended, I would have no hesitation in playing him if Glenn was not fit.

We returned for lunch to our old hotel and to watch our prospective quarter-final opponents Argentina and Uruguay clash for the first time in more than 50 years. There was no love lost between these two teams and Uruguay had already been warned that they would be kicked out of the competition if there were any repetition of their previous crude behaviour. It was no longer to matter, however, for they lost a moderate match by a single goal with 64 free kicks and 6 cautions. The only highlight for me was Diego Maradona who was in a class of his own. He is the sort of footballer who can win a match in five minutes of blinding skill. If we play them he will need to be watched but I was not thinking about that yet and if the time came I would have the reports of Dave Sexton and Howard Wilkinson who were at the match. I was told that this game was less dirty than Uruguay's previous games. I still did not like what I saw and some of the tackles that went unpunished by the Italian referee made a nonsense of Wilkins' sending off and Fenwick's suspension. There was no consistency. I wasn't sorry to see Uruguay out and, indeed, Argentina fully deserved their win.

Once the game was over we left for the Holiday Inn and it was all smiles when the players saw a return to first-class accommodation, complete with outdoor swimming pool. It had been logical to try a hotel near the training ground but now we had done the right thing. We could finish our preparations for our game against Paraguay in peace. I couldn't even hear the aeroplanes.

TUESDAY 17 JUNE: The sun was shining, the players were smiling and everything seemed to be back on course. I even had all 22 of my players training as we tried out a new practice pitch at the Club Atlantic. It was a beautiful club, with good security, and the players loved it. We sorted out our penalty takers in case of a sudden-death shoot-out, choosing Gary Lineker, Peter Reid, Trevor Steven, Peter Beardsley and Glenn Hoddle. Glenn would take them if they came within normal time – not that this seemed likely as there had been only four penalties in our favour in my four years as manager. One or two practised spot kicks. Hateley is one who loves banging them in, but others like Reid, Lineker and Beardsley preferred to save their skills for the game. I was not going to force them. We had our usual 'Friday' session on the eve of a game, with a few set-plays and finished off with a lively nine-a-side game.

I thought to myself on the way back that maybe even the hotel situation had worked out well as had we come to the Holiday Inn straight from Saltillo we would not have appreciated it so much and it gave us a boost at the right moment. We deliberately trained early that morning so that we could be back in time to watch the noon showdown between the World Champions Italy and the European Champions France. It turned out to be a disappointing match. France won easily and when the Italian team returned to the Holiday Inn, where they were also staying, manager Enzo Bearzot said to me: 'Dead minds ... nothing.' I felt for him. I had told the players to have plenty of rest in the afternoon and most of them chose to watch the televised second-round match between Morocco and West Germany in Monterrey. It was an awful game that did not surprise me in the least for we, better than anyone, knew of the problems the West Germans would face. It put our performances in context as the Germans won from a last-minute free kick.

My thoughts moved on to the game against Paraguay and, though I was confident that we would win by one or two goals to earn a place in the quarter-finals against Argentina, I was still concerned that we had not fully acclimatised to the thinner air of Mexico City, even though the cooler temperatures would help. It was as vital a match as the one against Poland had been but somehow there was less pressure. We had qualified, we had performed respectably and had come as far as we had been expected to. We had not been outstanding but any success from now on would be an achievement. I was well versed in Paraguay's qualities and weaknesses. Good in attack and not so good in defence. The way I read it their marking was loose, they would let us have the ball in certain areas and they would crack under sustained counter attack. Romero had not lived up to his reputation so far and our biggest danger could be the prematurely grey

Nuñez and the clever Cabañas who had scored 53 goals in 55 games for New York Cosmos in the United States.

I was happy with Butcher and Martin at the back for in nine games together they had never finished on the losing side and had conceded only two goals. I had also made up my mind about the substitutes. There would be no Robson and I decided to give John Barnes his chance on the bench as a possible replacement for Chris Waddle. I believed we would get through and I wanted to keep the lad involved. He had been tremendous with not a word of complaint, a really good squad member. He typified the sort of spirit I demanded and expected from them all. We had to have the right mood, passion and determination as we had had against Poland. Although we had been written-off then, no one had cracked. That was the commitment we were looking for again. I wanted to see them chance their arms with long-range shots for I felt that if we scored the first goal we would on our way.

We were saying goodbye to Howard Wilkinson in a day or so and I took the opportunity to speak to him and Dave about Argentina and France. After all we could end up playing both of them. It was my day for meeting up with Football League managers and when I bumped into Manchester United's Ron Atkinson, I braced myself for another conversation centred on our mutual captain. He surprised me, however, by saying: 'Bobby, Bryan is my player during the season and yours now. It is entirely up to you what you do with him and how long you want to keep him.' I appreciated that. I also met Watford's Graham Taylor who had come out for the second part of the tournament, showing his faith that we would stay in.

WEDNESDAY 18 JUNE: If we beat Paraguay we would be in the quarter-finals. It sounds simple putting it like that but the problem of altitude still concerned me. Would we run out of steam? Would the South Americans punish us if we did? Once again I was touched by the messages I received from all sorts of people around England, including one which read: 'Wishing you the best of luck against Paraguay.' Signed: Bert Humphreys, Chimney Sweep, Birmingham. The telephone was also ringing non-stop and at 9.15 a.m. I heard a voice I remembered. It was Mrs Porter, the cockney senior citizen who lived in Newcastle. She sounded quite flustered and explained: 'I've been dithering all day whether to ring you. I can't really afford it but if it didn't go well I would think it was my fault for not wishing you luck. 'I was really touched for she had loved watching us play against Poland and particularly her local Geordie favourite Peter Beardsley.

Fifteen minutes later we were on our way to the stadium for the midday kick-off. I was quietly confident and the good cloud cover, which was keeping the temperature down, helped allay my fears about the altitude.

Although the skies had begun to clear by the time we reached the stadium it hardly mattered for the players were enthralled by the wonderful atmosphere in the Aztec Stadium and the prospect of the game. The pitch was still poor but it did not detract from the excitement and as I looked around the dressing room everyone seemed more than ready. I was not as worried about Alvin Martin as some of the Press were. He knew that this was his chance and he looked determined to take it. There was no doubt that he had regained his appetite for the game. We were a little early at the stadium because of the presence of our escort, but had still arrived half an hour after the South Americans. The time passed quickly helped by a special visitor to our dressing room, Sir Stanley Matthews. He is a shy man and wasn't certain whether he should interrupt. I insisted and the lads were delighted to see him. He is not only a legend but a great personality and, as I thought it was a moment that the public at home should share, I let in the television cameras.

The game did not start well for us. Within five minutes the influential Peter Reid was hobbling having taken an awful blow on his already injured ankle. I saw it and knew that Peter was in trouble but he is a gritty character and was determined to play on in pain, though his game was clearly impaired. Paraguay looked ready to take advantage and their fast forwards gave us a hard time for the first 25 minutes. Howard Wilkinson and Dave Sexton had warned us that they were a happy-go-lucky bunch who would be playing as if they had nothing to lose. For much of the first half they did exactly that and we knew we had a fight on our hands. The turning point came when Terry Butcher, usually so solid and dependable, cut the ball back to Shilton without looking and let in Mendoza. Shilton made him go wide but a goal still looked certain when Mendoza cut the ball back for Cañete. Fortunately, Shilton was there once again to save. Even during this awkward period I was sure that we would come right and, just as we had done against Poland, we immediately followed up a Shilton save with a goal of our own.

We had our share of luck though. Gary Stevens advanced, only to hit Glenn Hoddle with his over-strength pass. The break went our way as the ball returned to Stevens who, this time, kicked a good ball to Hoddle who immediately swept the ball into the area where Lineker and a defender collided. From my position of almost pitch level, I thought that Steve Hodge had scored but I learned later that he had calmly pulled the ball back and Lineker, reacting brilliantly, had bounced up before the defender to get his foot in. When I saw it again on television I was pleased to notice that had Gary missed it, Peter Beardsley would have certainly scored.

The goal gave us confidence on the field and on the bench for once we have scored we rarely lose. We might have had a second goal almost immediately afterwards as Beardsley passed one of his superb first-time balls for Lineker to volley goalwards from close range only for Fernandez to save. The South Americans were shaken and suddenly they were no longer the happy, smiling bunch of devil-may-care players. They now found themselves in a different situation compared to the first phase. They attempted to intimidate the Syrian referee and tried to provoke our players. This went completely against all that we had learned about them and it was important that we kept our nerve.

It was still 1-0 at the break and we remembered our experiences of a year before as the oxygen was made ready and the cold towels were provided to bring down the body temperatures. Fred Street and Dr Crane were busy with Peter Reid's ankle, taking him into the small gym next door to test him out after removing the tight strapping. Fred came back to tell us that Peter was struggling. Shilton turned round and said to the greying Reid: 'Eh, old 'un. We effing need you.' I decided to give it a go but it was soon clear that Reid was not going to last and I warmed up Spurs' Gary Stevens. But, before I could replace him, Delgado had elbowed Lineker in the throat and our top goalscorer was carried off on a stretcher, struggling to breathe. The referee saw it but did not book anyone and it was left to us to extract the best possible revenge as Butcher drove Hoddle's corner for goal and when the goalkeeper failed to hold it Beardsley nipped in from Gary's usual position to score off the rebound. That was the difference between the two goalkeepers. Both were brilliant but ours held onto everything.

I could now send on Gary Stevens with a two-goal cushion. He must have wondered what he had let himself in for as the South Americans became increasingly hysterical and paranoid, falling over in a bid to get fouls, chasing the unfortunate referee and behaving in a disgraceful manner. Our players did remarkably well, keeping their cool and hitting the South Americans on the counter attack. We scored for a third and decisive time when Lineker, back in the action, sparked off a super move on the right with Glenn Hoddle changing feet to put in club-mate Stevens who, in turn, set up Lineker for his fifth goal of the tournament. It was well-engineered, displaying good movement and vision.

We might have had a few more had our finishing been a little steadier. I sent on Mark Hateley for the spent Beardsley but, on reflection, it should have been Barnes. However, you cannot win them all and I thought Mark's height and strength might have had greater effect than it did.

It was an enormously satisfying victory spoiled only by Alvin Martin stupidly getting himself booked along with the innocent Hodge who should not even have had a foul given against him. But Alvin performed well, as did everyone. Shilton had done everything that could be asked of him; both full-backs had shown their athleticism; and Glenn, after a quiet start, had a hand in all three goals. Steven and Hodge were wonderful and our two strikers had performed again. There was a great feeling as we went into our dressing room. It was another comprehensive three-goal win and while we had won the Poland game in 35 minutes this had been a sustained 90-minute performance. It had been hard work and we had worn them down. Who was it who said that we had overtrained the players? It was our fitness and stamina which had carried us through.

While we were celebrating in our dressing room, the official FIFA film crew asked if they could bring their cameras in to see us. Why not? Any film about the World Cup should include England, especially a winning England. I was taken to the after-match Press conference and it came as no surprise when the first question was about politics instead of football. England were to play Argentina and it seemed as if the rest of the world were rubbing their hands in glee at the prospect. We were going to have to play it as coolly in the build-up to this game as we had with the Paraguayans. Gary Lineker, now the tournament's top scorer, was doing more interviews than I and he raced onto the coach still in his match gear having had no time to change.

The players' enthusiasm was enormous. Having played a match you would have thought that would have been enough for them but they wanted to know who they might be playing when, rather than if, they beat Argentina. The chances were that it was going to be Denmark but we soon saw them defeated by Spain in a sensational 5-1 win. It was the most surprising result of the tournament and the fancied Danes were on their way home along with the reigning champions Italy, pre-tournament favourites Uruguay and the Soviet Union. I must admit that I would rather play Spain than Denmark but I was also impressed by Butragueño and his four goals. He looked a similar player to our front two.

We were now faced with a different problem as that opening question at the Press conference had shown. To be honest this was one we could have done without. No matter how hard I tried to avoid the political under-tones, I couldn't hide the fact that four years ago we had fought a war with Argentina. When I got the players together I told them of the inevitability of the line of questioning and told them not to become involved in the political aspects. The same went for me too. We were here to play football and I am a manager not a politician.

But, at the same time, I could not bury my head in the sand and I was well aware of the implications and the potential difficulties with the two sets of supporters. At least I knew I need not concern myself with the players. We had seen their discipline that very afternoon. The nagging anxiety was whether the Argentine supporters would provoke the so far well-behaved British. I was already praying that there would be no confrontation in front of the world's television cameras. It was still on my mind when I went out into Mexico City with the former Israel manager Joe Mirmovich and his friends.

THURSDAY 19 JUNE: I was both mentally and physically tired and I slept soundly before getting up to see the Italians off on their long journey back. I had already heard of the marvellous reaction to our win back in England where the whole country was talking about it and we all felt that we could give them still more to cheer about. It was now a question of keeping the players fresh and alert as well as fit and with this in mind we gave them all the day off, though Terry Fenwick asked for a training session and went off with Norman Medhurst. We let the rest sunbathe around the pool or go shopping.

There was no day off for me, however. Howard Wilkinson and his wife were due to leave on holiday within the next 24 hours and I wanted to have a last talk with him about Argentina. His reports were encouraging though with an obvious emphasis on Maradona. The reports did not suggest that we should mark him man-for-man and I was beginning to reject that option. Moreover, there was no one in the squad who was really suited for the task. Terry Fenwick was too likely to be booked and Spur's Gary Stevens is not as happy defending as he is going forward. My thoughts were that I should keep the same shape for if I were to change it now it might blunt the fine cutting edge that has developed over the last two games.

The one problem was Peter Reid's injured ankle and who should replace him if it did not improve. It was being assumed that Ray Wilkins would automatically return after his suspension but I had a gut feeling that Bryan Robson would be the one to sit in the hole and be the anchor man. It would not put his shoulder so much at risk as charging into the box and it is a job he could do to great effect. I was also aware of the psychological effect his appearance would have on the Argentinians. What would a fit Robson do to this side? It would add another goalscorer to the four already there. I could cry about it, with a fit Robson we would be 20 per cent closer to winning the World Cup. I mentioned my feelings to Bryan who was keen and eager to play but when I warned him that if Peter was fit he would not be in he generously replied, 'Quite right. You can't change that team.'

The other question mark was at the back. Alvin had played well but that booking meant that if I played him, both he and Butcher would go into a potentially explosive situation carrying the threat of suspension for the semi-final. For that reason I thought that Fenwick should return, but he was going to have to keep his head in this one. As it was the Queen's official birthday we were invited to the residence of British Consul John Morgan. It meant dressing up and lots of circulating but it was important that the officials wave the flag as we had excused the players in order to give them a full day off. I didn't mind at all but I was annoyed when the morning sunshine gave way to torrential rain and wrecked my hopes of a round of golf.

FRIDAY 20 JUNE: The volume of telegrams, mail and messages was increasing day by day. Sports Minister Dick Tracey was becoming a regular and welcome correspondent and after our conversation following the Morocco game, when he had told me to stick two fingers up to the critics, he sent the missive: 'Congratulations and thanks. That is *three* fingers to the cynics.' The three-goal win over Paraguay brought forth the sequel: 'Congratulations. Three more for the cynics. "England Expects" on Sunday. Every good wish.' It was all very encouraging to know that people from every walk of life were so much behind us.

The morning dawned bright, clear and sunny. We could feel the heat but trained hard all the same. I had studied the possible programme and this was going to be our last day of hard training with rest days becoming increasingly important as the matches followed hard on each other. This was not the time to pick up strains and injuries and we spent a good 20 minutes warming up, using a particularly good exercise that Bryan Robson had learned from the well-known physiotherapist, Richard Smith, in Amsterdam. We worked on knocking balls wide, headers and shots and finished with a nine-a-side game. All who had not played on Wednesday did an extra quarter of an hour while we were missing the injured Reid with his bad ankle and Lineker, resting a sore groin, altogether.

The boys had worked hard without moaning and, having watched the West Germans looking so cumbersome in Monterrey, I was more convinced than ever that our preparations had been right. We had gone to the top for advice, to experts in the Armed Forces who had to send troops out to fight in wars in much worse conditions than the ones we were experiencing. It was paying off. Here we were at the end of a long, gruelling and emotional season and everyone was scrapping for the right to play against Argentina. Those who were in were fighting to keep their places against those who could see the pot of gold just beyond their fingertips. How I admired and respected players like Chris Woods, Viv Anderson, John Barnes and Kerry Dixon. All of them good enough to be here and in the team. I owe them my thanks.

We had made a promise to the players' wives in Colorado that we would bring them out if we reached the semi-finals and that was a pledge we had to keep. Feverish work had been going on at both ends to arrange a charter aircraft. They had been successful and I told the players that, providing we beat Argentina, they could bring out their families for the last week of the competition. It was a chance of a lifetime and I felt that it was only right that the players should share it with those close to them. However, the players did not need a lift for they were on top of the world already from the last two results. I knew how they were feeling for I had felt like that at times during the last 30 years. Funny how much better Sunday lunch always tasted after a win on Saturday afternoon!

Peter Reid was certain he would be ready for the Argentina match and that meant my only change would be Terry Fenwick for Alvin Martin. On the bench I would have Chris Woods, Gary Stevens, Ray Wilkins and, perhaps to the surprise of some, Chris Waddle and John Barnes so that I was covered for the wings and down the middle if necessary. At a Press conference earlier in the day, in between fending off political questions, an American asked: 'Will Bobby Robson play?' For once I could answer in all honesty: 'He's got no chance at all.'

SATURDAY 21 JUNE: I awoke to the now familiar voice of my new friend Mrs Porter of North Heaton. For a moment I thought it was match day until she said: 'I thought you would have too much to do on Sunday, so I decided I would ring you now when you have a bit more time.' I told her it was eight in the morning and was instantly admonished for daring to hint that she did not realise the time in Mexico City. Although she told me for the third time how she could not afford the call she was more chatty than ever and told me how her grandfather, one of the cricketing Pococks, had played with W. G. Grace.

I didn't mind the call at all, in fact, I would have been disappointed if she hadn't telephoned. Anyway, we were due an 8 a.m. call to go to the Aztec Stadium for an early training session to be back to watch the first of the quarter-finals, France versus the favourites Brazil. But when we arrived we found the dressing rooms locked. We made our way on to the pitch where the groundstaff were cutting the grass and preparing for Sunday's game. They even had the strings out along the lines ready for marking and they had no intention at all of allowing us to interrupt. The head groundsman told us that FIFA had contacted them yesterday, but no one had been in touch with us. We tried to explain that we had permission to use the pitch and that the World Cup regulations permitted us to train on the pitch for 45 minutes. He would not budge and said that we could walk on the pitch in our trainers but no ball was allowed.

We telephoned FIFA but everyone was away, either at meetings or in Monterrey for the Mexico–West Germany game. There was only an office girl who exacerbated the situation by telling us that we could wait if we wanted until the Argentines had trained at 11 a.m.. We protested, we argued but still those dressing rooms remained locked and as we left I warned them that we would lodge a strong protest if our opponents were allowed to train and we were not. In fact, the pitch was lousy, worse than ever and I suggested to Bert Millichip that no one should be allowed to train on it. It should be kept for matches only.

We wasted an hour messing about but eventually spoke to someone about the Atlantic Stadium where we had previously trained. We were assured that there would be someone there to let us in. But the battle was far from over as that ground was bolted as well. Our security officer, Les Walker, told our police escort to break open the padlock but they refused and, instead, sent for a lock picker! The players were becoming irritated and even when the policeman's friend had done his work we could not get into the dressing rooms. We were forced to make our way up to the stands and down onto the pitch where we stripped in the open and worked for half an hour before returning to see the second half of the game. It was a disgraceful situation to find ourselves in on the eve of a World Cup quarter-final but then the Aztec was a disgraceful pitch! When we had walked across it Peter Shilton had lifted out one of the turfs while others had sunk, making it look like a cabbage patch. Anything hitting those bumps would fly dangerously. We could only hope that the bounces went in our favour.

The game between France and Brazil was one of immense quality. The passing and movement was a joy to watch with good individuals prominent in good team patterns. Careca scored a wonderful goal for the South Americans with the ball being transferred across the box until it found the free man. Brazil should have gone on and won from there, even after Platini had equalised. The favourites won a penalty that Zico insisted on taking even though he had been on the pitch for only a minute or so. Joel Bats saved it and set the pattern for the rest of the day. Both teams made and missed chances and I thought that the Brazilian goalkeeper, Carlos, was lucky to stay on when he fouled Bellone. Foul? It was more like common assault!

Justice was done, however, when the game was decided on penalties with Bats saving from Socrates and Julio Cesar while, of all people, Platini missed for France. Amazingly, the game in Monterrey between West Germany and Mexico also went to penalties with the host country throwing away their chance after Berthold had been sent off. All they needed to do was to be patient but Aguirre stupidly got himself sent off and the West Germans defended well through extra time to penalties. They then gave a classic display of how spot kicks should be taken, struck firmly into the corner of the net, which was the opposite of the casual way the Mexicans and Brazilians had taken theirs.

It made me think further about our spot kickers. There was every chance that our game against Argentina could go the same way. Fenwick would return to the side and be one of the penalty takers. I announced the team after dinner and was able to inform the players that Argentina had made a negative change in their formation to protect themselves. I hardly needed to warn them about Maradona but told them not to have a phobia about him. We would crowd him, push him across the field. We would keep our back four in position, not lose our shape and not dive in. I was quietly confident and once again sensed the players felt the same way. They had big hearts and wanted to win. We had won our last two games by three goals and, in my four years as manager, England had never lost by as much. This time one goal would be enough. I wasn't greedy.

Policing was going to be tight for the game. During the afternoon I had a meeting with the head of security for Mexico City and he explained that there would be four, fully-armed, plain-clothes men on our coach plus the usual support of armoured cars, police cars and helicopters. Just in case there was trouble, they would even have a decoy coach at the stadium and take us out of the back door. I just hoped that none of it would be necessary.

SUNDAY 22 JUNE: I busied myself carrying out the usual requests of the BBC and ITV before 9 a.m. and I also did a live radio interview with the extrovert Stuart Hall. We were then accompanied by the customary calvacade of police cars and motorcycle outriders to the Aztec Stadium. There was no sign of Argentina as we inspected the ragged pitch and the rapidly-filling concrete arena. There was time to chat as I re-emphasised that it was certain to be a close game and how hard we would have to apply ourselves to this difficult task. The first goal was going to be crucial. I told them that we must be ready for extra time and even penalties if necessary.

The state of the pitch was causing me concern and Peter Shilton was not the only one worried about the goalmouths. There were senior FIFA officials on the pitch but there was no heavy roller to flatten the bumpy ground and it was no more than a gesture when, half an hour before the kick-off, they brought on a little mower-roller. I had no fears about the game, however. Argentina might have had Maradona but we had a team.

The first half was flat and I was disappointed that we did so little in attack. Although they had the edge and were slightly the better side, they looked no more likely to score than we did. No one, perhaps with the exception of Peter Reid who took another tremendous knock in the first five minutes, could get going and our front two, Lineker and Beardsley, waited in vain for some decent service. On the rare occasions it came, they were closely marked and they couldn't hold the ball up long enough for our midfield to support them.

I was more worried, however, about the competence of the referee in that first half. We had handled Maradona well but our first foul of the match, almost ten minutes into the game, brought an instant booking for Terry Fenwick from the Tunisian referee, which was to inhibit our play. He had never looked comfortable despite his reputation as one of Africa's best referees.

I hurried into the dressing room at half-time because, though we had hustled, worked hard and chased, we had to find a way of playing more in their half while keeping our defence intact. We had four at the back marking two and I felt that that was where we could bring the ball out far more, especially through Gary Stevens. We hadn't got our two wide men, Steven and Hodge, working at all.

In the build-up to the game I had warned the players that Maradona had the ability to change an entire game in five minutes. How prophetic that proved to be. Five minutes before half-time against Morocco our team had changed shape, five minutes after half-time against Argentina our dreams were ended and my worst fears about both Maradona and the referee were realised. The first goal happened in such a flash but no one in the dug-out had any doubts at all. I immediately knew that it was a handball and I waited for the officials to sort it out.

Almost as quickly I realised that nothing was going to happen. Maradona had looked at the referee and seen him give the goal and was now celebrating that all-important breakthrough. Our normally passive players were going crazy. Hodge, who had played the ball back to Shilton, Hoddle, Sansom and Shilton himself were chasing the referee back towards the centre circle. Shilton, more than anyone, knew he had been cheated for the only way Maradona could have beaten him in that type of situation was by using his hand. I remained outwardly calm but there was a hollow feeling in the bottom of my stomach.

It certainly lifted Argentina and raised Maradona to new heights. Within four minutes of his unfair goal, he scored a second of staggering brilliance. There was no lack of discipline on our part, no errors, just the genius of one player who went through half our team to score the best goal of the competition so far. I thought that that was the end. We now needed to score three goals to win and we had not had a real shot on target. But we were not going to give up. I had selected our two wingers, Chris Waddle and John Barnes, as substitutes just in case we found ourselves trailing. This was the moment to use them. We also needed to keep as many goalscorers on the field as possible without affecting the shape of the team. So, reluctantly, I pulled off Reid who had taken another bad knock and sent on Waddle. Soon afterwards John Barnes went on for Trevor Steven. In between we kindled new hope. Argentina were retreating for all they were worth as Fenwick headed over from Hoddle who himself hit a screaming free kick, which goalkeeper Pumpido did wonderfully to reach from the wrong side of his wall.

But it was Barnes, once we could get him on, who almost saved us. The officials were so lax that it took ages to send both Barnes and Waddle onto the pitch but, once we managed it, we took Argentina apart. Butcher headed straight into the goalkeeper's arms and then, with ten minutes still to go, Barnes dribbled past two defenders and crossed for Lineker to head his sixth goal of the competition. Could we get a second to force the game to extra time?

The goal gave us hope and I knew it would do for us what Argentina's first unfair goal had done for them. We were so excited that we almost let Maradona through for a killer goal straight from the kick-off but we pulled ourselves together and launched a final, all-out attack that sent Argentina reeling. I had asked the players at half-time if they really wanted to win and this was their answer. Shots hit bodies, there were scrambled clearances and, with three minutes left, we had unbelievably bad luck when Barnes crossed again and Lineker, seemingly, had only to nod the ball in to send the game into extra time. Somehow, Lineker ended up in the net and the ball rebounded out of the muddle on the wrong side of the post. That was the first time I jumped out of the box. We did not even get the injury time that the Argentina timewasting demanded. Forty-five seconds after the forty-five minutes was up, the referee blew his whistle. We were out and Argentina could not contain their relief.

I was devastated but I still had to keep up appearances in my position as England manager and my entry into the dressing room was delayed by the usual television interviews. When I did open the door there were tears, anger and annoyance. They were sick and bitter and nothing I could say could help them. I was in a trance myself and the coach seemed more like a hearse on the return trip. There was no blame attached to anyone. We had done all we could. They had their Maradona – we did not have our Bryan Robson.

There were to be no protests or complaints. We had to take defeat with dignity the way we had taken victory. All the players wanted to do was to get home and our travel men, Cyril Broderick and Brian Scott, quickly made arrangements for a crack of dawn departure on Monday. The meal was more like the last supper but Ted Croker helped raise spirits with a short speech in which he said that he had never met a better bunch of players. I fully endorsed that and his remarks about our skipper, Bryan Robson, brought spontaneous applause from the squad. I told them there was no shame in defeat. They could go home with their heads held high. Everyone of them had been a credit to their country and two months had gone by without a single, sour incident.

I couldn't bring myself to watch the match between Spain and Belgium for the sparkle had, for the time being, gone out of the competition for me. What did it matter who Argentina played in the semi-final? I saw the Belgians win the penalty shoot-out and that did nothing to lift me at all. Imagine, Belgium in the semi-final. I would have settled gladly for a semi-final against Belgium.

MONDAY 23 JUNE: The reality of defeat is always at its clearest the following morning and the general lack of appetite over breakfast owed little to the drowning of sorrows the previous evening. Football people, by nature, are a resilient bunch for they suffer so many reverses that they tend to become hardened to them. This one hit a lot harder for there was no next Saturday, nor even next season and it was the end of a four-year era.

All I wanted to do was get on the plane with the players and go home. Saying goodbye to each of them outside the hotel was an emotional time for I had become closer to this group than to any set of players in my career. We had played pool, watched television and eaten together for almost two months and there was not one of them I didn't want to go up to, say thank you, see you next season and mean it. I felt particularly moved when I shook hands with Bryan Robson and Ray Wilkins. I could only imagine how they must have ached inwardly. They had come out as the two main outfield props and had then to watch the team lose their biggest game from the sidelines. They were obviously in despair but hadn't once shown it in public. They had been wholly professional in their outlook. Don Howe is another true professional. What an unselfish man. He was going back to look for a job having put aside all concern about his future to give everything he had to England's cause. We were closer than ever after he had shared the problems and worries and he had provided great moral support.

As the coach drove away I turned back to the hotel. Although Dave Sexton was there for another 24 hours while Ted Croker and the other members of the Committee were returning in dribs and drabs, it was still desperately empty without the players.

TUESDAY 24 JUNE: The unwinding process was going to be slow and painful but it was eased by a trip out to Cuernavaca, a town 40 miles south of Mexico City's smog and blessed with year-round, spring-like weather. I was made welcome at a superb country club and visited the luxurious home of one of the wealthier local residents.

WEDNESDAY 25 JUNE: Things began to improve. There was, after all, good football to watch. France were playing West Germany in Guadalajara and the other semi-final, the one we should have been in, at the familiar Aztec Stadium was between Argentina and outsiders Belgium. For the sake of the competition and my own, I wanted to see France and Argentina win. France had once again shown themselves to be one of the best teams in the world. They were loved by the neutral fans, blessed with ability and had provided one of the highlights of the tournament when they played Brazil. There was a true artistry about their football while the West Germans had achieved their results by sheer determination and their usual efficiency.

Early in the game West Germany took the lead with an awful goal when goalkeeper Bats let Brehme's shot squeeze under his body. It was the sort of goal you would expect to see in a park rather than in the World Cup but it was enough to change the whole course of the match. The Germans were able to sit back, defend and make counter attacks. The French were the better side, made all the second-half running but could not get the ball past goalkeeper Toni Schumacher. The Germans snatched a second goal in the last minute of the game when their best player, Magath, played a ball over the top for substitute Völler to score a fine goal. It was the second successive time that the West Germans had beaten France in the semi-final and it extended their record to five appearances in the final in nine attempts.

I must own up to feeling envious when I made my way to the superb Aztec Stadium for the other semi-final. How we would have fancied ourselves against Belgium! Even the weather was perfect, cool and overcast in contrast to the strong midday heat when we played Argentina. At least I had a decent view of the game up in the stand instead of having to look at players' ankles from down in the dug-out. I wanted to cast a critical eye over Argentina as a team though I could not help but admire the little genius Maradona. The setting was perfect for his talents with the full, colourful stadium presenting a wonderful spectacle and I was thrilled just to be there. I was glad I had not gone home especially when I watched Maradona play at his best in the second half, just as he had done against us. I remember looking up at the clock when he stretched for a ball and made his first mistake. It read 65 minutes 40 seconds. By then he had destroyed the brave Belgians single-handed, scoring a few minutes into the second half. This time there was no doubting the validity or quality of the goal. Only he or Gary Lineker could have scored it, for the ball was never his. Two defenders and goalkeeper Pfaff looked in control until an explosion of pace and a flicked left-foot shot carried the ball deep into the opposite corner of the net. The Belgians looked on in sheer disbelief and did so again when the entire 110,000 rose to his second, solo goal soon afterwards. I was off my seat as he ran at the defence, beating four tackles and finishing with an unstoppable shot.

Belgium were now in the same position that we had been in but there was no fight back from them. Maradona murdered them and the score should have been five-nil as he laid on chances for others and almost repeated his second goal. This time his shot went past the post. Goalkeeper Pfaff stood rooted to the spot, staring at his tormentor for what seemed an eternity before breaking into a huge smile. After all, it was no disgrace to be beaten by this man. In two games he had put himself among the greats, alongside the Cruyffs and Eusebios of this world. Another game like that in the final on Sunday and we would be talking of him in the same breath as Pele.

As I walked out of the stadium I shook my head thinking how close we had been, remembering the handball and the late chance. By a great irony, Valdano had had a first-half goal disallowed because of handball. Three days after that scandalous decision had robbed England, the officials were not taking any chances. But it was too late to help us! That's the luck of football and, despite the saying, you don't always make your own.

Outside the stadium I bumped into Kevin Keegan who, like me, was commentating for Independent Television. It was the first time I had met him since I had taken over as England manager and had left him out of the side. I had no argument with him and bore no grudges for the things he had said. It was water under the bridge and I went up, shook hands and talked about the player we both considered the best in the competition, Maradona.

THURSDAY 26 JUNE: The Football Association almost had to look for a new manager – whether they wanted one or not! A group of the ITV crew, Bob

Harris and I took advantage of a couple of quiet days to travel to the beautiful Pacific Ocean resort of Ixtapa. The big Pacific rollers were hard to resist as we swam into deeper water. Suddenly, a young lady ran along the beach, screaming and waving at us to come out of the water. I was too far away to understand what it was all about but there was no mistaking her actions. I decided that discretion was the better part of valour and began to make my way back. As we came closer we could see the fear in the girl's eyes and we heard her shout 'Big Fish'. That did it. The five of us moved faster than Maradona, scrambling ashore to turn and see the large black fin of a shark no more than 30 yards from where we had been swimming.

FRIDAY 27 JUNE: In spite of the shark, we went back to the beach before our flight to Mexico City and the real world. Those waves were too tempting, though we did give the horizon a hard scan first. Sharks, we were told, were the exception rather than the rule. Far from putting me off, Ixtapa is the sort of resort where I would love to spend a family vacation.

SATURDAY 28 JUNE: I was impatient for the final. I watched France, with only a third of their regular players, beat Belgium 4–2 after extra time, in the play-off for third and fourth places. I wonder what I would have done in the same circumstances. The temptation is to give everyone who hasn't played a chance, though I would have definitely started with Peter Shilton because I want him to become the most-capped goalkeeper in history. Others like Viv Anderson, Kerry Dixon and John Barnes would have played but, after the disappointment of losing a semi-final, how could anyone's heart really be in this game? I still thought it was a good, entertaining performance from both sides.

SUNDAY 29 JUNE: As soon as I woke up, even though I was looking forward to the World Cup Final between Argentina and West Germany, I couldn't help thinking what might have been. I wondered whether the result would confirm just how close we had been. From a professional point of view, I was looking forward to seeing how West German manager Franz Beckenbauer would handle Maradona. He had wider options than I, for man-for-man markers and sweepers are common practice in the German League. We had had perhaps only four in the last twenty years starting with Nobby Styles, through Peter Storey of Arsenal, Norman Hunter (for country, though, not for club) and Ron Harris who was perhaps not of international calibre. In the event, Franz nominated a midfielder, Lothar Matthaus, to do the job. He is a shortish, disciplined player with pace and was not going to be turned too easily. It was only partially successful for not only did the Germans miss Matthaus in his usual attacking role, leaving 33-year-old Felix Magath too much to do, but Maradona was still able to exert tremendous influence on the game. This time there were no spectacular solo goals but, instead, he displayed what a fine team player he can be.

Maradona was fouled by Matthaus for the first goal. The West German was booked and Burruchaga crossed for sweeper Brown to head a goal at the far post with Toni Schumacher failing to cut out the cross. Maradona played an even bigger part in the other two goals, losing his marker to open up the path to goal for Enrique and Valdano and then perceptively putting Jorge Luis Burruchaga in for the dramatic winning goal. Maradona never flagged, running, putting in other players and going close on a couple of occasions himself.

In the end I was glad that Maradona did not score for it meant that our own Gary Lineker finished up as the tournament's top scorer. Maradona was undoubtedly the man of the tournament, though I am not sure that I would yet put him in the same class as Pele. He is certainly close to the great Brazilian and there is still time for him to bridge that narrow gap for, at 25, he can make his presence felt in the next World Cup in Italy where he knows and relishes the conditions.

Having said that, I would not make him the Man of the Final for that honour undoubtedly went to Jorge Luis Burruchaga, an exciting 22-year-old midfield player who plays for Nantes in France. He has supported Maradona throughout the tournament but really came into his own in the final, capping a tremendous performance with the winning goal six minutes from the end. He, Maradona, Batista and Enrique formed the backbone of the World Champions.

The game was not a classic and, indeed, there were times in the second half when it went quite flat. When the West Germans were two goals down, it did not look as though they had the flair ever to get back into the game. They were only able to because the South Americans became sloppy and complacent. It was a hot day and they seemed to think they had done enough to win it. I have always been a great believer in going for the next goal. To be three in front is always better than two. Argentina lost their momentum. Twenty minutes later they must have been kicking themselves for the cushion of those goals from Brown and Valdano disappeared as Forster took over marking Maradona, freeing Matthaus to go forward. Argentina had shown a vunerability to crosses in the last half hour against us and when the West German goals came they were both from the position in which John Barnes had caused such difficulties. They came from two corners by full-back Andreas Brehme in the space of eight minutes with Karl-Heinz Rummenigge scoring his first goal of the tournament and substitute Rudi Völler the second.

It amazed me for, in spite of having big men like Batista, Brown and Valdano, who are good headers of the ball, Argentina allowed two corners to cross their goal unchallenged. At 2–2 it would have been good if Europe could have broken the stalemate and won in the Americas. On the other hand, I wanted Argentina to win comfortably to show the world how close we had been to the big prize. I would not like to have guessed who would have won in extra time but it was not necessary. How often does it happen that a team scores, relaxes and immediately concedes a goal? No matter how much you guard against it, no matter how much you emphasise the danger to the players it still happens. Didn't it nearly happen to us against Argentina when we scored? The West Germans will never forgive themselves for relaxing but Argentina can congratulate themselves on having hit back so quickly. The control, the pass and the vision of Maradona was followed by the pace and finish of the scorer.

Walking away from the Aztec Stadium I felt I could hold my head up high. Although we had finished in joint fifth place only, it was hugely encouraging for the country and for me. We were so close to being the best – only one disputed goal away from the World Champions. We were behind nobody. There was no team in the World Cup I would not have been delighted to play against. There was no team who could show us anything tactically. Neither did the final persuade me that I should alter my approach. I would hate to see five or six in midfield at home but I could see some value in having a marker in my squad ready to use against a top player. That would be my priority for I was aware of the need to contain in some instances while in others there was still a place for top-class wingers. The one thing I had certainly had emphasised for me in the past four weeks was the need for flexibility.

207

14. Reflections

The image of Diego Maradona's hand rising above Peter Shilton's and knocking the ball into the net will live with me for ever. I did not need to see the television replay of the incident for it was burned into my memory and I am convinced that that illegal goal robbed England of a chance of victory against Argentina and maybe even of the biggest prize of all – the World Cup. Yet, I feel no bitterness towards the Argentine captain. He acted instinctively and got away with it and had the boot been on the other foot – or rather the other hand – I do not suppose we would have argued with the referee. No, if I feel any anger at all it is directed towards the FIFA committee that selected a Tunisian referee and a Costa Rican linesman for a potentially explosive match. I expressed my fears when I first heard of the appointments because this was always going to be an evenly-balanced, tense match, even without the inevitable political undercurrents for, no matter how much both sides played that aspect down, you could not get away from the fact that the two countries had been at war only four years earlier.

Anything could have set it off with the obvious repercussions on the terraces. This was the spiciest match of the tournament, even more so than the Argentina versus Uruguay game in the previous round and, because of this, FIFA needed to put their most experienced man in charge, possibly as a test for the final itself. Personally, I would have accepted a competent South American referee just as I am sure that the Argentine manager, Carlos Bilardo, would have settled for a first-class European one.

My worst fears were realised less than ten minutes into the match when the referee showed the yellow card to Terry Fenwick for a foul on Maradona. It was a foul, certainly, but not only was it Fenwick's first foul it was England's. It was a decision right off the top of his head and an indication that he would throw a cloak of protection over Maradona. Throughout the tournament the standard of officiating had troubled me deeply. There was a tremendous inconsistency in decisions. I saw brutal tackles, vicious elbows and violent obstructions go unpunished while mild tackles were penalised and players succeeded in conning referees into booking opponents for nothing at all. Some simply could not distinguish between what was a foul and what wasn't. Often it was an official from a country where football is still emerging. It is fine to give them experience in the opening phase when mistakes still have a chance of being rectified, but not at the sudden-death stage.

The opening goal in our quarter-final match against Argentina was going to be crucial. When it came, it was such an obvious foul that everyone in the stadium seemed to realise it except the men who mattered most, the referee and the linesman. I haven't seen such a blatant mistake for years. I have certainly watched one or two players trying to get away with it but the referee has always spotted the offence and once or twice the culprits have been booked for deliberate handball and unprofessional behaviour. Instead of being booked, Maradona was lifted to such an extent that four minutes later he picked up the ball in his own half, beat Beardsley, outpaced Reid, cut inside Fenwick and dummied the best goalkeeper in the world, Peter Shilton. It was very special.

I didn't like to say it at the time in case it sounded too much like sour grapes after the best goal in the World Cup but, if the film of the event is rewound, it can be seen that the move began with an obvious foul on Glenn Hoddle, who had his legs swept from under him. There were other frustrating moments like the free kick that would have put John Barnes clear on the blind side of the wall only for the ball to hit the legs of the referee who was standing in the channel – he even had his back to goal. The referee was not biased against us, he just seemed to find the occasion a little too much for him. After all, it was a big moment for everyone, a quarter-final of the World Cup played in front of 110,000 people. He could not wait to blow his whistle at the end and get off the pitch.

It has been suggested that Maradona is a cheat. However, that is a strong word that I am not prepared to endorse. What he does is to make the most of any situation, often looking for the foul when sometimes he would be better off going for it in the way that he did in that second goal. Maybe it is for his own protection but as the best player in the World Cup, he should have put himself above that sort of thing. In his defence, however, he moves so fast that sometimes it only needs a touch to send him flying and that could mistakenly be interpreted as a dive. If he were mine, I would want him protected and anyone who tried to stop him unfairly, punished. I would be thrilled if he ever brought his tremendous skills to Britain where he would be able to display his full range of talents free from the cynical foul. Supporters in England would be amazed at his electric pace and the remarkable control that seems to keep the ball tied to his boots no matter how quickly he is running.

Within ten seconds of the end of the game I realised that our World Cup dreams had disappeared with one dubious goal and one miraculous one. I knew it, but my mind would not take it in. There were other managers who had suffered, especially those whose teams had lost on penalties. Some of those, as well as some who had just had enough of the severe pressure of managing a World Cup team, resigned even before they left Mexico.

That did not happen to me. My immediate reaction was to vow that I would be back to challenge again. I examined my decisions, my selections, my substitutions, my preparations and everything else that could have contributed to our exit from the World Cup. There was nothing that I would have changed. I still have no doubt at all that we were the best-prepared team in the competition. We were handed the short straw in terms of venues but we performed really well to beat Paraguay only six days after moving from the heat of low-lying Monterrey to the high altitude of Mexico City. There were those who criticised our displays in Monterrey and said we had overtrained but who had managed to play well in the extreme heat of Mexico? Yet, when it would have been the easiest thing in the world to have given up against Poland, we played the best football seen at that venue.

I am certain that we had the right players in Monterrey and Mexico City. There was no fit player left behind who should have been included. Although Gary Bailey was only three-quarters fit, we did not need him and it did not affect any result. There will be those who say that I should not have gambled with Bryan Robson but I had every right to take a chance with the best English player and if I had left him behind there would have been those who would have blamed our failure on that.

No one knew better than me the risk involved with Bryan. The best medical advisers had warned me that what had happened in Los Angeles against Mexico could happen again at any moment. I could have replaced him by calling up Stewart Robson of Arsenal or Paul Bracewell of Everton but I knew that the other players liked having Bryan around as much as I did. It looked as though the decision was the correct one when the skipper timed his return to fitness to the minute to take his place against Portugal in our opening match. When he survived a couple of heavy tumbles I was filled with hope, even though I eventually had to take him off because of his lack of match fitness.

I was not disappointed by Bryan's performance in that game any more than I was by the overall team performance in the surprise 1-0 defeat. No one had argued about team selection before the game, how could they after we had gone 12 months without defeat, including that three-goal win over Mexico, something no other team could do in the World Cup matches that were to follow. Those who shook their heads after the Portugal game about playing a winger and three against five in midfield conveniently forgot that our winger, Chris Waddle, was arguably our best player and had we taken our chances we would have won with something to spare. It was certainly no time to panic.

If it had been the right team for the first match, it was certainly the correct one for the second game against Morocco. Admittedly, we did not start well but I knew that, with a few adjustments at half-time, we would win comfortably. Then, in the space of five minutes, it went horribly wrong as Robson's shoulder re-dislocated and Ray Wilkins was sent off. Suddenly, I knew that we would be fighting for a draw. I had to make changes and, fortunately, the squad had enough depth and quality for me to take risks. I had known all along that I would have to find a place for Peter Beardsley after his performance in Los Angeles while Trevor Steven, Steve Hodge, John Barnes, Peter Reid, Gary Stevens and Viv Anderson were all knocking on the door and I knew that I did not have to worry about the morale of the team after their performance in the second half against Morocco. If we had gone behind in that match we would have lost and if someone had offered me a point at half-time I would willingly have taken it. It would have been a gamble to have kept the 4-3-3 system without Robson and Wilkins even though Reid and Hodge could have stepped straight in. Both were inexperienced internationally and they were certain to face a minimum of five in the Polish midfield.

I pondered on the formation for a whole day and when it became clear that we would qualify even with a draw my mind was made up. If we had lost against Poland we would have failed to qualify and there can be little doubt that the papers and the media in general would have started a public campaign for my dismissal. We were taking criticism from every quarter but I knew there was little wrong with what we had. Even if we had lost I had no intentions of quitting at that stage.

I was confident and calm. That is why the England job must always go to an experienced man for if I had cracked then the players would probably have done so too. It would have been an easy way out for everyone. I had gone through it all at Ipswich. Two days before we were due to travel to Holland for a European Cup-tie against FC Twente with a single-goal lead from the first leg, Don Revie's Leeds United slaughtered us 3-0 on our own ground. In that situation it is vital to the club how the manager reacts. He has to motivate the players. He must keep his head up and give a little whistle. I must have succeeded in doing so for we went to Holland and won 2-1. Without that experience and my confidence in footballers' ability to bounce back it would have gone wrong. I knew, however, that luck would turn our way. We needed to win one match only and that was something we

211

knew we could do. I played 4-4-2 and, though some saw it as losing faith in the original system, Trevor Steven and Steve Hodge got down the flanks and gave us width. For 35 minutes we played some of the best football seen in the World Cup. In that time we scored three times and I felt very fulfilled sitting on the bench. It was an even better feeling than when we had won in Brazil against all odds. I could not help feeling tremendously relieved for it confirmed everything I believed and restored our credibility. We were not just in the tournament but in with a real chance of winning it.

The only change I could contemplate for the next match against Paraguay was that of Alvin Martin for the suspended Terry Fenwick. I felt that everything was falling into place. We were happy to be playing Paraguay and moving up to Mexico City. Unlike so many of the other teams, we had a clean bill of health with no stomach ailments or upsets. Even the brief stay at the Vallé de Mexico hotel had worked in our favour for the subsequent move to the Holiday Inn lifted everyone's spirits at the right moment. The feeling was strengthened when we beat the South Americans so well. Our ambitions seemed well founded with Shilton virtually unbeatable, Lineker likely to score goals all the time and the midfield combining skill with hard work.

I wasn't fooling myself for I knew that Argentina, and Maradona in particular, were going to be tough but I thought we were a better all-round team and if we overcame them then we would be in the last four. But there were a lot of elements beyond our control such as injuries, the bounce of the ball, a moment of genius and especially referees. Officials are something you can't legislate for but you have to abide by their decisions and that is what we did. There were no official protests or complaints. The decision could have gone our way just as easily as it went for Argentina.

The people I felt most sorry for were the players. They had given their utmost for seven weeks and, in all that time, had caused me not one moment of concern. They were perfect ambassadors both for their country and for the game. I could not have wished for a better group.

Peter Shilton proved himself to be the best goalkeeper in the world and it would not surprise me if he were the best again in Italy in four years' time. It depends on how ambitious he is but, judging by the way he trained and worked for this one, I cannot see him deteriorating. His understudy, Chris Woods, will go to Graeme Souness at Glasgow Rangers a better goalkeeper than he was when he came out. Chris had to do a great deal of work and he did it without complaint. As for Gary Bailey, he stuck at it and, though his knee did not recover, he never lost his enthusiasm and he made up his mind that if anything happened to Shilton he would give us cover.

If Peter Shilton was the best goalkeeper in Mexico then Kenny Sansom was the undisputed king of the left-backs. He made only one mistake in five games. I was concerned about Everton's Gary Stevens when he joined us after being substituted in the Cup Final but he pulled his game together and he kept his place despite a strong challenge from Viv Anderson. What a credit Viv is to football. That was his second World Cup without making an appearance and it upset me that we didn't give him a game. He is unfailingly loyal and cheerful.

Terry Butcher had a very good World Cup. He is an outstanding defender and his consistency ranked him among the best in his position in the tournament. Terry reads the game well and wants to win every game. So does his central defensive partner Terry Fenwick. He always likes to be in the thick of things but sometimes his enthusiasm gets the better of him and he would be an even better player if he learned to discipline himself. His pluses outweighted his minuses even though Alvin Martin has the edge in the air. Alvin had his best England game of all time against Paraguay and would have stayed in the side but for his silly booking. I won't be satisfied with Alvin, though, until he plays as well for England as well as he plays for West Ham.

Trevor Steven and Steve Hodge returned home better players and both can play a big part in England's international future. They are young and bright and can only get better. They each had superb games against Poland and Paraguay but were a little less effective in the tension of the quarter-final.

At the other end of the scale Bryan Robson and Ray Wilkins will also be around for a while. Ray seemed worried that his international career had ended when he was sent off against Morocco. Nothing could be further from the truth. He is right for England and right for the squad. I expect him to be around at least until the European Championship Finals in West Germany. Had we enjoyed a fit Bryan Robson we would have functioned at 20 per cent above our excellent performances and, while Argentina had their Maradona, we were without our Bryan Robson. That could have been the difference. A fully-fit, on form Bryan Robson could have helped England to the World Championship. On the eve of the team's departure, Bryan came to me upset after hearing a Press story that he was supposed to have given me an ultimatum to play him or he would go home. It was a scandalous rumour for Bryan was the model of good behaviour. Had the story been true not only would Bryan have been on his way but he would not have been picked for England again. No one gives me ultimatums.

In the sad absence of Robson and Wilkins, Glenn Hoddle took on added responsibility. He played every minute of every game and did some clever things to catch the eye and worked harder than he has ever done before. But, judging him on the highest level, he did not quite fulfil his potential in terms of threatening the opponents' goal. He is good enough to be compared to Platini but Platini is always dangerous around the goal. Glenn has the talent and ability to be among the goalscorers as often as the French captain. That is what he should aim for now.

Peter Reid came into the squad late in his football life and, now turned 30, he will have to be looked at afresh. How I like this gritty, determined character. He says his piece openly and honestly and was liked and respected by his fellow players. He was hindered by a troublesome ankle but showed his toughness and keenness to play. Gary Stevens of Spurs is another for the future. He lost a year of football through injury but he returned and did everything that was asked of him. His natural athleticism should see him develop into a top-class midfield player.

Chris Waddle and John Barnes may have finished the tournament on the substitutes' bench but that does not mean I have given up my ideas about wingers – I am still satisfied that these two are the best in the country and when it came to picking my top 16 for the quarter-final, they were both there. Even my close friend and coach, Don Howe, was surprised at that and asked me why. I picked them because they opened up so many options with Waddle able to play on either flank and Barnes wide or down the middle. If we were losing I was prepared to use one or both and to risk losing by an even greater margin – the fact that I used the two of them is history with Waddle hitting one of the best crosses of the tournament from the right while Barnes laid on one goal for Lineker and almost saved the match with another. I knew it was successful because those who had previously scoffed at wingers then said I should have brought on Barnes sooner.

The choice of these two as substitutes meant that Mark Hateley and Kerry Dixon were left out. Mark had arrived in Mexico as my number-one centre-forward. A terrific header of the ball and with a cracking shot, he scored two goals against Mexico in Los Angeles that no one else could have scored but he was not able to fire on all cylinders when it mattered in the opening two games and he became a casualty of the change of system against Poland. He should not worry, he is going to be on the international scene for two more European Championships and another World Cup. He has a great deal to offer when he gains the experience to play at the highest level.

Kerry Dixon came along as understudy to Mark Hateley and then had to take a step further back because of the irrepressible Peter Beardsley. But I stand by my decision to take Kerry. He was one of those who serve by standing and waiting, a manager's dream. He was a perfect squad member who always kept himself ready for the chance if it came along. In the end, the tournament was not long enough for him.

Peter Beardsley was one of the reasons why both Hateley and Dixon were forced to take a back seat. He was a little star. I liked him against Egypt and then was convinced he should be in the squad when, through a series of mishaps, he played and performed brilliantly against the Soviet Union in Tbilisi. He was the eventual reason why Trevor Francis did not come. By the time he played against Mexico in Los Angeles, I knew I would sooner or later have to fit him in somewhere, even to the extent of reshaping the team. He has the temperament to match his ability and I am convinced that he has the necessary qualities to become a major name in the game.

He and Gary Lineker will be around for a long time to come and Mark Hateley will be there as well. England's goalscoring prospects look exceptionally good. Lineker was everything I hoped for and with any luck he would have had two goals against Portugal to add to the six he scored and had we stayed in the competition he would have added more. He looked likely to score every time he played. He is going to get better and with his electric pace, eye for goal and his ice-cool temperament he is going to be one of the world's great goalscorers. He will further his experience with his move to Barcelona.

These are the sort of players who have inspired me over the last year and the reason why the next four years could be so exciting for English football. They have helped to make a difficult job a wonderful experience. I have enjoyed every minute of the World Cup. I feel now that I am a more able international manager than at any stage in my four years. I have learned a great deal and particularly about how to cope with the sort of problems that simply do not occur when you are a club manager. When the World Cup ended I still had a year of my contract to run and there was no question of me asking for my release.

Whether or not I stay is up to the International Committee, but whatever they decide they should decide now, for I firmly believe that any appointment should be for the full four-year period between World Cups for the manager to have any chance at all of success. If they turned round and said that they were looking for someone new I would accept it immediately and not even ask them for an explanation, but it would upset me if they said let's see how we go in the next year. For if they made up their minds to change then it would be wrong for the country and unfair on the new man.

I feel that it is a job half done and there is a lot I would like to do, particularly in the area of the schools of excellence, not to mention the challenge of the European and World Cups. My appetite has been whetted. There are some tempting alternatives but I then have to ask myself what job can be higher than managing England? If I do stay on I shall recommend that my successor be found within the next two years and then appointed as my assistant to witness at first hand the pitfalls. It would give him and the country the same head start that the French and, to some extent, the West Germans have had in recent years.

With the players available, England have a bright future and, having gone so far this time, I am sure that we can go even further in the next World Cup whether Bobby Robson is manager or not.

England's Results Under Bobby Robson's Managership

Key: BC – British Championship; EQ – European Championship Qualifying Tournament; F – Friendly; RC – Rous Cup; WF – World Cup Final Tournament; WQ – World Cup Qualifying Tournament.

Denmark (0)2 (Hansen A. pen, Olsen J.) England (1)2 (Francis 2)	Copenhagen, 22 September 1982 Attendance: 44,300 (EQ)
England (0)1 (Woodcock) West Germany (0)2 (Rummenigge 2)	Wembley, 13 October 1982 Attendance: 68,000 (F)
Greece (0)0 England (1)3 (Woodcock 2, Lee)	Salonika, 17 November 1982 Attendance: 45,000 (EQ)
England (4)9 (Moes og, Coppell, Woodcock, Blissett 3, Chamberlain, Hoddle, Neal) Luxembourg (0)0	Wembley, 15 December 1982 Attendance: 35,000 (EQ)
England (1)2 (Butcher, Neal pen) Wales (1)1 (Rush)	Wembley, 23 February 1983 Attendance: 24,000 (BC)
England (0)0 Greece (0)0	Wembley, 30 March 1983 Attendance: 48,500 (EQ)
England (1)2 (Francis, Withe) Hungary (0)0	Wembley, 27 April 1983 Attendance: 55,000 (EQ)
Northern Ireland (0)0 England (0)0	Belfast, 28 May 1983 Attendance: 22,000 (BC)
England (1)2 (Robson, Cowans) Scotland (0)0	Wembley, 1 June 1983 Attendance: 84,000 (BC)
Australia (0)0 England (0)0	Sydney, 12 June 1983 Attendance: 14,000 (F)
Australia (0)0 England (0)1 (Walsh)	Brisbane, 15 June 1983 Attendance: 10,000 (F)
Australia (1)1 (Neal, og) England (1)1 (Francis)	Melbourne, 19 June 1983 Attendance: 20,000 (F)
England (0)0 Denmark (1)1 (Simonsen, pen)	Wembley, 21 September 1983 Attendance: 82,050 (EQ)
Hungary (0)0 England (3)3 (Hoddle, Lee, Mariner)	Budapest, 12 October 1983 Attendance: 15,000 (EQ)
Luxembourg (0)0 England (2)4 (Robson 2, Mariner, Butcher)	Luxembourg, 16 November 1983 Attendance: 12,000 (EQ)

France (0)2 (Platini 2) England (0)0	Paris, 29 February 1984 Attendance: 45,000 (F)
England (0)1 (Woodcock) Northern Ireland (0)0	Wembley, 4 April 1984 Attendance: 24,000 (BC)
Wales (1)1 (Hughes) England (0)0	Wrexham, 2 May 1984 Attendance: 15,000 (BC)
Scotland (1)1 (McGhee) England (1)1 (Woodcock)	Hampden Park, 26 May 1984 Attendance: 73,064 (BC)
England (0)0 USSR (0)2 (Gotsanov, Protasov)	Wembley, 2 June 1984 Attendance: 38,125 (F)
Brazil (0)0 England (1)2 (Barnes, Hateley)	Rio de Janerio, 10 June 1984 Attendance: 56,126 (F)
Uruguay (1)2 (Acosta, pen, Cabrera) England (0)0	Montevideo, 13 June 1984 Attendance: 32,800 (F)
Chile (0)0 England (0)0	Santiago, 17 June 1984 Attendance: 3876 (F)
England (0)1 (Robson) East Germany (0)0	Wembley, 12 September 1984 Attendance: 23,951 (F)
England (2)5 (Hateley 2, Woodcock, Robson, Sansom) Finland (0)0	Wembley, 17 October 1984 Attendance: 47,234 (WQ)
Turkey (0)0 England (3)8 (Robson 3, Woodcock 2, Barnes 2, Anderson)	Istanbul, 14 November 1984 Attendance: 40,000 (WQ)
Northern Ireland (0)0 England (0)1 (Hateley)	Belfast, 27 February 1985 Attendance: 28,000 (WQ)
England (1)2 (Steven, Lineker) Republic of Ireland (0)1 (Brady)	Wembley, 26 March 1985 Attendance: 34,793 (F)
Romania (0)0 England (0)0	Bucharest, 1 May 1985 Attendance: 70,000 (WQ)
Finland (1)1 (Rantanen) England (0)1 (Hateley)	Helsinki, 22 May 1985 Attendance: 30,000 (WQ)
Scotland (0)1 (Gough) England (0)0	Hampden Park, 25 May 1985 Attendance: 66,489 (RC)
England (0)1 (Hateley) Italy (0)2 (Bagni, Altobelli, pen)	Mexico City, 6 June 1985 Attendance: 8000 (F)
England (0)0 Mexico (1)1 (Flores)	Mexico City, 9 June 1985 Attendance: 15,000 (F)
England (1)3 (Robson, Dixon 2) West Germany (0)0	Mexico City, 12 June 1985 Attendance: 8000 (F)

USA (0)0 England (2)5 (Lineker 2, Dixon 2, Steven)	Los Angeles, 16 June 1985 Attendance: 10,145 (F)
England (1)1 (Hoddle) Romania (0)1 (Camataru)	Wembley, 11 September 1985 Attendance: 59,500 (WQ)
England (4)5 (Waddle, Lineker 3, Robson) Turkey (0)0	Wembley, 16 October 1985 Attendance: 52,500 (WQ)
England (0)0 Northern Ireland (0)0	Wembley, 13 November 1985 Attendance: 70,500 (WQ)
Egypt (0)0 England (2)4 (Steven, Omar og, Wallace, Cowans)	Cairo, 29 January 1986 Attendance: 20,000 (F)
Israel (1)1 (Ohana) England (0)2 (Robson 2)	Ramat Gan, 26 February 1986 Attendance: 15,000 (F)
USSR (0)0 England (0)1 (Waddle)	Tbilisi, 26 March 1986 Attendance: 62,500 (F)
England (2)2 (Butcher, Hoddle) Scotland (0)1 (Souness, pen)	Wembley, 23 April 1986 Attendance: 68,357 (RC)
England (3)3 (Hateley 2, Beardsley) Mexico (0)0	Los Angeles, 17 May 1986 Attendance: 45,000
Canada (0)0 England (0)1 (Hateley)	Burnaby, 24 May 1986 Attendance: 10,000 (F)
England (0)0 Portugal (0)1 (Carlos Manuel)	Monterrey, 3 June 1986 Attendance: 19,998 (WF)
England (0)0 Morocco (0)0	Monterrey, 6 June 1986 Attendance: 22,600 (WF)
England (3)3 (Lineker 3) Poland (0)0	Monterrey, 11 June 1986 Attendance: 22,600 (WF)
England (1)3 (Lineker 2, Beardsley) Paraguay (0)0	Mexico City, 18 June 1986 Attendance: 98,728 (WF)
Argentina (0)2 (Maradona 2) England (0)1 (Lineker)	Mexico City, 22 June 1986 Attendance: 114,000 (WF)

Summary:

Played	Won	Drawn	Lost	Goals For	Goals Against
49	26	12	11	87	27